# A HISTORY OF
# SIERRA LEONE
## 1400–1787

# A HISTORY OF
# SIERRA LEONE
## 1400–1787

BY

## A. P. KUP

*Lecturer in History in the*
*University College of Sierra Leone*

## CAMBRIDGE
## AT THE UNIVERSITY PRESS
### 1962

PUBLISHED BY
THE SYNDICS OF THE CAMBRIDGE UNIVERSITY PRESS
Bentley House, 200 Euston Road, London, N.W. 1
American Branch: 32 East 57th Street, New York 22, N.Y.

©

CAMBRIDGE UNIVERSITY PRESS

1961

*First printed* 1961
*Reprinted* 1962

*Printed in Great Britain at the University Press, Cambridge*
*(Brooke Crutchley, University Printer)*

# CONTENTS

## MAPS

# ACKNOWLEDGEMENTS

My grateful thanks are due to the Director and staff of the Institut Français d'Afrique Noire, Dakar, and the School of Oriental and African Studies, London, who permitted me to use their libraries and gave me much good advice. Also I owe an especial debt to Dr R. Kelfa-Caulker, the Rev. H. A. E. Sawyerr, the Rev. A. E. Hamelberg, O.Sp., and Mr D. M. Edmundson, all of Freetown, who helped me to translate words in dialect or in Portuguese.

I also wish to thank the following for permission to quote or translate from their publications:

The Hakluyt Society; George Allen & Unwin Ltd (*General T. P. Thompson* by L. G. Johnson); Centro de Estudos da Guiné Portuguesa (*Description de la côte occidentale d'Afrique: Sénégal au Cap de Monte, Archipels*, ed. by Mauny, Monod and De Mota (Bissau 1951)); Biblioteca Geral da Universidade de Coimbra (*Relação Anual das coisas que fizeram os Padres da Companhia de Jesus* by Padre Fernão Guerreiro, ed by Artur Viegas); Academia Portuguesa da História (*Duas descrições seiscentistas da Guiné*); Routledge & Kegan Paul Ltd (*Journal of a Slave Trader* by N. Owen); Librairie d'Amérique et d'Orient (*Description de l'Afrique* by Jean Léon L'Africain ed. by A. Epaulard); Agencia Geral do Ultramar (*Tratado Breve dos Rios da Guiné* ed. by L. Silveira).

A.P.K.

*Fourah Bay College*
*The University College of Sierra Leone*

# NOTE

*Sources indicated by raised numerals ([99]) in the text are identified on pages 195–202. Footnotes are indicated by symbols (\*, †, etc.).*

*Square brackets in quoted matter indicate an interpolation or explanation by the author.*

eone, an ancient character with a new name, had arrived to play
er part in European history:

his is what I have seen and learnt during the time I was in these parts;
ut there have been others after me. Of most importance were the two
rmed carvels which the King of Portugal had sent thither after the
death of the Infante Don Henry. Their commander was one Piero de
Sinzia [i.e. da Sintra], a squire of this lord's, whom he commissioned to
sail farther along this coast of the Blacks, and to discover new lands. With
this captain went a Portuguese youth, a friend of mine, who had been
thither with me as a notary. On the return of the caravels, I, Alouise da
Mosto, was in Lachus [i.e. Lagos, Portugal], a place near Cape de San
Vincenzo whither the said captain returned. My friend came ashore to
my house and gave me his observations point by point on the land they
had discovered, the names they had given, the places at which they had
stayed, all in due order...as set forth below.

...About 24 miles beyond the Rio Verde [i.e. the modern river
Mellacourie] there is another cape to which they gave the name Cape
Liedo, that is in our tongue [i.e. Italian] *Aliegro* because it seemed to
them that this cape, with the surrounding country, was exceedingly
pleasant.

Beyond this Cape Aliegro begins a mountainous coast which extends
for about six [leagues], and it is very high, covered with tall and peren-
nially green trees; at the end of it, about 8 miles out to sea, there are
3 islets, the largest of which is about 10 to 12 miles in circumference.
They named this the *Isola Salvaza* [i.e. the largest of the modern
Banana Islands] and the mountain *Montagna Liona*....

Beyond the coast of the *Montagna Liona* all is low land and fringed
with many sandbanks which run out to sea.

Thirty miles beyond the cape of this mountain there is another large
river, three miles wide, which they named *Fiume Rosso* [i.e. the Kag-
boro], because the river water appeared red, as the bottom was red
ground. Beyond this river there is a cape, the earth of which is red, to
which they also gave the name *Capo Rosso* [i.e. Shenge Point]. Off this
cape, about eight miles out to sea, there is a red islet, originally part of
this Capo Rosso, the *Isola Rossa* [i.e. one of the Plantain Islands]....

Beyond the Capo Rosso there is a gulf, at the head of which is a large
river [i.e. the modern Sherbro river]. They named this the *Rio de Sancta
Maria* because it was discovered by them on the day of Sancta Maria de
la neve [i.e. a Saint's day in the Catholic calendar, 5 August].

On the further side of the river there is a point with an islet a short
distance out to sea. In this gulf there are many sandy shallows which
extend for twelve miles along the coast and over which the sea breaks.
The sea currents are very strong, and there are great flood and ebb

# CHAPTER I

## THE FIRST REPORTS

*Serra Leoa* was tranquil and the inhabitants were satisf
Negros considered it a good country rich in everything;
who went to *Guiné* were not highly thought of if they had
in the same way as we [in Portugal] think poorly of anyon
been to France or Italy. People who subdued those pa
esteemed unless they had travelled there also because, b
lavishly supplied, it was the haven of many who arrived as
came out as men.[1]

European explorers had first sighted the coast of Sier
in 1446 when a Portuguese expedition, commanded b
Fernandes, passed the river Casamance. Sixteen years late
da Sintra—so called because he came from a town in P
named Sintra—bringing two armed carvels, mapped the
rivers and islands. Such maps were secret, and every na
every ship's captain almost—as they arrived here tried to
their knowledge to themselves; thus, throughout our period,
landfall was in a sense a new discovery. Even by 1800 books
still a luxury and what texts there were had been largely draw
usually without acknowledgement or textual criticism—from ol
authors in translation. Thus legends and misrepresentations beg
in the fifteenth century were still stated as facts in the eighteent
but amongst these fantasies, as we can now see, lay a remarkabl
core of accurate information.

Pedro da Sintra, once a page to Henry the Navigator, was
chosen by the king of Portugal to continue the work of his master
who died in November 1460. When the expedition returned to
Cape St Vincent, where Henry had built up what was virtually an
academy of navigation, it so happened that an Italian from Venice,
Alvise Cadamosto, who himself had sailed with Portuguese permission as far as the Casamance in 1456, was living at Lagos, a
few miles from the port of St Vincent in Portugal. In 1507 he
published an account of the west coast and, after describing his
own adventures, told of the work of da Sintra and explained why
the explorer named the prominent landmarks as he did; Sierra

I                    I                    K S L

tides. To this islet they gave the name *Isoletta di scanni* [i.e. Sandbank Island], on account of these banks.

Beyond the islet there is a great cape which they named *Capo de Sancta Anna*, because I believe they discovered it on that day [i.e. another Saint's day, 26 July].[2]

The dates of the discovery of the Sherbro river and Cape St Anne, as it is called today, are significant because, although the Cape lies further south than the river, the cape was named on 26 July and the river ten days later. The Portuguese, as they sailed down the coast, always hoped that one day they would discover a passage either through or round the great continent to the riches of unknown China—or Cathay as it was then called after a tribe with Mongol affinities which lived in the north. The East had been cut off from western European trade by the Muslim invasion of the Mediterranean in the twelfth century and its spices and silks consequently fetched tremendous prices in Europe at this time. Cape St Anne, running out to sea, is visible before one reaches the Sherbro river, but a legend existed from earliest times—and still persisted in 1800—that there was a river on the west coast of Africa which divided the continent, as the Danube did Europe, and eventually joined the Nile. At first the river Senegal raised their hopes; indeed it was named the Nile by the early Portuguese. Now, having sailed across the wide estuary of the Sherbro, the explorers could not afford to ignore the possibility that this at last was what they sought. But once more they were disillusioned; only in 1498 did Vasco da Gama reach India by way of the Cape of Good Hope.

The next to describe Sierra Leone are Valentim Fernandes, a German from Moravia who became a printer in Lisbon, and who obtained all his information at second-hand, and Pacheco Pereira who, born in Lisbon soon after 1450, was Governor of Elmina Castle, at that time Portuguese, from 1520 to 1522. Fernandes wrote in 1507 and Pereira some time between 1505 and 1508. The modern name *Sierra Leone* is a mixture of Portuguese and Italian; Cadamosto was an Italian and his description, the first to be published, was naturally influenced by his mother tongue. The name was perpetuated by subsequent Italian map-makers who were already famous in the sixteenth century. Fernandes and Pereira, however, both use the proper Portuguese form *Serra Lyoa*. Fernandes obtained his information mainly from a man called Alvaro Velho, a Portuguese trader who had his headquarters for eight years at Sierra Leone. He tells us that the Africans here called their country *Pymto*, after a village of that name which lay amongst the mountains:

The main villages in this country of *Serra Lyoa*, that is to say, of the Bulloms, are as follows:
  *Manguy*, village of some thousand inhabitants
  *Maguem*, village of 300 inhabitants
  *Pinto*, village...of 200 inhabitants
  *Bop*, village of 150 inhabitants.
Besides these, there are many others of 60, 40 and 20 inhabitants, and farms where rice is planted.[3]

*Manguy* (Mange) is still a common name for villages in Temne country. *Maguem* has not been identified, although *ma-* is a prefix used by Temne people for places found near water; perhaps it stood for *Maben*, now at the mouth of the river Gbagbai, or for Magbema which lies on an arm of the Bunce river. *Bop* is very likely the modern Gbap, headquarters of the Nongobah Bullom chiefdom. *Pinto* has now disappeared, but in 1607 William Finch, an Englishman, found a chief, Captain Pinto,* living 'within the second cove' of the Sierra Leone river—that is, at the modern Aberdeen Bay.[4] Fernandes says also that the country was inhabited by Bulloms and Temnes, that each village had a king called *Bee* and that the Temnes who lived inland owed allegiance to an overlord called *Obe Vrig*. This title corresponds to the modern Temne *Bai*. The Bulloms along the coast also paid homage to an overlord. All towns possessed their Societies, their Medicine Men and their idols called *cru*; the chiefs had their own 'medicine' which was known as *piso*. War was waged only after discussion amongst the elders and subsequent sacrifice to the war god called *yniell*, an image made from wood in the shape of some deceased and famous warrior. The dead, often decorated with a shield made from elephant skin and a spear and covered with country cloths, were buried in their houses. As today, the parents of brides were presented with a dowry, the price being recoverable in case of desertion. A woman's adultery was punished by fining her partner. The rich wore cotton cloths, but the poor only a fibre-covering round their hips. For certain crimes the Bulloms demanded capital punishment, but the Temnes had no such institution. If a

---

\* It is possible that Pinto is a corruption of the Temne place-name *Binti*.

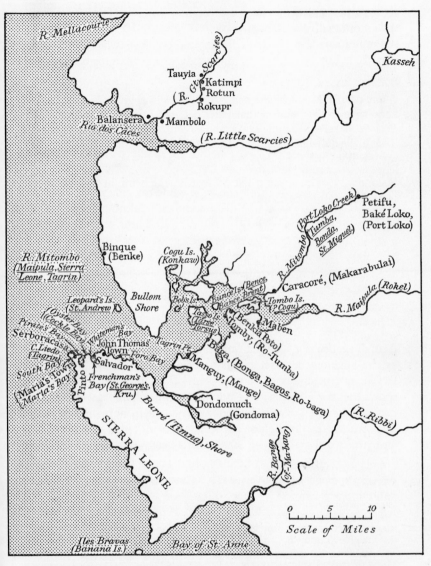

Approximate locations of the main places known in the sixteenth and seventeenth centuries. Modern names are given in parentheses after the contemporary names, thus: Binque (Benke). Alternative contemporary names are in parentheses and underlined, thus C. Liedo (Tagrin). Some names, e.g. Maria's Town, Bûrre and Pinto, no longer exist; others, like Foro Bay, have been given to places nearby.

leopard was killed the skin and teeth were given to the chief as a sign of loyalty, as they are now.*

Pereira, the last of our early sources, confirms what Fernandes was told, but he adds two interesting pieces of information; he says first:

Many people think that the name *Serra Lyoa* was given because many lions were to be found in that part, but that is wrong. It is because Pero de Sintra...when he saw a land so rough and wild, called it *Lyoa*. That is the only reason and no other explanation is true because he told me this himself.[5]

Secondly, Pereira gives a list of words which might be of use to later travellers. These were:

Bullom

| | |
|---|---|
| *emloam* | gold |
| *men* | water |

Temne

| | |
|---|---|
| *tebongo* | gold |
| *mancha* | water |
| *maloo* | rice. |

Actually *maloo* is a Malinka word and, as such, may have been used by the Susu on the coast at this time; otherwise Pereira's vocabulary is as true today as it was then. It is important because it shows that the Temnes and Bulloms had been here long enough in 1500 for their language to be commonly spoken; more important in this context, the Portuguese preoccupation with gold led Pereira to write this word first in both lists. Moreover, *tebongo*, as opposed to

---

* See *Man* (1909), no. 40, fig. 4; this figure resembles—except that it is standing—the description of early Temne and Bullom warriors. Fernandes mentions also certain gods and holy places and, allowing for his account being obtained at second-hand and for his knowing no Temne, these may be identified with reasonable certainty: 'There are certain houses or churches for idols where women do not enter; some are called *baa*, others *piçaa*, *piso* and others *cõ tuberia*.' *Ba* is modern Temne for 'a place'; there is a Poro devil called *Fisa* (cf. modern Temne *o fisa*: he is getting better). He adds: 'The women's idol is called *pere*.' Today there is a Bundu devil called *perea*; possibly *cõ tuberia* is a corruption or a variation of this word. Portuguese writers speak also of *china* and this word was copied, irrespective of differences of pronunciation, by English and French authors; it is probably the devil *sine* which is a word used also for a twin. The idols made of clay at this time are probably Sherbro; today only a bare handful of Temnes make clay figures and there is no tradition that this was ever otherwise.

*a-bono*, means jewellery; the latter word is used for gold in general. Sierra Leone is not rich in gold today, nor has it ever been; what the Portuguese bought from this country were mainly ornaments made from gold and brought in from elsewhere, from Fula or Mandingo country as it was in 1792.[6] Similarly, the fibre mats which every European nation bought here were known to the Portuguese as *bicas*. The modern Sherbro for a mat is *bik*.

As they sailed down the coast the Portuguese were often unaware of the local place-names, so that, like da Sintra, they marked the prominent features on their charts according to their fancy. The Sierra Leone river, however, is marked on early maps as *Tagurin*, *Taguyri* or *Tagrim*, with other variations. Port Loko Creek is often named *Mitombo* or *Bintombo*, whilst another tributary is styled *Maipula*.[7] These are all local names, probably Sherbro-Bullom. *Tagery*, according to Nylander,[8] a Church Missionary Society missionary on the Bullom shore in 1812, means spotted; there was in his time still a small town of that name, but the name has in fact been applied throughout the centuries to a bewildering variety of geographical features, whilst the word itself has undergone an anglicisation which has corrupted it. For instance, the Reverend Richard Madox, drawing a map of the river mouth in 1582, marked Tagarin Point where we know it to be today, but the modern Bunce river he named the Sierra Leone river. The estuary which will later divide into the river Rokel and Port Loko Creek— neither of which is on his map—he names *Tagurine*. Barbot, factor to the French African Company in 1678, wrote *Tagrin* where now lies what we call Cape Sierra Leone. In this he was probably misled by Dutch maps; Johan Vingboons, for instance, had done the same forty years earlier.[9] The Dutch in fact came late into the West African waters, but the English and Portuguese still kept secret their maps. The Dutch, therefore, encountering many names of which they had no record on their chart, became confused and tended to mix them up; and since the map-makers of Amsterdam were second to none at this time, the inaccuracies of their West Coast surveyors became widely propagated. Later maps, however, place Tagrin once more upon the north bank of the river as we know it today.

Corruption of local words is the inevitable misfortune of any race which opens its doors to strangers, but it so happens that Tagrin has an unhappy resemblance to a word used in the north of England to denote a marine store or one which visits ships in harbour with a boatful of wares for exchange.[10] It is possible that the word took on this later connotation, since ships did indeed trade with canoes at that spot.

Sailing further down the coast the Portuguese named the Banana Islands the *Bravas* or Wild Islands, perhaps because one of them has a rocky shore. The largest of the group they called *Isola Salvaza* or Healthy Island; this reputation it long maintained. Farther on lay a wide river mouth bordered by many palm trees and this was entered on the chart as *Fiume de la Palme*; very soon the Portuguese began to send small ships seventy miles up this river for trade with the Bulloms and, although the texts are not very precise at this point, such traffic in boats of twenty tons or more suggests that this river mouth was what today we call Shebar Strait and the river is the Waanje. Next in their path lay the Sulima river which the explorers called *Rio di li Fuimi* because, sailing by in September they must have seen the smoke from the rice farms being 'brushed' in the thick forest and so christened the river the river of Smoke. The Kife river they called *Rio das Galinhas*, for here one might buy fresh fowls. To the south they came to a long cape and above it a high mountain so they named the place *Capo del Monte* or, as we say now, Cape Mount. A few miles to the west lay a river whose shore was a favourite resort of monkeys, hence what we know as the Mano the Portuguese called the river of Monkeys—*Rio dos Monos*—although, said Pereira, other nations had different names for it. Local knowledge of that kind was not available to the very first explorers, but very shortly Portuguese traders settled in the country and by questioning them Pereira was able to discover a little more about the coast. He speaks of a river which he calls the *Ganboas* and says that he has been told that it lay some miles east of the Banana Islands and that small ships might sail one league upstream to a place called *Harhouche* where they could obtain small quantities of gold and slaves. This river is the modern Gbagbai, but *Harhouche* has defied identification. Similarly, he learnt that trade was conducted some seventy miles up-river from the modern Shebar by ships of under thirty-five tons which called at a town called *Quimanora*. It was a large town and the inhabitants were especially keen to buy tin or pewter. This was the modern Mano Bonjema, on the river Waanje, in Krim country—*Quimanora* being a corruption of Krim Mano. Mano

8

Bonjema and Matru are the only large towns in that area today which may be reached by water, but only Mano Bonjema has a deep channel navigable all the year round.

By the end of the century the coast was well charted and Alvares d'Almada, a Portuguese from Santiago, Cape Verde, writing in 1594, omitted the usual dull navigational aids which form the greater part of earlier Portuguese accounts. He wanted to encourage his countrymen to colonise Sierra Leone and so he wrote what was virtually a handbook describing the hospitality of the inhabitants, their history, customs and secret societies and the richness of the land in general:

Each village possesses its court of justice. This is a large house with an adjoining circular porch, called *funco*;* on a raised platform is seated the chief with his councillors on either side and a little below him. Under the porch, whose ceiling and floor are covered with finely woven coloured mats, is a sort of tribunal for the audience. The plaintiffs come forward, each accompanied by an advocate known as *Arões*. These lawyers, when they appear in court, deck themselves ingeniously with plumes and bells, and have their faces covered with grotesque masks, for they say that thus disguised they feel more at ease to speak boldly in front of their chief. They also carry lances on which they lean as they talk. Each one speaks in turn, until the arguments of one outweigh those of the other. The case is discussed in secret by the chief and his councillors (chosen from among the *solategi*),† and when the verdict is rendered the sentence, whatever it be, must be carried out on the spot; thus fines must be paid in full before the court adjourns. Sorcerers are condemned to death, beheaded and their bodies thrown outside the village to be eaten by wild animals. Those condemned to death for other reasons are offered for sale; whoever pays the price, five or six gold crusados, acquires the right of life and death over the culprit.

Rulers are chosen by the elders strictly according to lineage. At the death of a ruler, the funeral rites once over, a group of elders rush into the house of his successor, bind him, and take him to his future residence. Here they set about buffeting for a while; then all around keeping the strictest silence they untie him. They bathe him, clothe him as befits his new dignity, and lead him to the court-house (which is called the *funco* and is near the chief's compound) where all the nobles are gathered. One of the eldest *solategi*, or nobles, proclaims that he has been chosen to rule in the place of his father or of his brother as the case may be. The speaker goes on to say that if a short while ago some of his subjects did not hesitate to behave towards their new ruler exactly as tradition

* Modern Temne for a rice store.  † ? modern *santigi*.

9

demanded it was only to impress upon him how it behoved him too to maintain tradition in the future, to mete out punishment, and—no less important—to reward faithful service without regard to person. Like a sceptre a weapon called *Queto* is placed in his hand; the same weapon is used to behead criminals.* Rulers are held in great veneration by all their subjects.

*Solategi* are named on merit by the ruler. An assembly being convoked in the court of justice, or *funco*, the candidate is led in and seated on a wooden stool. The pluck of a goat is brought, and with this the ruler strikes the cheeks of the new *solategi* until his face and chest are smeared with blood. Rice-flour is then sprinkled on him and to end the ceremony the ruler places a red cap on his head. *Solategi* act as advisers to the ruler. When called upon to take an active part in a court case they are entitled to a quota of the fines imposed. They retain all their privileges even when in another ruler's domains.

The common people are terror-stricken by the belief in a 'demon' called Contuberia† which is supposed to visit their villages. His visits are always announced, and all are forewarned to stay indoors as long as he is heard to roam about. This demon is none other than a group of *solategi*, who all quite naked with the ruler in their midst disport themselves. By blowing on a wooden instrument they sound a loud blast, and with the aid of sticks and bells create a pandemonium. Should but a dog bark or any other animal be heard from within a house, the occupants are made to throw out the animal immediately, to be killed on the spot. Should a person inadvertently pass the streets, only the intervention of the ruler can save him from being beaten to death; and that by casting on the person's head his own cap. Such a person becomes automatically a *solategi*, and a member of the society.

All young maidens are made to pass a period of a year or more in seclusion in a large house set away from the others, and guarded by an elderly noble of good repute, who also instructs them. Parents supply food, but may not see their children nor talk to them. While in seclusion the girls are known as *menda*,‡ they are given new names, and finally when they leave they come out dressed in all their fineries, and in procession go through the village on to the dancing ring. Here they give a display of dancing to the accompaniment of musical instruments called *bombalo*§ of various sizes played in unison. Parents come to admire their

---

* If Fernandes was correct, this custom refers to the Bulloms because the Temnes exacted no death penalty. See p. 4 above.

† Fernandes also mentions this: 'There are certain houses or churches for idols where women never enter; some call these *baa*, others *piçaa*, and others *cõ tuberia*...the women's idol is called *pere*.'

‡ *toma ra-Mena* = dance of women with white caps.[11]

§ Cf. Temne: *ta-maboro*.

children, and young men on this occasion declare their choice of a
future bride, offering a token-gift to her parents, and something also
to the old man who served as their guardian during the period of
instruction.

This people bury their dead within their houses, and they bury them
with such gold ornaments as they are wont to carry: in their ears,
around the arms, and through the nose. Their ear-rings or *ma-suko*
weigh up to thirty crusados [approx. 3·5 gr.]. The weeping which follows
varies according to the status of the deceased; and an important part of
post-funeral duties is reserved for feasting. Rulers are buried along the
foot-path outside of the village, and the reason given for this is that
having administered justice they should be buried where all can see.
A hut is later erected over the grave. These Africans practice circumcision.[12]

By now, much to d'Almada's disappointment, Sierra Leone was
being neglected by his countrymen. There were several reasons
for this. First, until 1480 the Castilians, not yet united with their
neighbours to form what was soon to be the new nation of Spain,
had also claimed the Portuguese possessions in Africa. In this
quite unfounded demand they were encouraged by the Dutch, and
many of their pilots were of that nationality. But these enterprises were directed mainly against Senegambia and, especially,
the gold trade of Elmina, so that Sierra Leone tended to be ignored.
Although the Portuguese began to build a fort on the Sierra Leone
river about the year 1482, it was soon demolished, and when India
and Brazil were discovered the Portuguese government tended to
ignore this country in favour of the richer lands of the New World
and the Far East; what trade there was with Sierra Leone was
centred upon Santiago, the largest of the Cape Verde Islands,
although a flourishing settlement grew up about 1470 at Cacheo
which, being to the windward of Sierra Leone, was advantageously
placed for trading here, to the subsequent embarrassment of
the English: 'Ye Cacheo Trade to Serri-liona will be lost if the
Portugueezes Company continues', wrote Zachary Rogers, factor
to the Royal African Company, in 1682 to his directors in London.[13]

Secondly, the Portuguese government leased commercial rights
along the coast to official contractors. (These leases usually began
on 24 June, the end of the financial half-year in Portugal, although
some started on 1 January.) The contractors were not always
Portuguese; many were Jews, some were Spanish, others Italian.

The coast was divided into 'Trades', or districts; the Trade of Sierra Leone was one of the five sub-divisions of what was known as Upper Guinea, so that the richer countries to the north tended to cast Sierra Leone into obscurity. In 1510 this Trade was let for three years for a payment of 1,616,000 reis.

A third reason for the eclipse of Sierra Leone was smuggling which was almost universal, and the many efforts made to prevent this, all without success. For example, ship's captains were ordered to sail direct from Cape Verde to their destination without trading on their own account *en route*. Merchants of Santiago were forbidden to sell anything on the coast except what the islands of Cape Verde themselves produced, so that they should not compete with Portuguese home products; trade between Cape Verde and Sierra Leone was strictly forbidden at one time. Mainly the Portuguese brought with them for trade brass bowls—often of the kind used by barbers, who were surgeons in those days and used them for blood-letting*—linen, cotton goods, red cloth and cornelian—which is a semi-transparent reddish stone often used in modern signet rings.

Obviously, apart from official contractors and their agents, there were many other resident Portuguese, renegades called *tangomoas*† not trusted by their own countrymen. Often they lived several miles inland, intermarrying with their neighbours, trading without a licence, learning the local language, and acting as interpreters and agents for any Europeans who would pay them enough. D'Almada describes how they actually helped French and English interlopers to appropriate the Portuguese trade. Many became rich and in 1513 we hear how 'certain passengers who went to Serra Leoa and lived amongst the negroes' had bribed Gonçalo Lopez, Customs Officer for Guinea, to allow them to remain. Two years later two people were fined 8000 reis 'as penalties for going to Serra'.[14] Altogether their influence was much greater on the coast after a few years than that of the official Portuguese.

Finally, by about 1560 events in Europe and Sierra Leone had combined to increase the hostility of other nations to the Portuguese here and to depress ordinary trade. The religious wars in

---

* It is possible that brass reached West Africa quite early by an overland route, and it was probably in Nigeria, at least, before the Portuguese came.

† Fernandes tells of a Temne idol called *Tschyntrchin*—by other writers called *chinchin, china*—whose priests were called *tangomas*. There is possibly a connection between these two words.

France and the Reformation in England enabled French and English privateers to add religion as well as the argument of force to their requests for a share in the African trade. John Hawkins now inaugurated the transatlantic slave-trade which quickly made him the richest man in England; soon others began to follow him, not only in England, but also in the Netherlands when the Dutch began to break into the Spanish and Portuguese monopoly in South America; for this purpose they established bases in the Gallinas and at Cape Mount in the seventeenth century. Moreover, there arrived in Sierra Leone, as we shall see elsewhere, invaders who ravaged the coastal belt for three years. About 1570 they settled down to an uneasy period of armed truce which lasted for nearly one hundred years. Such wars naturally curtailed ordinary trade, but both invader and vanquished regularly sold their captives into slavery with the Europeans. Even so, the coast of Sierra Leone was never a principal source of slaves; as one Englishman wrote towards the end of the century: '...this place is the last and most comodious for a merchaunt to provide himself in before he goe over with the Indies when he hathe his complement of negros'.[15] Consequently, hindered by official restrictions, undercut by rival European traders as well as by their own *tangomoas*, and with little hope of big wholesale purchases, the Portuguese began to neglect this country, and D'Almada, when he returned from Sierra Leone, did his best to convince his government of the folly of this state of affairs:

So abundant are the natural products of this land [i.e. Sierra Leone] that it is difficult to mention any one thing that is lacking, blessed as it is with all kinds of food, fine rivers, fruit trees such as oranges, lemon and lime, also sugar-cane, palm trees in plenty and timber of good quality. Should a colony be established here it might well equal Brazil in profits; for if in Brazil the main trade is sugar and cotton, here besides cotton one has: ivory, wax, gold, amber, and pepper whilst it would be quite easy to set up sugar mills; iron and wood being at hand and labour far from scarce.

A colony here would be of particular interest to His Majesty because ships bound for India would find an ideal winter shelter in the river Mitombo, where they could furnish themselves with all things necessary for the rest of the voyage. Indeed who can predict all the benefits that would accrue from a colony such as this? I for my part can testify that many people from the island of Santiago—to which I too belong—have declared that much as they are attached to this island they would gladly migrate to Sierra Leone, and only to Sierra Leone, at His Majesty's command. Fourteen years ago [i.e. 1580] this people deputed me to treat with His Majesty about their migration to Sierra Leone. Dr Gaspar d'Andrade was then governor of Santiago and I having broached the subject with him in secret he pointed out that I would best serve the interests of His Majesty by staying on the island, and argued that were we to go ahead with the project, it would ultimately bring about the complete abandonment of Santiago. Alas! the good things of this land, at such a convenient distance from Lisbon; merely fifteen to twenty days, are slipping through our fingers, while the French and the English are gradually monopolising the trade. It grieves my heart to see us let go by such a safe investment....Christendom would be bound to gain from a settlement in this region, in as much as the losses of our Holy Faith in Europe [i.e. the European Reformation in religion] would be compensated for by conversions among these nations, not to mention the riches which would flow into His Majesty's Treasury.[16]

Despite the jealousy of the merchants at Cape Verde, d'Almada's glowing account was in a certain measure responsible for the despatch by King Philip III of Spain of Sierra Leone's first resident Christian missionary. Balthazar Barreira, a Jesuit and a personal friend of King Philip, landed on the Sierra Leone peninsula on 25 September 1605. Despite his age—he was born in 1538—he set himself the arduous task of converting as many as he could to his own faith. When he left four years later he had baptised several chiefs, acquired land at the mouth of the Sierra Leone river on which it was proposed to build a fort, and constructed several churches made of wood. His first impression—which he has left for us in two memorable letters published originally in his own lifetime—was one of horror at the state of his countrymen: 'The Portugals in these parts lived liker Ethnikes [i.e. heathens] then Christians, neither having sacraments nor the Word of God in many years past, so that they had almost quite forgotten them.... I confessed some Portugals here which in ten, twentie, thirtie yeeres had never been Confessed....'[17] Yet every Portuguese fleet carried one or more priests and so one must conclude that for the previous thirty years few, if any, official ships had called at Sierra Leone. In 1664 Coelho, who had twenty-three years' experience as a merchant on this coast, wrote of the Portuguese in general: 'We who make the voyage to Sierra Leone never used to go except in launches, starting from the port of Barranceira*.'[18] New routes

* Balansera is on the river Great Scarcies.

from Europe which avoided this part of the coast were now required because trade was directed, as d'Almada says, towards the Indies and South America. Also shipwreck and starvation had attended many approaching the West African shore too closely, for currents were strong and the winds uncertain. A Dutch account of 1600 says:

But they that desire...to goe right forth, to the Gold Coast of Myna, hold their course by the Ilands of Canaria, and sayle Southward, untill they have past by the Ilands of Cape Verde, leaving them commonly on Bagh-boord,* or as the wind serveth them, being under ten, nine or eight degrees,† then they begin to make towards the Land, and to hold their course South and by East...to seeke to get above all Bassis‡ and shallowes...; for they that fall upon Saint Annes shallowes, lying under sixe degrees,§ have much labour and pain before they can get off them again;...for in one place you shall have three fathome deepe, and then againe ten fathome, and then againe, the streame drives you still to Land, so that many men by meanes of their negligence know not what to do....Now, sayling further, and comming under seven and sixe degrees, there commonly you find calmes, specially...in Aprill, May, and June, whereof men are in great feare. It fell out so with us, that beeing under those highthes, we were twentie dayes driving in a calme, without winning any great highth, and that which we wonne with the Current, the next day we lost it againe with a contrary wind; so that you must beware of the Land in any hand, specially, those that goe to Brasilia....I once found a ship thereabouts, which...beeing not able to fall into his right course, hee was constrayned to leave it, and in stead of sayling to Brasilia, he was forced to goe to Saint Thomas, so that under those highthes, you can doe nothing with the wind, but onely by the current, which alwaies runnes East with the bough.

They that sayle to East India, also shunne this calme as much as possible.[19]...

On such long voyages, Sierra Leone was regarded rather as a place of refuge than as a natural port of call. The fine harbour and convenient watering-place at King Jimmy were of more interest to the larger expeditions sent out by the joint-stock companies of this time than were the relatively small returns to be made by local trade; this was left to the individual interloper.

* I.e. to port.                          † I.e. of latitude.
‡ I.e. shoals; a word derived from the Portuguese.
§ This is a miscalculation; the shoals of St Anne lie between 7 and 8 degrees. At the end of the seventeenth century Barbot complained of the inaccuracy of Dutch maps—see p. 21 below.

The English had begun a little earlier than the Dutch to seek an entrée into the trade with the Far East and the New World. For instance, Sir Francis Drake called at the Sierra Leone river in 1580 for water on his way back to England after sailing round the world; whilst the casks were being filled he carved his name on a rock near the watering-place. In 1582 Edward Fenton spent several weeks in the river on his way to Brazil. Like many others, he missed his landfall altogether and ran on to Cape Mount; beating to windward again, he fell upon the shoals of St Anne before he arrived in the estuary at dusk on 9 August. The next morning, he says:

I wente...in my Pynnasse, as well to view the wateringe place, as speciallie to sownde, for the bringinge in saffe into harbour of our Shipps and, a Longe the Sowtherlie shoore of Sereliona within a quarter of a mile founde, 7, 8, 9, 10, 15- and 16 fathoms, In the after-noone, waighed Ancour and cam into harbour...in good saffetie and Roode in 10 fathom water within fawconett* shott of the Wateringe place....

The xvii^th daie, I wente to fishe. and into a Baye, where growes upon trees infinitt nombers of Oysters...which in respect of the stroungness and plentie of oysters, I named it Oyster Baye.

Satterdaye The xviii^th daie, abowte xi of the Clock in the forenone we discovered a Canow cominge from theast parte of the river, which showinge a desier of conferrence. by a flagge of Truce. We admitted therof with the like signe from my Shipp, Wheruppon they cam aborde beinge iii Portingalls havinge traffique in this River for Negroes, Rize and Oliphante teethe; the only traffique (as they informed me) they have in thies partes: And being robbed (as they said) of their Carvell iii or iiii monthes before by certein frenche men, repaired to us for succour of some Barke or Pynnasse....The Barke Elizabeth beinge then to be Caste...as thought insufficiente to be carried or do further service, but to be burned there in harbour: we entred some conferrence with theim a farr of for the byinge of the Barke, for the which they offred 60 bushells Rize and 400 weight of Oliphante teethe....[20]

A certain class of Portuguese renegade had always traded with his country's enemies, but now that Portugal had become part of the Spanish empire there was an added incentive. These Portuguese told Fenton that Tagrin was the chief town on the north side of the river and that King Farma's capital was 'Carrnorre'† which was

* A type of gun.       † ? Carracoré.

'stronglie fortified with tymber'. The natural products of Guinea
were gold, pepper, ivory and slaves. Sierra Leone provided gold
ornaments—the invaders who came to this country in the 1560's
from the south specialised in digging up the graves of those they
had conquered because it was customary to bury important persons
with jewellery—but because there were no mines these were soon
exhausted. Pepper, after the more piquant Indian variety became
popular, was still bought but only in small quantities. The French
specialised for a short time in this trade though by the end of the
sixteenth century it was no longer plentiful in Sierra Leone.[21]
Ivory too became rare in the seventeenth century because of the
wanton slaughter of the elephant herds; in 1678 the English factor
for the Royal African Company at Bunce said: 'I never knew a
Ton of Teeth brought down this River in my life.' This meant
that slaves and, as a subsidiary, the kola-nut offered the only
profitable return—although small quantities of soap and other
products of the oil-palm were also taken out. Slavery was never a
big trade here as it was elsewhere on the coast; the Portuguese
bought especially kola-nuts, mainly in the basin of the Great
Scarcies, which they found valuable when buying slaves further
north, but they kept this secret well into the seventeenth century.
The rice which Fenton speaks of is interesting, because this is the
first hint of any large-scale production that we have and it is likely
that the Portuguese had by now imported improved strains from
the Far East.

Fenton was able to read Drake's name at the watering-place and
he decided to go one better by fixing there a copper plate inscribed
with his crest, his motto of 'rien sans Dieu', his initials and the
words:

> Edwardus Fenton armiger pro
> Elizabetham reginam Angliae, classi
> praepositus ei quae regiones
> Chinensem et Cathaiam disco-
> -operire destinata est. August 26 1582.*

In 1600 the English still had very little idea of the coast; captains
often disagreed as to where water might be found and whether

---

* 'Edward Fenton Esquire, appointed by Queen Elizabeth of England to
command the fleet sent to discover the lands of China and Cathay.' In fact
Fenton disobeyed his instructions and sailed for Brazil looking for private
plunder.[22]

Sierra Leone—by which they meant only the Sierra Leone river—
was a suitable port of call:

Mr Hawkins told that Sir Francis Drake even in this monethe and
within 2 dayes of this tyme watered at ye Serra Liona and found no
annoyance at all, Mr Wood sayd that it was a villanows place for while
Sir Francis dyd ther stay to water they set on ye potage pot with ryse
every meale. Mr Hawkins added that his uncle had commended this
place unto hym, the generall replyed that hear his uncle had lost many
men.*

The ordinary seaman having no such worries exercised his super-
stition; Ned Stocks, Fenton's chart draughtsman, frightened his
messmates by telling: 'How ye lions in Affryk kept 100 together in
a schole and that they had fyrst spoyled and did now keepe 2
villages, and that yf a lyon be hedged abowt with thorns he wil
rather be taken than pryck his foote to come away....'†

In 1607 William Keeling, bound from England with three ships
to the East Indies, was driven by storms just south of the equator
to turn for home, but he was too short of water to be able to make
the whole journey without a fresh supply. Some argument followed
as to where they had best put in until Keeling, having presumably
no map, produced Hakluyt's *Voyages* from his cabin and convinced
his officers that Sierra Leone would provide the nearest watering-
place. This book, it was said at the time, saved Keeling's owners
£20,000. The ships arrived in the river on 5 August and left on
14 September, yet, although they bought one small gold ear-ring
and a half-moon of gold, together worth less than £1, several
thousand lemons as an anti-scorbutic, and an elephant's tusk
weighing sixty-three pounds, they met no other ships in the river
and seem to have encountered no European inhabitants. But
Barreira and those Portuguese he had confessed were in the
neighbourhood at the time; presumably they were lying low, uncertain of the English fleet's intentions. The English had not come
for trade and so did not explore the river when they might have
found the Portuguese settlements. Following what was by now
almost a tradition they carved their names by the watering-place
where they read the names of 'Sir Francis Drake, which had bin

---

* Thomas Wood, one of Fenton's pilots, had sailed with Drake; there were
about twelve of Drake's men in this expedition including William Hawkins,
nephew of John Hawkins, who was one of Fenton's lieutenants.[23]
† Stocks died at Cape Mount.[24]

ther seven and twentie yeeres before, Thomas Candissh [i.e. Cavendish], Captaine Lister with others'.

Bartholomew André, an influential Portuguese merchant on the river at this time, may well have watched the English from the woods. He had an extensive trade up and down the coast and on 20 February 1606 had written to his king a long letter describing the commercial possibilities of this country: 'Until now I have never told Your Majesty what I do here because none who have visited me in the past have ever come to settle; but God has sent his priests of the Company of Jesus*...and seeing how well they have begun...and taking into consideration the advantages of having this country settled by Your Majesty's subjects, I now take a different view of the situation.'[25] It is evident, from his opening remarks, that André was no renegade to trade with his country's enemies as had those who bought a boat from Fenton nearly twenty-five years before. He continues:

One may reach this country in twenty days or less...there is much fine gold here and Your Majesty's subjects buy it yearly in the form of bangles, ear-rings and rings for the nose. Much more could be bought if the nobles did not collect it so that it might be buried with them.... A reliable Fleming confessed to me that ships from Holland alone carry 2,000 pounds weight a year from this coast, besides what is taken secretly.... To facilitate this trade the Hollanders wanted to build a fort and trading station in the narrow entrance to the Sierra Leone River but...the King of Sierra Leone...immediately drove them away....

I cannot say whether there is any silver in these parts but it is rumoured that on the River Nuno not far from here where the Portuguese go to load dyes there was a man called Araújo, a goldsmith who found veins along the river which he smelted in the forest so as not to be seen by the Africans. He made bracelets which he sold to the Negros but, because he was afraid...that they would kill him, he went to the Rio Grande....

To speak particularly of Sierra Leone...there is sugar cane...cotton grows well and the timber is good so that we can build as many ships as we need. There are also trees from which we gather tow for caulking ships' bottoms; it is much superior to ours because it stays green and does not rot; from this same tree we make fuses.... There are also various types of gum...which we use for painting ships,...many trees from the fruit of which oil is taken; one kind is bitter and serves as pitch and another is edible...on the coast...much redwood for dye.... If there is no abundance of cattle...it is not because they cannot

* I.e. Father Barreira and others.

flourish here as well as...elsewhere in Guinea...but because the Negros have no interest in cattle rearing. Indeed they do not sow enough rice to last them the whole year.[26]

In spite of André's optimism no settlement was made, although a ship was sent out with builders and masons to erect a fort near the mouth of the river; this was destroyed by a French ship when it was scarcely begun and the scheme was abandoned. About sixty years later came Jean Barbot, Agent General of the French Royal Company of Africa in Paris, but later, for religious reasons, a refugee in England: he wrote at length of the Sierra Leone estuary, but he warned his readers that the spring at the watering-place was not always healthy:

There is a tradition, that this tract of land from cape Verga to the north-side of the Sierra Leona river, which is the utmost extent of Nigritia to the southward, was formerly subject to a king called Fatima, residing up the inland, and ruling over several petty kings his vassals and tributaries; among whom were Temsila, Teemserta and one Don Miguel, converted to Christianity, and baptised by a Portuguese jesuit missioner, called Barreira, about the year 1607.*

The tide at sea from cape Verde to that of Tagrin, along the coast of Nigritia, sets N.W. and S.E. as in the British channel.

What I am to speak of in the next place relates to the kingdom of Sierra Leona, where Guinea, properly so called, commences some leagues to the northward of that river....

What I shall say of the product of the land, manners of the natives and religion profess'd in the country of Sierra Leona, may be applied in all those particulars to the territories and inhabitants of that part... lying betwixt cape Verga and the river Mitomba, or of Sierra Leona, which shall conclude this book of the coasts of North Guinea.

The north parts of this river Mitomba, from the point of the bay or mouth westward, and up the bank, are subject to two petty kings, to him of Bourre on the south, and to him of Boulm to the north; this last in my time was call'd Antonio Bombo. The former commonly resides at the village Bourre, which consists of about three hundred huts or cabbins, and five hundred inhabitants, besides women and children.

The Portuguese missionaries formerly made some converts at Boulm, among whom was the king; and they still continue to send missionaries thither, from time to time. The word Boulm, in the language of the country, signifies low-land; and others pronounce it Bolem and Bouloun. The coast, on the side of Boulm, is low and flat, in comparison of the

* See ch. IV below.

opposite shore of Bourre or Timna; near which are those famous mountains of Sierra Leona, being a long ridge, and reckon'd the highest of either North or South Guinea, except those of Amboses in the gulph or bight. There are so many caves and dens about these mountains, that when a single gun is fired aboard a ship in the bay, the echo is so often and so distinctly repeated, as makes it sound to persons at a distance like the report of several guns, the clap being so loud and smart, which was often pleasant to me to hear; whereas, on the contrary, it was dreadful in thundering weather, the echo repeating each clap of thunder with as much force as the real; insomuch that till us'd to it, not only I, but all the company aboard, did quake at the horrid rattling noise breaking forth from so many parts, thunder being here very frequent, and extraordinary fierce. Hence the Portugueses call them Montes Claros, that is, mountains that have a clear sound or echo.

Not far from these mountains there runs out into the sea westward a hilly point, much lower than those hills, forming almost a peninsula, over which the Blacks carry their canoos on their shoulders, when they design to launch out to sea, because it saves much trouble of rowing round from the bay thither. This point is call'd Cabo Ledo or Tagrin, and by others Tagaraim, lying exactly in 8 deg. 30 min. of north latitude, according to our exact observation;* contrary to all the Dutch maps, which are faulty in this particular of latitudes all along the coast of this part of Guinea, laying down all the coasts thirty degrees† more northerly than they really are. These mistakes ought to be carefully observ'd by Europeans trading along the coast of Nigritia, and part of those of Guinea properly so call'd, accounting every port, cape and river half a degree nearer to the north than the Dutch maps represent it: for the over-shooting of any port or place there, is of great consequence, it being no easy matter to recover the same by plying to the windward....‡

The river of Sierra Leona runs down from a great way up the inland. A certain Black would needs persuade me, that the source of it is in Barbary....Besides, it is reasonable to suppose, that the river of Sierra Leona has a communication up the country with other rivers, or with some branches of the Niger....§

This river has several small islands and rocks at the entrance into the bay, which look like hay-reeks. The chief of them are the islands Cogu, Tasso and Bences; on the last whereof the English have erected a small fort, which has nothing considerable but the advantage of the situation,

---

* This is correct.     † He means minutes, not degrees.

‡ In August 1615 two Dutch ships under Cornelius Schouten had in fact overshot the river Sierra Leone, finding themselves at the Banana Islands—which they called the Islands of Madrabomba—then uninhabited; an error, as Barbot rightly says, of half a degree.

§ The exact course of the Niger was not discovered until 1830.

on a steep rock, of difficult access, which is only up a sort of stairs cut in the rock, and is a store-house for the royal African company....

About four leagues from the watering-place stands the village Bagos, close to a little wood; and to the eastward of it is Tomby, where is a curious prospect, and before it the English ships usually ride; the island Tasso appearing from thence at a great distance, and looking like firm land....

The Portugueses have several small settlements in this country, particularly one near Dondermuch, or Domdomuch;* but very little correspondence with the English of Bence island, being jealous of them in point of trade....

The country all along the sides of the river Mitomba is well peopled, and has many hamlets and villages. On the north side of the bay, being the coast of Boulm, are three villages; which are those of Binque, Tinguam, and of Young Captain Lewis.† The soil is very fertile, and therefore the Blacks have added to the name of Boulm, signifying lowland, that of Berre, which imports good; and thus Boulm Berre denotes good low-land.

The king of Boulm favours the English more than either the Portugueses, French or Dutch; though there are many of the first who live dispers'd up and down this country.

The Blacks of Timna are much in the French interest....

The village of John Thomas, who is governor of that part of the country, stands in the wood, E.N.E. from the place by the French call'd La Fontaine de la France, consisting but of a few huts, built round, much like those described at Gamboa.

The bay of France, where this fountain or spring of fresh water rises, is about six leagues up the river from cape Tagrin, and easily known by the fine bright colour of the sandy shore, looking at a distance like a large spread sail of a ship. The strand there is clear from rocks, which renders the access easy for boats and sloops to take in fresh water. At a few paces from the sea is that curious fountain, the best and easiest to come at of any in all Guinea, the source of it is in the very midst of the mountains of Timna, stretching out about fifteen leagues in a long ridge, and not to be come at without great danger, as well for the many tygers and lions living on them, as for the crocodiles resorting thither. Some persons who would have made a farther discovery of the country, could not go above two English miles along the channel of one of the springs, not daring to venture any farther, by reason of the dismal and dreadful prospect they saw before them.

* Barbot's map places this on the south shore opposite Bunce Island; probably the modern Gondama, on Waterloo Creek.

† I.e. running from west to east; the last being near the modern Tagrin Point. Binque is the modern Benke.

The fresh waters fall down from the high hills, making several cascades among the rocks, with a mighty noise, sounding the louder in that profound silence which reigns in the forest; then running into a sort of pond, overflow and spread about the sandy shore, where they gather again into a basin, or cavity, at the foot of the hills; which not being able to contain the vast quantity of water continually flowing in, it runs over upon the sands again, and thence at last mixes with the sea-water. This, in my opinion, is one of the most delightful places in all Guinea; the basin which receives this delicate fresh water being all incompass'd with tall ever-green trees, making a delightful shade in the most excessive heat of the day; and the very rocks standing about it, at a small distance from each other, do no less contribute to beautify that piece of lanskip, and add to the pleasure of the place. I us'd, whilst there, to take the advantage of having my dinner and supper carry'd thither frequently. Here a large ship's crew may easily fill an hundred casks of water in a day.

As sweet and fresh as this water is, it must be observed, that it has an ill effect upon the sailors, if taken in the beginning of the rainy season, but more especially in April, because the violent heats of the summer having corrupted the earth, and kill'd abundance of venomous creatures, the violent rains which ensue, occasion mighty floods, and these wash down all that poisonous matter into the springs and channels of this fountain, and consequently give a malignity to the water. This has been experimentally found by many to their cost; but it happens only in the winter, or rainy season. It is also requisite to be sparing in eating of the fruit of this country, and to avoid drinking of the water to excess, because it causes a sort of pestilential distemper, which is almost certain death, at least very few escape.

The duty for liberty of watering and wooding here, is not above the value of four French crowns, in several small wares and toys, paid to captain John Thomas, the chief commander there.

The wooding-place is about an hundred paces N.E. from the fountain, or else to the eastward, as the Black commander thinks fit. The felling of wood here is very laborious, the trees being close together, and linked from top to bottom with a sort of creepers, by the French called Lianes; otherwise the wooding would be easy, the carriage to the water-side being short.... These people make very curious mats of rushes, and other weeds, and dye them of several colours, which are much valued by Europeans. On these mats the Blacks lie at night. It is questioned whether the Portugueses taught them, or they the Portugueses, to make these mats.[27]

Barbot also wrote of the district just south of Sierra Leone. It will be noticed that the goods he recommends for barter are much the same as the Portuguese had brought two hundred years before:

Rio Cerbera or Sherbro is a large river coming from very far up the inland to the sea, through the country of the Boulm-Monou, a land full of morasses and swampy grounds, and loseth itself in the ocean near Cerbera island: some call it Madre-Bombe; others, Rio Selbore; others, Rio das Palmas, from the Portugueses; from whom perhaps may have been derived the other name of Cerbera, given it by some.*

This river is very large and navigable for ships of burden for twenty leagues up to the town of Baga, belonging to the prince of Boulm; and for brigantines and sloops of seventy or eighty tuns, drawing but seven feet and an half water, to thirty miles above Kedham or Kidham, which is up the river two hundred and fifty English miles,† though very difficult to sail up, for the prodigious thickness of rushes, with which the banks are covered; being in some places so very narrow, that the channel is choked up with them on either side, and must of necessity be sounded all along with poles; and still grows shallower and shallower upwards, there being scarce ten, or nine feet water in many places in April and May, the fittest time for the voyage up the river to trade for camwood, which is there extraordinary plentiful and cheap....

It is well inhabited all along the banks, and the natives are very civil people....

The English have a factory at Bagos or Baga, about twenty leagues up the river on the North side of it....

The country is very fertile in rice, and abounds in all the same kinds of plants and animals I mentioned to be in the island of Cerbera and adjacent places,‡ and is also very populous.

The Blacks commonly wear a frock of striped callico, as do those in Cerbera island, having all the same customs and manners.

The town is behind a large wood, and cannot be seen from the road; but the inhabitants come out in canoos about ships riding there, and bring plantains, palm wine, honey, rice, chickens, and sugar-canes. The town is very large and populous, but the houses very mean and low, except a great one standing in the middle of the town, where the principal Negroes make their assemblies and receive strangers.

---

* Elsewhere Barbot says: 'The English call it Sherbro, the Dutch, St Anna or Massa-quoja; the Portugueses, Farulha and Farelloens; and the French, Cerbera.'

† A great exaggeration.

‡ I.e. 'rice, maiz, ignames, bananas, potatoes, Indian figs, ananas, citrons, oranges, pompions, water melons, and the fruit Cola, by the English called Col, poultry in plenty, and breedeth great numbers of elephants, who often repair to the villages.'

The inundations of this river, at the proper seasons, contribute very much to fertilize the soil.

The proper goods to purchase the Camwood and elephants teeth in Sherbro river, are chiefly these;

Brass basons and kettles,
Pewter basons and tankards,
Iron bars,
Bugles,
Painted callicoes,
Guinea stuffs or cloths,
Holland linen or cloth,
Muskets, powder, and ball.

A ship may in two months time, out and home, purchase here fifty tun of Cam-wood, and four tun of elephants teeth, or more.

The Cam-wood is a much better sort of red wood for dyers use, than the Brazil, and accounted the best in all Guinea. It will serve seven times over, and the last time is still effectual.

From the south point of Rio Cerbera to that of Galinhas, the coast stretches E.S.E. eleven leagues, flat, low, swampy and marshy land, all over cover'd with trees, and inhabited.

Rio de Galinhas, by the natives call'd Maqualbary, has its source in the lands of Hondo....

The Europeans trade in it, and carry thence dry hides and elephants teeth, which are brought down the river from Hondo and Karoodoboe-Monou. This last country is about forty-five leagues from the sea-coast, a crafty bold nation, perpetually at war with their neighbours at the east, the Hondoes; and both depend on the king of Quoja, who resides at cape Monte.[28]

This long and accurate account by a Frenchman represents the contemporary change in the balance of power along the coast. Barbot copied much of his description from Dapper, a Dutch surgeon who wrote in 1666 during the time of the Dutch ascendancy which followed the decline of Portugal.* Now the initiative had fallen to the French and English; William Bosman, chief

---

* Dapper is a mine of information and as such represents almost the last of the old school of writers. Typically, John Ogilby who copied him into English 'augmented with observations' is one of the few writers at any time to mention rock gongs in Sierra Leone; he says: 'To the South end of Serra Lions, near the Islands Banannes, appears to Ships sailing by, a very high Mount...called Machamala...the skirts of whose overshooting Edges...which hang like... Penthouses...with the Points towards the ground within 4 or 5 feet, like Isicles from the Eaves of a house,...when struck, yield a pleasant twang like the strings of an Instrument.'[29]

factor for the Dutch at Elmina, speaking of the district in the south of Sierra Leone in 1700, wrote of the difficulties of trading there because of being outnumbered by hostile English merchants:

*Rio Sestre* is a very fine and pleasant River...but what adds to the charms of this river...is the multitude of villages along its banks; amongst which is that of the King, situated about three miles up the river and composed of about thirty houses....

These countries seem to live in perfect peace with other countries; for all hereabouts we hear of no other wars than a few skirmishes which formerly happened with the inland *Negroes*....

This, Sir, is all I have to say concerning *Rio Sestre*, which I should have gone further up and have more particularly visited the country, if any body had been with me to take care of our trade, or we had not been bound further; but the *English* ships generally come so thick upon this coast that without utmost diligence in my post I could not expect to do anything.[30]

In fact, as competition had increased the profits of the expanding trade upon the coast, the new interlopers had begun to make more permanent settlements; in so doing they had induced the local population to settle villages nearer the coast and navigable rivers where intercommunication was easier.* The French, first of the newcomers, built a fort on an island at the mouth of the river Senegal in 1638; this was the beginning of St Louis. The Dutch had a settlement in the Gallinas which they abandoned about 1640 when their interests took them to the East Indies; however, they kept their forts to the south which they had taken from the Portuguese, and struggled to hold on to their official monopoly until 1795 when the Dutch West Indies Company was liquidated. The Portuguese in the late seventeenth century still traded extensively in Cacheo and the Great Scarcies river; this left the English little option but to settle in the Gambia and Sierra Leone. The Royal African Company, founded in 1672, was soon established on Bunce Island in the north and in the south on York Island; simultaneously there began to appear descriptions of Africa written in English. Generally these were translations, often without acknowledgement, of works in other languages and

---

* The *Description de l'Afrique...traduite du Flamand d'O. Dapper* (Amsterdam, 1686), p. 251, said of the Sherbro river: 'Les Anglois et les Hollandois ont leurs tentes et leurs magasins dans le village de Baga, mais les Anglois sont ceux qui negotient le plus sur cette rivière.'

they add little to what we know already. The ordinary Englishman who worked in the forts and factories, or who set up on his own, was frequently illiterate and those visitors who did publish their impressions or make even manuscript notes which have survived wrote generally from a merchant's point of view. These accounts are invaluable for their descriptions of European settlements here, but they tell us almost nothing about local affairs.* In any case none of them shows the scientific curiosity—so much in advance of its time—of Fernandes, who recorded details of African societies so carefully, or of Richard Madox whose interests covered navigation, the classics, zoology and a little anthropology, or of Dapper whose stories of tribal movements were so painstakingly collected and where possible checked from earlier writers.† After Dapper there were no giants until the nineteenth century.

\* See ch. III below.  † See ch. IV below.

# CHAPTER II

# EARLY VISITORS

For nearly two thousand years, since the voyage about the year 500 B.C. of the Carthaginian Hanno who is supposed to have gazed in awe across the dark waters beneath his ship at the volcanic flames of Mount Cameroon, there was a tradition of secrecy surrounding the lesser-known parts of Africa. Living in the north, the Carthaginians guarded well the Straits of Gibraltar, allowing few to pass from the Mediterranean into the unmapped waters of the Atlantic, and they purposely excluded the Greeks and Romans from the southern Mediterranean ports. A certain Roman captain once shadowed a Carthaginian ship bound for the lead and tin mines of Brittany and Cornwall; the Carthaginian ran his ship aground and sank her, leading the Roman vessel also to destruction rather than share his secret destination with a rival. Similarly Hanno never gave any reason for his voyage to the west coast of Africa since he did not wish to have to say that he had come for trade, probably in search of gold; this would have set other rivals in the field. But it is unlikely that Hanno ever sailed even as far south as the Canary Islands. The story of his heroic voyage to the equator, which still lingers on, is, it seems, a myth invented by a later Greek author as a literary exercise and drawn from earlier writers. Sometimes—notably in the case of Herodotus—the author's sources are still recognisable. As the story unfolds it becomes more and more fantastic and words are used which no Greek writer of prose would ever employ; they have only a poetic usage. That such a fantasy should have been for so long accepted proves only that Africa remained a mystery for many centuries.

A short consideration of plain fact will show that such a voyage was at that time almost impossible. Because of the climate on the coast the only possible months for such an excursion are between March and October. It was in fact easier for a sailing ship to run from Egypt by the east coast route to the Congo than to make a voyage from Gibraltar to Senegal. This is because on the east coast the winds are more favourable and water more plentiful. Indeed, Roman coins have been found in Rhodesia, Madagascar and the

Congo where they followed the established trade route. None has been discovered in the west north of the Congo. A ship of those days could sail perhaps eighty miles a day, and because of contrary winds and currents a voyage down the west coast between March and October would require some three months on the outward passage and four for the return journey, so that Hanno probably turned for home about the middle of June. It is true that, just before they went about, the expedition found crocodiles in the rivers and that they are not found today north of the Canary Islands. But the forest then stretched further north than it does today; trees help to conserve moisture and without them the Romans could not have used North Africa—now a desert—as their granary, nor could the Carthaginians have captured elephants there to train for battle against their enemies. It was the Arabs coming from the direction of Egypt with their armies, and especially with their flocks of goats in the eleventh century A.D., who devastated the north of Africa.

Towards the end of the outward journey Hanno's men heard on shore the music of flutes, cymbals and tambourines as they lay at anchor in the dusk. The first two instruments are not now heard south of Morocco although cymbals made from copper were introduced to the countries south of the Sahara by the Arabs about 700 A.D., more than a thousand years after Hanno was dead. The description of the coast is sufficiently clear in the first few paragraphs of the account—before fantasy upsets geography—for some of the places mentioned to be identified today. These include the islands of Mogador, the Atlas Mountains and a bay, probably the Bay of Sous. If Hanno had sailed further south he could scarcely have failed to see the Canary Islands, but he never mentioned them, and our Greek story-teller had consequently never heard of them either, so that they do not appear in the account as it has come down to us today.

Finally it must be remembered that it strained even the resources of the Portuguese to reach Cape Bojador in 1434, nearly two thousand years later when they had the advantage of compass, bowsprit, rudder and several masts, improvements all developed in the thirteenth and fourteenth centuries A.D.* These early

* The bowsprit, a Roman invention revived in the thirteenth century, enabled a ship to sail closer to the wind, which would be a great help on the return voyage north. Two or more masts meant easier sailing in a beam wind and

Portuguese, sent by Prince Henry the Navigator, were just as secretive as Hanno about the real object of their exploration, for they would not admit that it was gold, not the extension of Christianity, which spurred them on in the first place. But facts betray them; Barreira, a Jesuit and their first resident missionary in Sierra Leone, did not arrive in this country until 1605, nearly one hundred and fifty years after Pedro da Sintra had mapped the Sierra Leone coast in 1462.*

Somewhere in the heart of Africa were supposed to lie huge quantities of gold; the king of the ancient state of Ghana was said to own a nugget so vast that he used it to tether his horse. Mansa Musa, king of the Mali, added to this legend when, setting out for Mecca in 1324 with the accumulated wealth of years, he arrived in Cairo with one hundred camel-loads of gold which he proceeded lightheartedly to spend. As a result, in the Mohammedan kingdoms along the Mediterranean and in the Christian kingdoms which began to emerge in Europe in the fifteenth century, plans were made to reach the source of these fabulous stories. Each nation hoped to keep the secret to itself; in Europe maps were guarded carefully and at one time only one family in Portugal, known to be loyal, was permitted to make maps for that country. When Pereira, Governor of the Portuguese castle of Elmina from 1520 to 1522, wrote an account of the west coast he was censured severely for disclosing so many nautical details; he died later in poverty, whilst his maps remained unpublished until 1892. Nevertheless, foreigners did find means of obtaining information; Portuguese pilots would sometimes desert—Hawkins usually employed such men for his voyages to this country—and sometimes charts would be captured at sea, as in 1495, when a French ship, piloted by a renegade Portuguese, captured a Portuguese vessel homeward bound from Elmina.

Such charts would be of little help today for they made great use of prominent landmarks which have long since vanished. 'This

more speed. The Portuguese carvel—built of planks laid end to end as opposed to the older overlapping clinker-built vessels—had a square stern with lateen rig (i.e. rigged with triangular sails like a modern Bullom boat, which is the direct descendant of the carvel) on a tall mast amidships and two smaller ones aft; it was much more seaworthy than anything that had gone before. For a modern account of Hanno's voyage see *Première Conférence Internationale des Africanistes de l'Ouest*, ed. R. Mauny (Dakar, 1951), vol. II, p. 144.

* Alvaro Fernandes, a Portuguese, had sighted the hills of Sierra Leone from the north in 1446.

river', wrote Pereira of some estuary in the Mellacourie area, 'has at its mouth an island and also several very tall trees towards the North West...a little farther on is a village.' Usually, the Spanish and Portuguese accounts of this part of the world are merely navigational aids provided with maps of the principal landmarks only, together with details of the shipping and personnel of their own empires; English, French and Dutch accounts are much more discursive. This is because, unlike the latter, Portuguese voyages in the fifteenth and sixteenth centuries were essentially part of a royal business run by the Portuguese royal family, whereas in England—where the least formal arrangements of any prevailed— the enterprises were undertaken by joint-stock companies respon- sible in a much less official way to their shareholders. It is true that the English companies exercised their monopolies under royal permission—there are whole volumes filled with complaints from the Portuguese ambassador in London about this royal encourage- ment—but they were not under such strong control as that demanded by the Portuguese royal house of Braganza whereby, after 1514, colonial trade was run by royal factors—*Vedores da Fazenda*—to whom individual merchants had to pay up to 30 per cent *ad valorem* on all trade abroad. Thus Portuguese accounts of the west coast were virtually government reports and as such they were couched in official language. The difference between these and the reports of English companies reflects in a way particular characteristics of the two nations which were partly the result of their respective positions upon the map of Europe. Portugal and Spain had beaten off an invader, moreover one from Africa, and in so doing had developed an absolute form of monarchy whose worth had been well proved in the struggle; naturally further expansion was left to that successful leadership. England had suffered no invasion since 1066, had no contact with Africa, and had still in the mid-fifteenth century a medieval type of kingship whose weakness was to be proved in the Wars of the Roses which ended in 1485.

Because of the way in which they developed politically, the greater part of trade from newly discovered lands fell first to the Portuguese and the Spanish and subsequently to the French, English and Dutch and to no one else in such great proportion. Even the order in which their merchant explorers sailed to this coast, became predominant, and then gave way to other European rivals reflects the sequence in which the mother countries attained national maturity at home. The banner of Islam had been carried into south-western Europe in A.D. 711 and within a few years was set over the whole Iberian peninsula as far east as the Pyrenees. This peninsula, long divided by race, government and language, soon mounted a counter-attack—Lisbon was recaptured in 1147—and by 1250 all but Granada had been reclaimed for the Catholic faith. The new Christian kingdoms of Portugal, Aragon and Castile, now united in marriage as well as arms, were forced to pursue an aggressive role or perish; choosing to fight, they quickly exercised a resolute central control over the military orders of knights and over the Church in general. The royal councils of Aragon and Castile—two States united by a marriage contract in 1469—became professional bodies, staffed by lawyers; to these were added the councils of finance, of military orders and of the Inquisition. From this there was born the mighty sixteenth-century nation of Spain; in 1492, when the Moors were expelled from Granada, Castile suddenly emerged as a world power. The Portuguese, already interested in the riches of the East, very soon turned their particular reconquest of the peninsula into a movement of expansion overseas. If a sixteenth-century writer is to be credited, they believed in the circumnavigation of Africa in ancient times, but more especially—fired still with the crusading spirit which had led them to fight for so long the heathen in Europe—they wanted to know how far south in Africa the Islamic kingdom of their enemies held sway and whether a Christian ally might be found in Prester John, whom European travellers had reached in the fourteenth century. Their first overseas possession, Ceuta, opposite Gibraltar, was occupied in 1415. The Spanish colonial territories differed from the Portuguese in that they were in the New World and that they needed settlement, not trade, to produce wealth; but sixteenth-century Europe had no emigrants to spare* and so from the first Spain relied upon indigenous labour. This soon ran out and in 1503 the first slaves were shipped from Lisbon; after 1515 they came straight from the west coast of Africa.

In France and England similar political developments were

* About 1600 approximate populations were: Spain eight million, France sixteen million, England five million, Portugal one million, Netherlands three million; altogether this is rather more than half that of the United Kingdom today.

occurring, but at a later date because from 1350 to 1450 these countries were locked in combat during the Hundred Years War. In France it was not until 1460 that the States General and the *Parlement* of Paris—respectively the fiscal and supreme judicial tribunals—sank into insignificance in the face of royal omnipotence; in England administrative reforms, begun earlier but hindered by civil war, were hastened on by the new dynasty of Tudor kings after 1485. Only towards the turn of the century did Henry VII feel confident enough to formulate any conscious foreign policy or have the leisure to give attention to overseas exploration; thus, when Portuguese merchants already had some hundred years' experience of the coast of Africa, traders from the north were still relative strangers there. But, unlike the States General and *Parlement*, the English Parliament survived as a check upon overmighty princes; consequently there was never such absolutism in that country as there was in Portugal, France or Spain and although Elizabeth I might join a trading venture as a partner, such expeditions were never a royal monopoly. However, Spain in her great might seemed to prove that wealth from overseas trade meant power and those who wished to preserve a balance between the nations of Europe must either find colonial possessions for themselves or ruin those of Spain; both methods were tried.

The Dutch and to a certain extent the Germans and Italians were an exception to the contemporary trend in Europe towards an absolute form of monarchy. When France invaded Italy in 1494 that peninsula entered upon a period of foreign intervention which ensured the existence of half a dozen principalities and a republic (Venice) for some 350 years. Skilful Italian map-makers and sailors, like the Columbus brothers, whose recent forebears had held a virtual monopoly of the spice trade from the Far East—in 1514 Turkish aggrandisement at the eastern end of the Mediterranean from whence they delivered their cargoes conspired to ruin them—now preferred to settle in Lisbon and to work for Portugal or Spain, whose sea-lanes to the east were the only link with this profitable commodity.

The Dutch, at first very satisfied with their profits from the sale of salt fish to the rest of Catholic Europe, later became occupied at home in religious wars with Spain. Also, by their business acumen and without stirring from their own counting-houses, they were able to make Antwerp the centre in Europe of the spice trade and to build up the main exchange for the silver bullion imported from the New World by Spain. Moreover, their natural outlet by sea was to the north rather than to the south. But in 1580 Portugal became subject to Spain and the Dutch were no longer welcome in Lisbon; consequently they too turned their attention abroad and by 1600 became powerful merchants in South America and in Java. Although they were the last of the big nations to enter the African trade, they were soon well established on the coast.

Until 1700 money was scarce in Europe and the sale of monopolies seemed the best way for a sovereign to enter trade and to acquire some of the profits for himself—by granting permission to trade in a certain commodity within certain areas in return for a portion of the profits. Every European nation interested in West Africa experimented with such companies and each time they proved a failure. By 1700, therefore, they had become discredited and only in the next century was this area opened legally to individual traders who were not required to hold shares in some West African company.

At the beginning of the seventeenth century, when Portugal was still annexed to Spain, 80 per cent of the Spanish profits in such trade were consumed in running the administration, whilst the Portuguese monopoly managed by royal factors in the sixteenth century had been grossly over-organised and corrupt. An English account of this system in Lisbon says:

The Custome howses of the Indies doe maintaine ther officers namely Purveior Treasurer of the howse Treasurer of the Spices Porter Judge of the Ballances (?Seyzers) waiters and Provost....Ther are alsoe other inferior Officers....Ther is on Judge called the Judge of Indies Myna and Gwynnie who determineth all causes in the said howse whose office and place is very rich and of great worth.

Of the house where the customs duties were paid we are told:

In this howse all sortes of cloth comeing out of the realme of Portugall into Lisbone doe paie Custome 5 per Centum. In tymes past yt yelded yerelie rent 350000 Crownes. In this howse is alsoe paid 1/10 and the retenth of all marchaundezes that come into the realme out of other Countries in the whole 20 uppon every 100. In those daies duringe the kinge of Portugall those marchaundize paid on per Centum towardes

34

the maintenaunce of certaine shipps of warr to keepe the Coast but at this present K.P. [i.e. King Philip of Spain] as it is truelie reported hath raised the imposition...to 6 per Centum....

There was also a 'House of Slaves':

Their are 3 howses...videlicet the said howse of the slaves wher is paid the ¼ and the 1/20 of such slaves as come from Gynne Etheope and other places and ther is the howse of the proprietors and the third is the howse of the weightes where is paid the Custome of honye oyle Rossin Cunies and such like...this howse mainteineth a Speechmann which overseeth all thinges a Treasurer a Clarke and some other officers.[1]

The other houses in this great monopoly were those for: 'all kind of Fleshe', 'imposicion of wynnes', 'Madera or Fusticke', 'the retenth of Fishe', 'Fruites', and 'portage'. All these demanded their various customs from any merchant trading there whilst speed and efficiency could most probably be obtained only by additional payments to the officers concerned.

Furthermore, although a percentage had been levied by the Portuguese kings to pay for the naval escort protecting merchants' ships, this was seldom provided. Ninety per cent of the Portuguese government ships in the Atlantic were defenceless cumbersome carvels, or poorly armed pinnaces, seldom exceeding one hundred tons—many with open decks providing no protection against tropical storms—and described by a Portuguese Jesuit in the seventeenth century as 'schools of cowardice'. Thus corruption, inefficiency and high taxation encouraged Portuguese traders to operate separately or to interlope, as it was called, whilst the lack of armed protection did not prevent foreigners from doing the same.

Since 1503 Spain had been bringing home huge quantities of bullion from her silver mines in South America, but it was not until 1523 that Jean d'Ango, a Frenchman from Dieppe, captured two of them. This made the Spaniards' secret public for the first time, and by the 1560's Englishmen were lurking off the north-west coast of Europe, in the Caribbean or down this coast in the hope of enriching themselves and their sovereign at the same time—for profits were enormous. John Hawkins's raids upon this coast and in the West Indies were not so much piratical as diplomatic attempts to persuade Philip II of Spain to give him the right to protect these waters against the French, thereby giving England an entrée into this lucrative trade without having to become an interloper.

However, before 1530, the Portuguese were able to trade along the west coast of Africa without serious opposition, although one hears of French ships in these waters at the end of the fifteenth century; indeed it has sometimes been said that the latter nation, and not the Portuguese, were the first to erect forts along this coast. This is not so, but a legend grew up in the seventeenth century, when Colbert, Minister in control of economic affairs under the French king Louis XIV, was anxious to provide France with an empire. In order both to enhance further the brilliance of his monarch's splendour and to forestall any international objections to his plans, he was willing to assert that French occupation had preceded that of any other nation, thereby giving him a chance to claim what would have been called in the nineteenth-century scramble for Africa a 'sphere of influence'.

Soon after the French there came the English and then the Dutch to challenge Portugal. John Tintam and William Fabian were probably the first Englishmen to pass this way in 1481, but nothing further was done for almost another fifty years. English interest in Africa at this time was due to a decline in trade at home; between 1350 and 1450 there had been developed a large export trade in woollen cloth to the continent of Europe, but now English traders were driven from northern Europe by the German Hanse merchants whilst the Hundred Years War had spoiled trade in the south and west of Europe. Accordingly they began to look for markets elsewhere, but in 1481 England was in the throes of a civil war which ended in 1485 with the accession of Henry VII. It was not until trade had recovered from this war and the Tudor dynasty was fixed firmly on the throne that the next English voyage was made by William Hawkins. Yet in 1562 the English still knew little about this coast and when they met the Portuguese ambassador to discuss their differences Martin Frobisher was one of the few Englishmen who could describe conditions here. After that date one or more expeditions left England every year in the winter so as to arrive in the dry season, and by 1569 these interlopers, as the Portuguese regarded them, had so strained relations between the two nations that all property in Portugal belonging to Englishmen was confiscated. After 1580 when Spain annexed Portugal rivalry became greater still, not only along this coast, but also on the sea-routes of the Spanish treasure galleons returning from the rich settlements in the Americas.*

Altogether eight nations competed for a share in West African trade during the seventeenth century: Portugal, France, the Dutch United Provinces, England, Denmark, Sweden, Brandenburg and Scotland. In the same century, West Africa was the centre of two major wars. Between 1641 and 1648 the Dutch attacked the Portuguese settlements in Angola and in September 1664 the Dutch Admiral de Ruyter, as part of his campaign against the English on the coast, destroyed the fort on Tasso Island; this began an Anglo-Dutch war in Europe which lasted until 1667. Generally, the Scandinavian countries and Scotland played only a minor part and there is no record of them in Sierra Leone.

After 1640, when the Spanish–Portuguese coalition—begun in 1580—had come to an end, Spain forbade all commerce with Portugal. But Portuguese vessels had always provided slaves for the Spanish empire in South America and, now that they had become a nation in decline, other nations sought to break into this monopoly. At this time also the first sugar plantations were started in the West Indies and showed a large profit in the space of a very few years so that the possession of colonies there became a primary object of the French and English governments. The sugar was cultivated by slave labour and unless France and England were to depend entirely upon the Dutch, who had succeeded the Portuguese as the chief entrepreneurs in this business, it was necessary to engage actively in this trade on their own behalf.

Until 1640 English slave-traders on the coast were comparatively rare. Hawkins's voyages between 1562 and 1569 were not immediately followed up by other Englishmen, as they might well have been, because the only market for slaves was in the Spanish colonies and Spain at that time rigorously excluded foreigners. In 1620, when Richard Jobson, exploring the Gambia, was offered slaves by an African merchant, his reply summed up what must have been the view of the average Englishman of his time. 'We were', said he, 'a people who did not deale in any such commodities, neither did wee buy or sell one another, or any that had our owne shapes.'[2]

Twenty years later this would not, alas, have been true, because

* Simultaneously a number of English mathematicians began to make magnetic experiments with the compass; e.g. William Borough and Robert Norman published a book on the mariner's needle in 1581.

the middle years of the seventeenth century witnessed the greatest rivalry amongst European nations for the slave trade. In 1621 the Dutch West India Company was formed to trade between Africa and the New World. In 1633 the French formed the Company of Senegal and in 1664 Colbert, the French Minister of Finance, followed the Dutch example and amalgamated the French West India and East India Companies into one huge concern. In 1618 there was founded in England the Company of Adventurers of London trading to Gynney and Bynney—that is, Guinea and Benin—which lasted in one form or another until 1660. Although this company made a speciality of redwood, used for dyes, which it developed in Sierra Leone and Sherbro, it always suffered badly from interlopers and from international rivalry. In 1660, when King Charles II returned to London after his exile, the royal family became interested personally in the possibilities of such trade. In their exile they had seen the splendours which the rich Dutch merchants had gathered into their houses from both sides of the world and so, in 1662, was founded the Royal Adventurers into Africa, a company whose main object was to search for gold. In 1663 this company received a new charter and in it the slave trade was mentioned for the first time as a principal objective. In that same year, too, was built the first English settlement upon the banks of the Sierra Leone river; fortified buildings on the mainland at Sherbro—probably Bendu—were also taken over. A report from the Royal African Company, founded in 1672 to take over from the previous company, says that they negotiated for two factories, one at Sierra Leone and one at Sherbro, which had been let out on lease.[3] The lessees were private traders who from 1667 were allowed to trade by licence within the limits of the company's monopoly. The Portuguese long continued to claim a monopoly over this coast and even in the Anglo-Portuguese treaty of 1654— by which time the Dutch had seized most of their forts—the Portuguese as a Catholic nation granted formal permission for their allies to use the English Bible, to worship according to the English Church in their own houses or on board ship only, and to have a special burial ground.[4] Yet in spite of such regulations, it was quite impossible to stop interloping by people who had heard stories in Lisbon of the coast of Africa. In 1569 a report 'for trade betwixt England and Portugall' noted dryly: 'The number of Merchants that trade Spaine and Portugall dwelling in the Cittie of London,

Bristow, Hampton, and other places Westwards is 120 knowen...."[5]
In fact ships' captains were deliberately concealing their desti-
nations from the authorities, since they knew that they would be
forbidden to sail from England if they announced that they were
bound for Guinea. On the other hand, Queen Elizabeth refused
point-blank to prohibit her merchants trading there, although
she might write to Portugal, when that country's ambassador complained that his master, having all the expense of building forts
and of exploring the African coast, reaped few of the rewards,
that she was 'rather sorry'[6]. Nonetheless, those who concealed
their destination from the Lord Admiral—of which subterfuge
that officer, today represented by the Admiralty, was quite aware,
complaining dryly that it 'gyveth us cause to mistrust that they
meane not so playnely as they wolde seeme to pretende'[7]—were
forced to conceal it from everyone else, so that we know almost
nothing of such voyages. Only those who sailed with official
backing have left us any real memento and since these arrived late
in the field we must rely mainly upon Portuguese accounts for the
period before 1600. Nonetheless, the Portuguese government
had virtually abandoned Sierra Leone as a main centre of trade
within fifty years, leaving it to the Santiagans at Cape Verde, who
had certain permanent privileges, and to interlopers of their own
or other nations.*

The origins of the Company of Merchant Adventurers, the first
English joint-stock company trading to Africa, have been traced as
far back as 1536 when William Hawkins, father of the more famous
John, made three voyages to Africa and Brazil. Because, unlike
the Portuguese, he did not traffic in slaves, he secured the goodwill
of the inhabitants on the coast who helped him, and other private
traders later, by keeping him informed of the whereabouts of
Portuguese armed galleys. In 1553 another expedition, consisting
of the ship *Primrose* and a pinnace, was sent out by a group of
Adventurers who had their headquarters in London. These
Adventurers, because of their enterprising discoveries, considered
that they should have certain privileges of trade, but they claimed
a monopoly neither of trade nor of territory as the Portuguese

---

* As late as 1568 two contractors were farming the shore between Cape Verde
and Sierra Leone, saving the rights of Santiago; but their interests lay in the
gum trade to the north and, especially, in the gold trade of the Gambia. Pepper,
once taken up all along this coast, was no longer bought once the lucrative trade
with India was developed soon after 1498.

were doing. In fact they said that the Portuguese were being unnecessarily uncooperative in adopting such an exclusive attitude. They regarded their own voyages as:

worthie attempts, so much the greatlier to bee esteemed, as never before enterprised by Englishmen, or at the least so frequented [i.e. frequently], as at this present they are, and may bee, to the great commoditie of our merchants, if the same be not hindered by the ambition of such [i.e. the Portuguese], as for the conquering of fortie or fiftie miles here and there, and erecting of certain fortresses, think to be Lordes of half the world, envying that other should enjoy the commodities, which they themselves cannot wholly possess.[8]

This expedition of 1553 gathered more than four hundred pounds of gold, thirty-six butts of Guinea grains—that is, pepper—and about two hundred and fifty ivory tusks. Obviously the profit was enormous, especially since, after Henry VIII's disastrous Anglo–French wars, the coinage had been repeatedly debased so that the same amount of silver could be made to produce more and more coins. This meant that, whereas the Adventurers' original capital outlay was made in debased currency, the gold collected from the coast was fine gold. Consequently other expeditions left every year between 1554 and 1557. It was said that a copper or brass basin made in Europe could be exchanged on the coast for an amount of gold worth £30. Not unnaturally Queen Elizabeth herself now decided to associate with these profitable voyages and in 1562 she became a partner, providing four ships, including the *Primrose*, and £500 worth of provisions. Subsequent net profits, divided in the ratio of one-third to the queen and two-thirds to her merchant partners who had provided £5000 worth of trade goods, amounted to about £8000. It is no wonder that the Portuguese ambassador, who complained so strongly that year of English inter-lopers, received no satisfactory reply from Elizabeth; indeed, although the ambassador was not officially informed, at the end of that same year the queen repeated the experiment in partnership with Sir John Hawkins who took some three hundred slaves from the coast. In 1564 another slaving expedition was sent out, the queen providing the ship *Minion*. Other vessels were the *John the Baptist* of London and *Merlin* of Bristol. This was a failure; amongst other disasters an accidental explosion caused *Merlin* to sink. These voyages of 1562 and 1564 had the most adverse effects upon the hitherto joyful relations of English seamen and the

Africans on the coast. English ships were no longer welcome after they had begun to obtain slaves 'partly by the sword, partly by other means'—the vagueness of this report is sinister enough; the Africans now regarded the English as no better than the Portuguese. The Portuguese, in their turn, confronted with such rivalry in what before had been virtually their personal monopoly, made it their business to keep a check as far as possible upon all English ships bound for the coast and to prepare a hostile reception in the shape of armed galleys. Consequently few English ships were sent out specifically to the coast between 1568 and 1588. But expeditions sailed in 1588 and 1590, fitted out by London merchants, to Benin where they were able to avoid the only monopoly then held by Englishmen which belonged to the Senegal Adventurers in the north of Africa. In 1592 Thomas Gregory, a west-country merchant from Taunton, received a royal charter to trade to Guinea. He brought to Sierra Leone linen, woollen goods, iron-work, copper bracelets, glass beads and coral, exchanging these for pepper, ivory, palm-oil and cotton. It is expressly mentioned that no gold was seen and as a result the company seem to have lost interest. The next company formed was that of the Adventurers of London trading to Gynney and Bynney (that is, Guinea and Benin), incorporated in 1618. But the English Parliament of 1621, during their struggle to reduce the powers or prerogative of the crown, singled out the company's monopoly as one of their special 'grievances'. This hostility at home, coupled with various attacks by private traders on the coast who chose to ignore their privileges, led the company to withdraw in 1629. And so, in 1630, was founded the Company of Merchants Trading to Guinea with a monopoly from Cape Blanco to the Cape of Good Hope with exclusive rights of importing African goods into England. But in 1631 it was already in debt; in 1652, during the English civil war, two of its ships were seized on the coast by Prince Rupert, who, driven into exile with his brother-in-law King Charles II, singled out the company's ships for attack because the shares of the Royalist stockholders had been confiscated and given to Commonwealth men. In the following year the company complained that the Swedes had expelled their factors from various factories on the coast which lay within their sphere of monopoly. This is the first English company to mention any factories and it was they who built the first in Sierra Leone—at Sherbro. However, because the company was in such low water in 1657, it was agreed that the East India Company should take over the forts for five years to be used as places of refuge in case of attack or other disaster on their way to India.* The rights of trade it leased to private individuals. When the exiled king returned in 1660 he chartered a new company, the Royal Adventurers, with Prince Rupert as its first governor. Like the previous company, they offered to sublet to private traders; in 1668 this offer was taken up by a daughter-company, the Gambia Adventures, for seven years at an annual rent of £1000. Unfortunately this would not even pay the debts which the Adventurers had already contracted; for example, they had promised their predecessors £20,000 as compensation for their forts; the debt was still owing in 1709. In 1671 they became insolvent and, being liquidated, were succeeded in 1672 by the Royal African Company with an initial capital of £100,000; this company lasted in one form or another until 1752, when it was succeeded by a regulated company which did not require its members to be stockholders as the former joint-stock companies had done.

The financial crisis in England, which resulted in the Stop of the Exchequer in 1682, when payment on government bills was postponed, was essentially a domestic crisis and so it affected only those concerns which engaged primarily in home trade; many of these went bankrupt. Foreign trade, however, as undertaken by the three great concerns, the Royal African Company, the East India Company and the Hudson's Bay Company, continued to flourish until the effects of the Anglo-French war made themselves felt in 1691.

In 1702, being now in low water, the Royal African Company embarked upon financial methods which were virtually fraudulent; calls were made upon their shareholders for which bonds were issued but, at the same time, the company continued to issue dividends so that the stockholders merely received back part of the sums which they had just subscribed, whilst at the same time they ranked as creditors for the full amount. Another crisis of 1708 reduced the value of the company's stock, which had sold from 1701 to 1706 at about seventeen, to just under five, and by 1712 it

* Sherbro is not mentioned in the East India Company records at this time, but only Cormantin, Cape Coast Castle, Wyamba, Anto and Cantacorry; all these lay to the south and, where the India Company found any buildings at all, the houses were in bad repair—India Office Lib. MSS.: Home Misc., nos. 4, 29, 40, 42, 43 and O.C. nos. 25–27 *passim*.

had fallen to two. Moreover, the reorganisation of the company's affairs in 1691 and in 1713 meant, in practice, that no dividend had been paid since 1692.

As a result of this kind of financial dishonesty and with the great increase in industrial activity, there grew up a strong hostility to the exclusive rights, or monopolies, of the joint-stock companies whose shareholders alone had the right to transport certain goods to various parts of the world. Thus, in 1752, the Royal African Company was wound up and instead there was set up a regulated company composed of all merchants who traded to Africa.

Early records of Dutch trade with West Africa have not survived, but about 1602 they had a settlement at Cape Mount, although the garrison was shortly afterwards murdered by a local king. An attempt was made at this time to settle in the Sierra Leone river, but the Portuguese there persuaded the king against them, threatening to take their own trade elsewhere if the Dutch came; however, by 1609 they had some twenty ships in the Guinea trade, soon to be operated from their base at Mouree, founded near Elmina in 1612. Ten years later they had forty ships, and nearly all the gold coinage of the Dutch United Provinces was minted from Guinea gold. In 1621 the West India Company was formed with a monopoly from Newfoundland to the Straits of Magellan in the Antarctic, from the south of the Canary Islands to the Cape of Good Hope, and from the west coast of America to the tip of New Guinea. This was three years after the beginning of the Thirty Years War—the last religious war in Europe—and together with their East India Company, founded in 1600, the West India Company may be regarded as the Protestant Dutch nation's answer to Pope Alexander VI's gift of the non-European world in 1493 to Catholic Spain and Portugal. Like Europe, the whole globe became an arena where rivals contended for riches in this world and bliss in the next.

In 1644 the Dutch had a garrison of one hundred and thirty in Guinea and thirty in Cape Verde, as well as four hundred at St Paulo de Luanda. Although the Portuguese still controlled the slave trade from Angola across the Atlantic to Brazil and Spanish America, by 1621 the Dutch had secured two-thirds of the trade from Brazil to Europe. There were twenty-nine sugar refineries in the northern Netherlands at that time, where there had been only three or four in 1595, and these were kept supplied by the product of slave labour upon the plantations across the Atlantic.

In fact, by now Dutch commercial prosperity was built entirely upon overseas trade. Their flourishing industries of cloth-making, brewing, sugar-refining, oil-refining and shipbuilding all relied upon imported materials. Even the corn for everyday domestic use came from abroad; all this was quite different from their economy of the previous century. But the Dutch sea-lanes up and down the English Channel were liable to attack by English shipping whilst their land frontiers were bombarded by French armies; indeed, from 1660 they were under constant economic and political pressure from these two nations. In 1660 they had a merchant fleet estimated to be twice the size of that of England and nine times as large as the French. A hundred years later, the tonnage of shipping cleared from British ports had risen from 450,000 to 650,000 tons, whilst the tonnage of English-owned ships had been multiplied six times. Similarly, French exports increased, and between 1722 and 1782 the merchant fleet of Bordeaux, France's most prosperous port at this time, rose from one hundred and twenty ships to three hundred. As the seventeenth century drew to a close it became steadily more evident that England and France wished to have their economic expansion centred upon the New World and so their main policy from 1660 to 1760 was to fight for a share in the new colonial trade, which of course included West Africa and which, since the collapse of Portugal, had become almost a Dutch monopoly.

Hand in hand with this revolution in trade went a considerable advance in technical knowledge. The English Royal Adventurers, founded in 1662, had had to import printed cloth from Holland which originally had been exported from England in its plain white state, because the secret of dyeing in this particular manner had not yet been perfected in England. Their successors, the Royal African Company, founded ten years later, seldom did this because by 1700 the English seem to have surpassed the Dutch in that art. From then on the cotton industries of Lancashire, using Jamaican cotton and learning how to copy the patterns of Indian chintz by printing upon calico, built up a very prosperous trade, especially to Africa.*
In 1680 there came an invention for smelting minerals and consequently we find the Royal African Company sending home samples

* England captured Jamaica in 1655.

of iron ore. About the same time great attention was paid to the problems of the rapid deterioration of ships' timbers in the tropics and several proposals were put forward; one suggestion was to impregnate the wood 'with a bitter sulphurous matter' to discourage the worms; another was to use rolled lead on the hull and keel.[9]

The first travellers had arrived in some doubt as to whether they had brought with them the most suitable equipment for trade and travel in such a far-off place, because they did not know what they might find. In the early days it was all a matter of trial and error; Richard Beaumont, about 1600, drew up a list for intending travellers of what 'a shippe that gose of a Longe Voyage is to have'; it was necessary, he said:

to have all the Caske Iron bound as well pease Caske as those that holde Liquor, to have 30 tonne of water Iron bound. To have two Bread roomes, one abaft the other and to reserve one for homewardes. Bread will last two yeares or more, soe good Care bee in bakinge choosinge and stowinge. Beefe and Porke will last two years and more, pease for Eight moneths, and Oatmeale for eight moneths. Poore John* for ten moneths, put upp in Caskes the tayles and Fynes cutt off. . . Cod for first spendinge or harbour Victuall, Butter and Cheese, for 5 moneths if the Ferkins be tight and full of pickell,. . . it may last a yeare and more. 16 dozen of Tallow Candles with a good quantitye of Trayne oyle [i.e. whale oil] for Lampes. . . sacke eight Tonnes, white wyne 4 Tonne, Syder a good quantitie for it is a lastinge Liquor. . . Vinegeere som tyme to wash the shippe with all. . . aquavitye one Tonne and ½, and 140 cwt. of Billitts [i.e. of wood] will last two yeares. . . . To have for every peece [i.e. gun] 45 shott, and the weight of soe many shott in Powder for there will be much spent in exersizeinge, allmost all must be double cased, 1 cwt. of Match [i.e. fuse]. . . .[10]

For a daily ration Beaumont suggests fish, two pounds of beef, half a pound of pork, one pint of peas, two ounces of butter and four of cheese, the whole to be washed down with a gallon of beer. It is distressing, but typical of the age that apart from the vinegar, used to keep away fevers, no other form of medicine is recommended. On the whole it is a wonder that a ship's crew survived at all. The water alone would kill any modern sailor: 'The 24 of Aprill [1583] we fell upon the coaste of Guinea, which beginneth at nine degrees [i.e. of latitude]. . . there wee finde a most extreame

---

* A fish, probably salted hake.

heate, so that all the water in the ship stinketh, whereby men are forced to stop their noses when they drinke....'[11] In 1679 the Factor at Sherbro complained:

Your Honours were pleased to order Mr Thurloe to send a Box of Medicenes for this River which he did well performe, furnish't with 2 roules of plasters and 2 potts of Unguint with a small Bottle, a quarter full of quicksilver. But for a sick man nothing to comfort him.[12]

It is hardly surprising that at the end of this century one European died on this coast, on an average, every ten days, and it has been estimated that a white man's expectation of life here could accordingly be put at five years.

It is not known for certain how ships of those days kept their powder dry. Beaumont recommends double-sided cases because salt spray and a climate so much damper than Europe, even in the dry season, must have been a great problem to a sea-gunner when there were no cartridges and all guns were muzzle loading. Possibly it was heated on a plate over a fire, or poured on to a succession of plates previously warmed until it dried out—hence Beaumont's advocation of seven tons of firewood to be taken on board. Ships on this coast were constantly purchasing firewood and not all of it can have been used in the ship's galley.

The voyage out from England, using the current which flows south to Cape Verde and the north-east Trade Winds, took about eight weeks. The homeward trip, against wind and current, was more difficult and casualties often occurred from fever, thirst and even hunger if the ships were too long becalmed. Beaumont wisely recommends that half the bread supply should be reserved 'for homewardes'. Also, whilst latitude could be fixed reasonably well, it was not until the seventeenth century that an accurate way was found to ascertain longitude. This was sometimes as much as 30° in error, so that navigation, unless in sight of land, remained a very hit-or-miss affair. Thus in 1582 when William Hawkins, at supper one night, saw from his ship high land in the distance and announced that it was Sierra Leone, he was answered by a neighbour that 'he wold reason with ye best mariner in Ingland it cold not be that'. The ship's chaplain who overheard the argument wrote piously in his journal: 'I pray God be our pilote, our Master and our leader and al, then shal we not err.'[13] In spite of this many captains, homeward bound, preferred to sail west into the Atlantic so as to catch the equatorial current running parallel, but in the opposite direction, to the north-easterly current which flows from Sierra Leone to Elmina. By this method, one also avoided having to beat to windward against the north-east Trade Wind. In the days of sail, wind and current were of prime importance. In the early seventeenth century when great battles were fought between rival trading fleets, the whole of the Atlantic was required for manœuvres. Thus when the Dutch Admiral Piet Heyn, cruising in September 1626 off Florida, heard of Portuguese and Spanish ships at Bahia in Brazil which he wished to attack, it was necessary to approach them by way of the Azores, and the round trip took him six months.

The change which took place before 1650 in the general direction of trade from a north to south route, when gold, ivory, spices and hides had been imported to Europe, to a westerly, transatlantic one, when slaves became the main cargo—drawn principally from the Gold Coast and the Niger delta—grew more pronounced as the eighteenth century progressed. Indeed, since no nation could be said to keep a firm hold on it, and because it was assisted by the neglect and disrepair of the forts along the coast, formerly kept up by a few nations to protect their own particular interests slavery became more and more extensive. The Dutch were ready to sell to all and sundry, whilst the Portuguese in the New World would buy from any source whatever; by doing so they avoided heavy State taxes. But, as we have seen, economic and political pressure drove the Dutch into a decline; in 1763, by the Treaty of Paris which concluded the Seven Years War, Britain was able to drive a hard bargain with France, and so gradually the lion's share of the trade fell to England.*

The French and Dutch had less interest in Sierra Leone than the English or the Portuguese, although in 1625 a Dutch fleet, finding themselves driven from the Portuguese colony of Bahia in Brazil which they had held for a few months, sailed across to Sierra Leone for a refit. Most likely they chose the Gallinas for this

* In 1725 ships from the English port of Bristol carried 17,000 slaves and London ships probably slightly more; by 1750 Bristol and Liverpool had the largest share, but at the end of our period Liverpool—more easily reached than London by a sailing ship from the New World—was carrying two-thirds of the total number transported in British ships. This naturally hastened the ruin of the Royal African Company, whose headquarters were in London.[14]

47

purpose, for they had a factory there which they abandoned before 1666, although Coelho, a Portuguese amber merchant, said in 1664 that at Robaga in the Sierra Leone river were two wooden houses occupied by eight or ten Flemings and their launches.[15] The French had no fort at Sierra Leone although there was a settlement up the river at Burré, on the south bank near Gambia Island, for much of the seventeenth century. In 1785 Gambia Island itself was occupied, rented by the French from Panaboure Forbana, king of the island, for one hundred bars a year and a grant of £1200 per annum for two years to educate his son Pedro in France. This settlement was abandoned in 1793 when almost all the garrison died of starvation during the Anglo–French war because the British colony at Freetown made it impossible to revictual them.

On the other hand, ships of many nations called at King Jimmy, at the mouth of the river, for water. When Walter Charles, the Royal African Company's factor at Bunce Island, had evacuated the fort there in 1728 in the face of a local rebellion fomented by a Portuguese descendant called Signor Lopez who lived in a town set on a hill to the east of Fourah Bay, he found that Lopez had pinned a notice to a tree at this watering-place, on the edge of a bay known then as Frenchman's Bay, later as St George's Bay, and now called Kru Bay. The notice is of interest not so much for what it says as for the site chosen for it—presumably the most public possible—and for the postscript added in another hand:

Lopez Placcard was written on a Sheet of large Paper, and nail'd upon a Board, it was address'd to all Captains and Commanders of Interlopers.... The substance is a strange Medley, but still the worse by means of the Weather which hath tore the Paper and defac'd the Writeing. It is sign'd by Lopez at bottom; but what is very remarkable, underneath is an Advertisement to the French, Sign'd Saint Amant, whereby that Gentleman adviseth all of his Nation, to be upon their Guard against the evil practices of the Natives, and by no means to trust them etc....[16]

This seems to imply that visiting French ships, unless sufficiently well armed, were loth to call upon their countrymen at Burré because it was too close to the English at Bunce Island who regarded all Frenchmen as interlopers. These were the days of the sailing ship, and the one great fear of Edward Pierce, English factor at Bunce in the 1670's, was that the French or Dutch might establish a factory to windward of him in the Iles de Los, and so intercept ships from Europe before they reached Sierra Leone; it is a constant theme in his letters home. Trade was bad enough as it was; by now the Portuguese had abandoned Port Loko as a settlement, visiting Sierra Leone only in launches from Cacheo and the river Scarcies, and many resident traders, even Englishmen, found it more profitable to move northward.* Pierce wrote of these disasters in 1678 when trade on the Sierra Leone river was already almost non-existent: "'Tis to be supposed that when the English first settled in this River that here then lived (as wee have some years since knowen) very eminent traders in this River that brought the windward trade hither, butt what of these are not dead are removed to those parts...and I never knew a Ton of Teeth brought down this River in my life; yet I hope in time we may procure a trade of Redwood...."[17]

Relations between foreigners in Sierra Leone were governed by day-to-day, often personal, rivalry over trade and also by international politics in Europe. About 1600 André, the most influential Portuguese trader in Sierra Leone, told the king of Sierra Leone that if he allowed the Dutch to build a fort, as they wished to do, he would take his own trade elsewhere. Permission was refused. In the sixteenth century there were no navies to protect merchant ships sailing into unknown or hostile waters, and when French and English armed merchantmen arrived together as interlopers upon this coast in 1557 they combined against the Portuguese on principle. Yet England, forced into it by her queen's Spanish husband, was actually at war with France at this time. But to break the Portuguese monopoly would be mutually advantageous, whilst to fall defeated upon a strange coast occupied by a line of hostile forts would be disastrous. It was therefore necessary not only to avoid defeat, but also to take every care to preserve one's ship as far as possible from excessive damage during the heat of battle; the lessons learned from these engagements helped to defeat the Spanish Armada sailing to invade England in 1588. Nowadays one accepts the broadside fired by a man-of-war as normal, but this was not always so; Henry VIII was the first to fit heavy guns so as to fire in this manner—previously they had fired straight ahead—and the first English engagement of this kind took

---

* The Portuguese settlement at Cacheo was still the northern limit of those who traded locally from Sierra Leone in the eighteenth century.[18]

place off the south coast against the French in 1545. It was not a success and consequently was not used again in English waters until the Armada came, when it won the day against the old-fashioned Spanish method of sailing alongside the enemy, boarding him, and engaging in hand-to-hand fighting just as soldiers did on land. But it was practised on this occasion by the opposing fleets in 1557, and no doubt on many other occasions too, because it was less destructive to the ships concerned. A usual preliminary to boarding was to ram the enemy, when both ships might well be holed or seriously damaged below the water-line; it is unwise, however, to be left sinking though victorious in a shark-infested sea three or four thousand miles from home.

In the seventeenth century and later, when larger navies were maintained by the European powers, it was no longer the armed merchant ship which was a menace to the settlements along this coast. Attacks now came from hostile naval squadrons; they were nearly always successful so that henceforth trade rivalry usually stopped short of open war. Raids on Sierra Leone were carried out by the Dutch and French navies on various occasions, but each attack was the result of international war in Europe. The Dutch Admiral de Ruyter, landing at King Jimmy on 12 September 1664, proceeded up-river and attacked the English stationed at that time on Tasso Island. This was a prelude to the second Anglo–Dutch war in twelve years. On 17 July 1704 the English factory, now at Bunce, was bombarded by the French; in September 1794 the new settlement at Freetown received similar attention from the same enemy. On each occasion the settlements were pillaged and each was the result of Anglo–French hostilities, first in the reign of Louis XIV and then during the French Revolution to preserve the balance of power in Europe and to save Britain's mercantile and colonial interests overseas.

More serious than international differences, because it was a constant worry to any official on the coast, was the rivalry between European traders who did business on their own account in defiance of any monopoly of a chartered company. Like the Portuguese in the sixteenth century, the Royal African Company of England, in the seventeenth, regarded all such persons in Sierra Leone, whether foreigners or fellow countrymen, as interlopers. For example, a company's agent reported to his directors in London:

# Early Visitors

## At Sherbro, July 1680

Just before ye *Freind* ship, came in an Interloper called Richard
Franks. He came by Gambia, Rio Noones and Serre Leon:* there,
getting one of Your Honours' servants from Mr Peirce,† brought him
away with him and came in here to gett red wood, which, if any had layen
in Lymberman,‡ he would have made bould to have it, as one of his
men told us afterwards.[19]§

In 1687 John Case, factor at Bunce, complained that 'a Dutch
Interloper gott Teeth'[20] and in the following year he wrote home
to report that, on his way to Rio Nunez, he 'was taken by a French
man with foure of the Companye's vessells'.[21] In 1692 Wilkinson,
another interloper, settled in the Sherbro river, right under the
noses of the company's servants where he was joined by one of the
local chiefs. Later the directors in London wrote to complain of
a private trader settled on Tasso Island when the company still
occupied Bunce; they spoke plainly of their displeasure at 'those
Vagabonds and Banditti who have settled in your parts', encouraged, it seems, by previous factors on Bunce Island.[22]

No doubt the factors had been bribed, for the profits from interloping were enormous whilst, unlike the established companies
with their expensive garrisons on shore, overheads were small.
Barbot, a Frenchman with a long experience of the whole coast,
tells how he was approached by someone whose name he carefully
omits:

## Sherbro or Cerbero River.

In the year 1698, I was often importuned by one...who had just
before made three voyages successively to that river, to be concerned
in a new venture thither, under his conduct; but being then deeply
ingaged another way at the coast of Calabar, I did not accept of the
proposal, which was to fit out a little ship of about seventy or eighty
tuns, not drawing above seven feet and a half water; the cost and out-set
of which he computed at five hundred pounds, and with another five

* Until the nineteenth century Sierra Leone meant only the hilly promontory
on the south bank of the Sierra Leone river.
† The factor at Bunce.
‡ The name of one of the factory stores in Sherbro. See following note.
§ In 1699 a factor at Sherbro referred to Limberman factory and to Banta
factory.[23] The latter is a tribal name, being a branch of the Temnes; perhaps
the majority of slaves taken were of that tribe. There is no reason to suppose that
Limberman has any connection with the Limba tribe—though they were known
to Europeans in the sixteenth century; limber is a military and naval term for
certain wooden parts of a gun-carriage and ship.

hundred pounds of the goods mentioned in the description of that river, he was positive to bring back for that cargo, as he had done at his last voyage, forty-five tuns weight of Camwood, then sold in London at ninety pounds a tun, and five tuns of elephants teeth, though he had ten tuns at his former voyage, which yielded then two hundred pounds a tun; and ingaged to perform that voyage in ten months, out and home.[24]*

A knowledge of the winds, currents and geography of the coast was essential in these enterprises and this no doubt was why Barbot was approached. But those who had the most knowledge, and consequently were most dangerous, were company servants who deserted. Not only did they know the company's secrets, but they often set themselves up with a basic stock-in-trade filched from the company's own warehouses. For instance, in 1721 the English Royal African Company's clerk in London noted: '*Memorandum* that John Moore ran away from Kiddham left there by Mr Callow and had in his hands of the Company's effects by the said Callow's accounts £581. 3s.'[25]

Because trade on the coast was conducted usually during the dry season, the company's vessels came out towards the end of each year to pick up the accumulation of stock; deserters naturally knew when they might be expected. Wilkinson, who settled in 1692 on the Sherbro river, was joined by two such deserters. Laurence Devenport had been the Sherbro surgeon and Richard Case was probably the brother of John Case, at that time factor at Bunce. These three managed to get out a ship of their own before the *America*, the company's vessel, arrived and so they carried off all the best bargains for that year.[26]

Often the agents in London engaged men who were obviously unsuited to serve in the tropics and it is from these that the class of deserters was largely drawn. Less understandable is the employment by the factors in Sierra Leone of persons engaged locally who were obvious rogues; naturally they cheated the company from the very beginning. For instance, about 1704, the Bunce factor took into his service a man called John Leadstone who quickly deserted and set up on his own. When the French fleet arrived in this river, during the Anglo-French War, on 17 July 1704, he piloted his country's enemies up the estuary to Bunce where they lay off and bombarded it into ruins. Later, he brazenly admitted to the factor

* The first voyage, therefore, produced a gross profit of £5,050.

that he had taken eleven hundred bars of iron from the island when he deserted.[27] But the company could hardly have expected any other behaviour if they had properly considered Leadstone's earlier history. Trading privately to the north of Sierra Leone, he had been taken into slavery by a local king from whom he had been redeemed by the Portuguese for a sum which he was made to repay by 'servitude'. The Portuguese took him to Cacheo and there the governor, being sorry for him, entrusted him with certain trade goods. This kindness he had repaid by stealing what he could, by murdering the governor's surgeon and by running away to Sierra Leone.[28]

By 1715 he had descended to piracy: 'This 16th of September last John Leadstone came up in his Boat to Tarse Island and took away from me per force Two men slaves in irons belonging to Your Honours and Embarqued them directly aboard.'[29] By 1721 Leadstone had retired to Whiteman's Bay, where he was known affectionately by others of his kind as 'old Captain Cracker'.

There was nothing new in this method of making a living on the coast and, because the forts were difficult to defend from attacks by sea, it was usually successful. For example, in 1683 the French pirate, Captain Jean Hamlin, arrived in these waters from the West Indies; he and others were driven across the Atlantic by the preventive measures taken there to put down privateering and piracy which had already grown to enormous proportions. Cruising off Sierra Leone for seven months, disguised as an English man-of-war, he captured seventeen Dutch and English ships. Others followed his example and the Royal African Company reports at this time are full of complaints: 'John Graham a Pirate took two Shipps....Another took a shipp at Gambia...a Pirat there at Sherbrow another in Frenchmans Bay....Pirates put bad Principles into our servants.'[30] All these were in the space of six weeks in 1684. A pirate famous in these waters was one called Captain England who had begun his buccaneering days when he was captured by a pirate named Winter. In 1718 he overpowered the *Cadogan* snow* off the Sierra Leone river and quickly seized four more vessels here. To one of these, the *Pearl*, he transferred his flag, renaming her *Royal James*. He ended his days in poverty in Madagascar.

* A two-masted sailing ship. England, Davis and Roberts were all contemporaries of R. L. Stevenson's Long John Silver, see *Treasure Island*, ch. XI.

Captain Rackham, a desperado who operated usually in West Indian waters, took two large merchantmen here in 1719. This expedition is of note because he had with him Anne Bonny, one of the few women pirates known to history. In 1720 he was taken and hanged in Jamaica, when his body as a convicted buccaneer was buried below high-water mark.

Howel Davis, the mate of the *Cadogan*, now turned pirate so as to save his skin, became friendly with a French rover known as le Bouse, and together they sailed into the Sierra Leone estuary at the end of 1719. Here they sighted a tall ship which the Frenchman coveted since his own was much inferior. Bearing down on the stranger, they remarked that she seemed to take no notice of their attack and that she made no effort to identify herself. However, when they were within range, she let fly with a broadside and, simultaneously, hoisted the black flag of piracy. In fact the strange ship was a pirate herself, formerly the *Rising Sun*, commanded by Captain Cocklyn. Cocklyn and his crew of twenty-five had been marooned on this ship by their commander, Captain Moody, also a pirate, and, arriving in Sierra Leone, had attacked a sloop commanded by Signor Joseph, an African lately come from England. His ransom had provided them with food and ammunition so that they soon captured several other ships in the estuary. About a month later Moody's crew mutinied, their principal reason being that they took a dislike to their captain because he was a 'gentlemanlike commander'. They put him and twelve others in an open boat which they had taken from the Spanish off the Canary Islands and left him to his fate, choosing as their next captain le Bouse who now, together with Davis, joined his old messmate to terrorise the whole river. They took amongst other prizes the *Despatch* belonging to the Royal African Company. Davis, it seems, had once commanded a ship chartered by this company and had been, so he thought, badly treated by his employers; he now wanted to burn the *Despatch* in revenge, but one of her crew, John Stubbs—'a witty, brisk fellow' we are told— ingeniously argued him out of it saying:

Pray, gentlemen, hold, and I will prove to you, if this ship is burnt you will thereby greatly serve the Company's interest. The vessel has been out two years, is old and crazy and almost eaten to pieces by the worms; besides, her stores are worth little, and her cargo consists only of a little red wood and *Malaghetta* pepper; so the company have little to lose if she be burnt; and they will save all the men's wages, which is three times the value of the vessel and her cargo.[31]

And so, letting her go, the pirates decided to attack Bunce Island instead and a few days later, after a furious bombardment, the defenders retreated leaving the pirates in sole occupation for seven weeks.

In 1720 Davis fell into an ambush on the island of Principe and was killed at the first volley, but not before he had taken several vessels, including the *Princess*, a London merchantman whose mate was a tall dark Welshman called Bartholomew Roberts. Like many others he turned pirate as the only alternative to walking the plank. In 1720 he occupied Bunce for a few hours whilst he rifled the warehouses. William Smith, surveyor to the Royal African Company in 1726, has left an account of Roberts's attack: 'Roberts having three stout ships under his command, put into Sierra Leone for fresh water, and finding a trading vessel in the Bay of France, took her thence and carried her into another near the Cape, which is very deep and has a long narrow entry. This the author in his survey has called Pirate's Bay, because when Roberts had rifled that ship, he set fire to her; and part of her bottom was to be seen at low water when Mr Smith was there.'[32] Soon Roberts became notorious, especially in the West Indies which he made too hot to hold him, so that in June 1721 he came once more to Sierra Leone; but within a few months he was killed at sea by Captain Challoner Ogle, R.N., of H.M.S. *Swallow*, whilst carousing after a successful venture.

As yet the Royal Navy kept no regular patrol in these waters, but sometimes the company would ask for protection either in time of war or during a period of especially outrageous piracy. In war, they would act as convoys not only to the company's ships, but also to private traders sailing to and from these waters. At such times, the directors in London would ask the factor in Sierra Leone to see that the private traders behaved themselves; any disorder was to be reported to the directors together with the miscreants' names, but the factor was not to embroil the company in such disputes and at all times was to give protection to all English ships lying under his guns.[33] The Navy seems to have neglected its duty at times, being lured away by the prospect of indulging in private trade on its own account instead of giving protection to other traders. For instance on 12 December 1700 the directors wrote: '...this is only to advise you that upon Notice of some Pirates that infest your coast, wee have prevailed with the government to send a man of war the *Rochester*, a stout ship and excellent sailer, Captain Maine, Commander, who is to cruise on the North Coast of Guiney untill April next to protect and countenance your trade...and to that purpose he will advise with you....'[34]

In October 1721 the directors wrote to Robert Plunkett in Sherbro: 'We cannot help being of the same Opinion as you in regard to the Men of War ordered to the Coast of Africa as to their making Trade themselves, more than taking care of the Company's Ships and Trade to defend them from the Pirates, and therefore we have it under consideration whether it would not be for the Company's interest to fitt out some Cruizers of their own. But... we shall not do anything in it at present....'[35]

In fact the company never did anything about it and ships continued to be lost, either to pirates or to men-of-war of other nations, especially on the homeward journey. Outward bound, it was possible to sail in convoy, but naturally vessels did not complete their loading at the same time and so sailed home usually alone.

A particularly strong pirate base grew up on the south side of the Sierra Leone estuary, probably in Whiteman's Bay. Here lived what a visitor in 1721 described as: 'The private Traders, settled on the Starboard side, were about thirty in number, loose privateering Blades who, if they cannot trade fairly with the Natives, will rob, though not so much to amass Riches, as to put themselves in a capacity of living well and treating their Friends.'[36] Perhaps the most famous of these was 'old Captain Cracker', as John Leadstone, now retired, styled himself; he lived surrounded by a large harem. His house could be seen from the bay and here, in front of his porch, he kept three cannon and a flagstaff with which he saluted pirate craft as they entered or left harbour. His old age was unusual, for most of his colleagues were callow upstarts. For instance, when Roberts was taken fifty-two men were hanged subsequently at Cape Coast Castle; their average age was twenty-eight, but some were under twenty-one. Roberts himself, who was struck dead through the throat by a handful of grape shot, turned out for his last fight in a typically flamboyant manner, 'being dressed in a rich, crimson damask coat, a large red feather in his hat, a gold chain round his neck with a diamond cross hanging to it, and two pairs of ornamental pistols hanging on a silk sash over his shoulder'.[37]

The trial of Roberts's men on 28 March 1722 brought piracy in these waters virtually to an end; in 1730 it received its *coup de grâce* when French merchants from Nantes and Le Havre fitted out an armed expedition, burnt the pirates' ships and hanged all those who did not escape.[38] This, following upon the end of effective occupation by the Royal African Company when Charles had withdrawn from Bunce Island in 1728*, left Sierra Leone to the more peaceful private traders. They were settled on Bunce Island, the Banana Islands, York Island, the Plantain Islands and—for a while until they were driven off by the outraged local population—on the mainland, especially in the Sherbro area. But the Seven Years War, begun in 1756, ruined nearly all of them; John Newton, who worked for a slave-trader on the Plantains in 1745, wrote in 1763, the year peace was signed: '...there are still upon that part of the coast a few white men settled (and there were many more at the time I was first there) whose business it was to purchase slaves, etc. in the rivers and country adjacent and sell them to the ships at an advanced price.'[39] The chief difficulty of these traders was that they were usually in business in a small way and so could not afford ships of their own. They had to rely upon casual vessels to carry off their produce and they preferred to haggle with several captains at once so as to get the best price. There were, for instance, two brothers in Sierra Leone who, after a period of trading up and down this coast, finally settled here in 1754. The elder, Nicholas Owen, who kept a journal, traded mostly in Sherbro and up the river Jong; his brother Blayney operated also in the north-west of Sierra Leone.

At this time France and England were engaged in the Seven Years War and trade here suffered as usual. In May 1757 Nicholas wrote:

It has been seldom known such a scarcety of shiping upon this coast as at this pressent time and such a bad time of trade; from Siera Lone to Cape Mount there [is] not above 3 or 4 sail of ships that come for trade, which is of bad consequence to us that lives in the country, depending upon quik returns of goods and the blacks keeping up to thier old price, let it be war or pace [i.e. peace—Owen was an Irishman], besides the great expences of our houses and kings, which is not much less than 50 crowns† per month....[40]

* See below, pp. 83 and 106.
† A crown was a Portuguese silver coin, in 1761 worth 2s. 8d.

In August Owen complained of the fall in prices:

July has past without any thing meteral, saveing the great decay of trade in these parts occasion'd by the French war and scarcety of English shiping, which has rendred the price of a slave 10 bars less then usual, so that the common price abard a ship is 70 bars.[41]

Yet only two years before he had written:

Our chiefest busness is the purchaceing of slaves, which is very trouble-some. In the first place you are obliged to treat...them all [i.e. the slave-dealers] to liquer before you purchase any thing or not; at the same time you are liable to thier noise and bad langague without any satisfaction.... Our common goods here for a prime slave is as follows—ships' boats indeed give more—goods for a slave up the river Sharbrow in the year 1755 (country money) stands thus:

|  | Country Bars | Which changed into ship's bars stands thus: | | |
|---|---|---|---|---|
|  |  | Bars | Shillings | Pence |
| 4 guns | 20 | 16 | 0 | 0 |
| 2 kegs powder | 6 | 4 | 0 | 0 |
| 1 piece blew baft [i.e. coarse cloth] | 10 | 6 | 0 | 0 |
| 1 kettle | 4 | 2 | 2 | 6 |
| 2 brass pans | 2 | 1 | 2 | 8 |
| 1 doz. knives | 1 | 0 | 4 | 6 |
| 2 basons | 2 | 1 | 2 | 6 |
| 2 iron bars | 2 | 2 | 0 | 0 |
| 1 head beads | 1 | 0 | 3 | 4 |
| 50 flints [i.e. for guns] | 1 | 0 | 2 | 0 |
| 1 silk handkerchief | 1 | 1 | 0 | 0 |
| Country bars  50 | Ship's bars | 33 | 17 | 6* |

This is the general goods on the coast of Guinea for slaves, considering your price in the country when sould on board this pressent year which is B80 [i.e. 80 bars], so that your profits is considerable if the price stands with shiping. Dye wood is much the same in trade, commonly giveing 3 country bars per...112 lbs, which will amount to 6 on board a ship.

* These sums are incorrect in Owen's original, reading 20 and 36 bars 1s. 6d. respectively. It is unlikely that he could not add, since his livelihood depended upon it; probably the figures have been misread. A bar at this time resembled our modern *Kissi Penny*; cf. 'their gold is current in what the Traders call *Bars*, little twisted lengths, or in Rings, 4, 5, 6, 7 or 8s. value'.[42]

In August 1757, however, they looked in vain for the Royal Navy, because the British empire was scattered now across the world and the resources of the Navy were scarcely adequate to protect even the major settlements from the French. In spite of an Act of 1752 which had provided for the company's forts to be inspected by men-of-war sent out by the Admiralty, the trade upon this coast was no longer of sufficient value to warrant the attention of ships which, already hard-pressed, could be more profitably sent elsewhere: 'All people here is surprized that the government has not sent out any of our men of war upon these coasts in these troublesom times to secure our marchant ships, when in pace we are sure to have 3 or 4 ships of force every year, we have lost lately 7 or 8 sail upon this coast and are still in fear of more by the Frinch priviteers and ships of war, so that it is hardly safe to venture out in boats.'[43]

By now the company had given up its forts and trading stations on the coast and those private ships which came to Sierra Leone preferred to trade directly with the inhabitants and to cut out the European middleman wherever possible. The company had tried to do the same years before but not always with success; in 1692 they wrote to York Island: 'we are fully assured that if our Agents and Factors did truly espouse and mind our interest as they ought to doe, we might have the choice of the commodities of those countries at the best hand and not be beholding to Robert Gun or any others who make great advantage by buying of the natives at the best hand and selling to you at much higher prices, though (wee understand) they purchase them with the same goods where-with you trust them'.[44] But three years later, in 1695, the directors wrote to Gunn promising him friendship and asking him for favours; presumably Corker, their agent on York Island, had told them that middlemen were indispensable. In wartime they were not; few goods could be imported by the residents since they could get no escort for their vessels and when a ship did arrive the news quickly spread 'to the great determent of us traders, who depends upon the good will of the natives for our trade, for the least affront now will keep them from your house, since they know there's a vessell at hand with the best of goods'.[45] The day of the individual general merchant, which had lasted ever since Portuguese times, was now virtually ended. Owen might dream in his more philosophical moments of returning home with his pockets well stuffed with gold and of being known in every great man's house as the 'African gentleman', but profits were not what they had been even in his early days. To make a fortune now people went to India and anyway the slave trade was entering its last phase; within a lifetime it was to be abolished. It had never been as big a venture in Sierra Leone as it was elsewhere and the Owens never traded in more than a very few at any one time. Moreover, ordinary trade-goods sold only in small quantities in this country; the Royal African Company's consignments to York and Bunce had never exceeded £5000 in any one year and the average amount had been about half that[46]—or merely the cargoes of five ships such as Barbot had been invited to subscribe to in 1698.

But although the slave trade was never a major business in Sierra Leone, this country was inevitably affected by the American War of Independence (1776–83) which, by depleting merchant shipping, left the whole of the Caribbean as well as the southern states of America very short of slaves. In 1728 two ships calling at Bunce for wood and water had been 'bound down the Coast for 300 slaves'[47] which they were to take to Jamaica and the Leeward Islands, but there was never any question that some of these should be taken up at Bunce. Nonetheless, there was a good harbour here and during the American War slavers soon found it a convenient port of call, especially since the headquarters of European settlement was nearby on the Banana Islands. Bolland, who traded from the Bananas at this time, was said in 1792 to have made 'a great deal of money' from this trade[48] so that by the end of the century a variety of national flags might be seen in the Sierra Leone river, especially at Christmas-time when the slave caravans arrived from the interior. An Englishman, Samuel Gamble, captain of the *Sandown*, a slaver trading from London to the West Indies and chartered for £125 a month, kept a log-book remarkable for its information and also for its fine water-colour illustrations. He records that before he left England the Press Gang—short of men to fight the French—relieved his ship of some of her crew, whilst excisemen also came aboard to seize a puncheon of rum which the remainder had broached in dock, thereby violating the regulations. At last the *Sandown* left Portsmouth in a West Indian convoy of seventy-six sail but, having parted from them off the Scilly Isles, she was attacked by a privateer at the Iles de Los; at length, after all the crew except the captain and the surgeon had fallen sick in the river Nunez, they arrived at Freetown in January 1794. *Venus, Sandown's* brig, was used to make excursions up the creeks at Cape Mount to take on slaves and bring them back to the parent ship. On Saturday, 4 January, Gamble wrote that he saw 'the *Harpy* of London and 7 craft of different sizes'. Sailing up to Bunce he met 'the *Eleanor and Eliza*, Captain Hallsa of New York, the *Morning Star*—of Bristol, a French Prize Brig and several other craft'.[49] Altogether, this is a typical voyage of the period.

It is evident from the number of ships in the river when Gamble was here that even after the war owners continued to make fortunes by supplying the planters on the other side of the Atlantic with slaves at inflated prices. Stocks had fallen very low; in Jamaica alone 15,000 had died, mainly during the first two years of the war, simply because not enough ships got through the blockade to supply the island with sufficient food.[50] Even so, few of the slaves taken up in the Sierra Leone river were local people; Bolland traded mainly to the south—Sherbro and beyond; the Liverpool Company which, after protracted and difficult negotiations, was permitted to settle on the mainland near Whiteman's Bay in 1785, kept their chief agent on the Iles de Los; the caravans brought down by the Fulahs at Christmas-time came from the northern interior.* Nonetheless, it was not to be expected that the new settlement at Granville Town in Kru Bay would be looked on with anything except suspicion by the local rulers in 1787; more than twenty years hard work was needed before its future was assured.

---

* Mandingos were becoming popular and fashionable as domestic servants, especially in Havana.

## CHAPTER III

# FORTS AND SETTLEMENTS

The earliest fort built by Europeans in Sierra Leone was put up by the Portuguese between 1482 and 1495. It lay nine miles up-river from Tagrin Point, probably at the junction of the Port Loko creek and the Rokel river, on an island known still as Tombo. Except that it was fortified and that King John II of Portugal (1481–95), who had ordered its construction, later had it destroyed 'for certain reasons',[1] we know almost nothing about it. The date suggests that it was built to defend the Portuguese against French and English competitors who were beginning to find their way to the coast for the first time. But King John had ordered his explorers to erect stone crosses in each newly discovered territory as a sign of Portuguese occupation and the fort may well have been built to protect the stone cross. Almost certainly the building was of wood because Pereira, a man associated with the founding of Elmina Castle in 1482, says that the castle 'was the first stone building in the region of the Ethiopias of Guinea since the creation of the world'. The timber for Elmina was cut and shaped in Portugal so as to save time, but even so it was nearly two years before it was completed. Perhaps the fortress at Tombo was dismantled and the best of its timbers shipped to Elmina. Except for an attempt in 1488, soon abandoned, to build at the mouth of the Gambia river, and a small fort erected at Conakry before 1460 the fortress at Tombo was the only one built by the Portuguese north of Elmina before the middle of the sixteenth century. The Dutch map of Johan Vingboon drawn about 1639 bears only one name in the Sierra Leone estuary and that is *Tomba Bages o Portu Real*[2] (Tomba Bagas Kingdom of the Portuguese). In fact Tomba, or *Rotumba*, a town then in the country of the Bagas, who are Temne by origin, and nearby Robaga* remained the chief trading centres until about 1630 for all visitors who had business with the Portuguese headquarters at Port Loko. Today at Romakapit, the next village up-river from Rotumba, there is a well made from dressed laterite blocks, and the foundations of a ruined house, also an upturned

* *Ro-* is Temne for a place or town.

62

cannon buried in the ground on the river bank possibly used as a bollard to which ships could secure themselves when at anchor. Half a mile further on is a town called *Benkia Poto,* a Temne name meaning White Man's Benkia. Here is an isthmus with high ground at the water's edge sloping, in the narrow neck, to a swamp; the ground then rises again and here, so one is told by those who live there today, used to stand a gallows. Across the narrow neck was a wall. In both villages tradition says that the buildings are Portuguese and that the wall was to keep out their African neighbours; if they are indeed Portuguese, they are much later in date than their other settlements. It is perhaps more likely that sites once occupied by the Portuguese and which received their names at that time were subsequently taken over and built on by eighteenth- and nineteenth-century traders.

Besides the official contractors who had bought their trading privileges from the Portuguese government, although they were not themselves necessarily Portuguese, there were many un-licensed traders scattered about Sierra Leone. Some of these settled inland and although such men must have reached Port Loko at an early date other nations were very slow to learn of its existence. Commodore Beaulieu, a Frenchman who visited the estuary in 1619, did not know of it although he heard that the Portuguese had lately murdered the crew of a St Malo barque 'some seven or eight leagues above the Sasena' which place he knew as the residence of the king of Tagrin.[3] This murder must have been done in Port Loko because it was too far up-river to have been Tombo, but as we have seen, Vingboon was also unaware of this town; only at the end of the seventeenth century does this settlement begin to appear regularly on maps. Shenk and Valk's map, published in Amsterdam in 1680, marks *Alagoas*; in that same year John Ogilby in his *Africa*—a translation of the Dutch work of Olphert Dapper written ten years earlier—wrote of a village called *Os Alagoas* 'whither the Blacks will let no White People (besides the Portugals) come'. The Frenchman d'Anville in 1729 called it *Alagoas aux Portugais*; presumably he meant the Portuguese swamp or lagoon, since *logoa* is the word for a swamp in Portuguese and from it is derived the name Lagos. The nine-teenth-century *Collection of Temne Fables* by Schlenker says 'Port Loko is in Temne called *Baké Loko,* which signifies literally "wharf of the Lokos"'. In 1887 T. G. Lawson, Government

Interpreter,* said that it was the port from which many Loko slaves were shipped.[4] In fact in the sixteenth century† the Lokos under the Mani kings were a very powerful nation—in the 1580's they were at war with the Limbas and supplied the Portuguese with slaves taken in these wars; in the seventeenth century the Loko nation declined and so in turn filled the slave ships with their human cargo; later they recaptured the town from the Temnes, but by then the name had come to stay. This was mainly because as Portuguese power diminished along the river during the 1630's, they were unable to keep secret their extensive trade in Port Loko so that other nations came to this town where at that time the Temnes were selling the Lokos to the slavers.

Before the first quarter of the seventeenth century the Portuguese went to any lengths to keep their secret and so Martin Frobisher in his *Declaration for the trafique to Guinea* in 1562, inaccurate in many respects, may perhaps be forgiven for saying: 'First...that the King of Portugall hath no other Castell, fort, or House of Traffique upon the coastes between Cape Verde, and the Kingdom of Binny but onlie one small fort at Cape Trepontes called Ashien‡ and the other 20 leagues beyond called Castell de Mina.'[5] Frobisher referred of course to the official contractors; he could hardly be expected to know much about the host of unofficial *tangomoas* who traded along the tidal creeks setting up their main depots at places where shipping called most frequently. After 1580 when Portugal became part of the Spanish empire few Portuguese captains or Spanish slave-masters in the New World objected to buying slaves from an unofficial source because, by doing so, they avoided the royal tax levied upon all licensed Spanish slave-dealing. Hence settlements arose in the Sierra Leone estuary, where the watering was convenient, and at Bonthe where food was often bought by passing ships and the chance seized to do a little trading at the same time.

When Edward Fenton's fleet was in the river in 1582 it was visited by three white men; the English account says that one of them had been born in Venice yet the author calls them all Portuguese. This shows that the Portuguese monopoly was still

* At the end of the seventeenth century de Lisle's map marks *Os Alagoas*; another marks *Las Magoas*, obviously a misreading of the former. The Temne for a white man is *apótó*.

† See below, ch. IV, p. 120.

‡ Ashien = Axim.

being successfully upheld in Sierra Leone because there was no question in the Englishman's mind that the Portuguese would permit any resident to settle amongst them unless they considered him as one of themselves. In any case we are told that the Venetian came from Cape Verde, a Portuguese possession, but his ship had been 'spoyled by a Frenchman and...broken agenst a rock'.[6] About 1602 the Dutch tried to build a fort in the Sierra Leone river but Bartholomew André, an influential Portuguese resident trader, threatened Felipe, king of Sierra Leone, that if he allowed this he would leave the country. Consequently Felipe discouraged the Dutch, who returned to their factory at Cape Mount, where André soon made arrangements to have them betrayed and murdered.[7]

Because of such threats by foreigners, the Portuguese now began to think of building a fort at the entrance to the estuary in what we now call Kru Bay. In 1606 King Felipe wrote to King Philip III of Spain (the second of Portugal), probably at the instance of Father Barreira, a Jesuit, offering land at the river mouth on which to build defence works. The offer was accepted and Philip granted the land to Pedro Alvares Cabral; part of this bargain stipulated that one-tenth of the revenue received from the fort was to be paid to the Church.[8] The project was a failure because the contractor, Balthasar Pereira, was outwitted by a French captain, as a Portuguese account explains:

At the entrance to the river, which has so many sandbanks that one needs an experienced pilot, and at the very foot of the Lion Mountain, there is an ideal watering place for ships, well sheltered in a bay; here moreover one may replenish one's vessel with whatever provisions are needed because the inhabitants are friendly and the soil fertile. There is a reef of rocks on which one might easily build a fortress to guard the watering place and the entry to the river because the channel runs close to the watering place and sandbanks block the passage on the far side so that no incoming vessel would be able to keep out of range of the fort's guns.

To this site came one Balthasar Pereira in a ship loaded with merchandise and building materials to erect a fortress on behalf of Pedro Alvares Cabral, Lord of Sierra Leone; but the project came to nothing all because of an insignificant French ship without artillery and with a crew of only some twelve or fourteen. I will recount the details of this humiliating event in the hope that it may serve as a lesson to others.

The Portuguese were about to start building, having experienced no opposition from the inhabitants, when a French vessel appeared. Our men showed little concern because the captain came ashore immediately in a small boat to call on the Portuguese captain and present him with many delightful things from France. These good relations lasted several days, and the Frenchman often dined aboard our ship. One day he invited Captain Pereira to dine with him and the former accepted with no more qualms than if he had been in the city of Lisbon. He was accompanied by twelve men—not a large enough escort—and after they had been made merry with French wines and other delicacies the French Captain said that he was anxious to visit some neighbouring area where he had incurred the hatred of the inhabitants but that he feared to do so without the protection of heavy guns. Would Pereira, he asked, with so much guns and powder to spare, be ready to exchange some for a few pieces of the best French cloth? When the Portuguese hesitated, he was warned that if he did not do so, he would be held prisoner in the French vessel which would sail away with him on board. At this, our Captain gave in, urged on by his two sons—soldiers as unworthy as their father—one of whom he ordered to fetch the guns. No sooner were they delivered to the Frenchman than he threatened to turn them on the Portuguese vessel unless the remaining artillery was also handed over. He added that he would begin by hanging the Portuguese captain and his escort. To save his life—which nevertheless he was to lose a few days later—the Portuguese surrendered his vessel. The Frenchman then cast ashore all the Portuguese sailors with nothing more than the clothes in which they stood. Most of them died of hunger or disease....[9]

In fact the next fort built in the river was a Dutch one at Robaga. It is uncertain whether the Dutch Admiral de Ruyter called in 1664 because his countrymen had a factory there at that time, or whether he left behind some of his crew to build it. If the factory was there earlier, it may explain why one of the only two principal English factories on the coast in 1651 was at Sherbro rather than in the Sierra Leone river: 'The Council states their opinion that 20 leagues on each side of the two chief factories, or residences by the sea coast, the fort of Cormantin, and the river Cerberro,* near Sierra Leone, may be granted to the present Adventurers....'[10] At any rate Coelho says that eight or ten Dutchmen and their slaves who traded in ivory were in occupation in 1669 and that the building consisted 'of two houses made of timber and some

---

* One of the earliest references to the name Sherbro as a geographical location; on the other hand *Fenton's Journal*, 1582, mentions a King Sherabola at war with the king of Sherbro.[11]

towers'.[12]* This was the period of the great Anglo–Dutch wars and Coelho tells us that the building had suffered greatly in recent fights with the English. The Dutch also built a factory in the Gallinas area, when they were trying to break the Spanish monopoly in Brazil early in the seventeenth century—to sail any farther south before crossing the Atlantic was to increase the distance from the next watering-place on the other side of the Atlantic. This they abandoned presumably before 1651, although they continued to trade there and in 1682 when the English Royal African Company had a disagreement with the chiefs of Sherbro the latter threatened to take their custom to the Dutch; it would seem that they were regular visitors at this time.[13]

It is often said that the Portuguese introduced missionaries to Sierra Leone in the sixteenth century, yet when Barreira, a Jesuit, came in 1605 there was no Christian tradition amongst the kings here, many of whom came to be baptised by him. Moreover, he said that the Portuguese on the river had had no opportunity to attend Mass for thirty years. Barreira built a wooden church on the south bank of the river, probably near Kru Bay, where the first Mass was said on 29 September (St Michael's Day) 1605. Other churches were built on the Bullom shore, where Barreira held his first Christmas service, in Salvador, a Portuguese settlement on the south bank of the river, where the first Mass was held on 1 January 1606—this was the largest church built by Barreira—on the Island of Tombo and in the chief town of the kingdom of Bena—eight days' march from Tombo—where the first Mass was held on 7 May (Ascension Day). A Jesuit mission remained here until 1617. In 1647 twelve Spanish Capuchins landed in the Gambia and three of them came on to Cacheo but, because the commander there was Portuguese, they were not welcome and were kept virtually as prisoners. Two of them, therefore, sailed for Sierra Leone but one, Father Antonio, quickly fell sick and returned to Bissau where he died. The other, Father Seraphim, lived in Sierra Leone for some ten years, dividing his time between Tombo and Port Loko. Probably Barreira's wooden churches had collapsed by this time and Father Seraphim built two more in Port Loko and Tombo, calling them both churches of St Anthony, presumably in memory of his dead colleague. Father Seraphim also died in Bissau.

* In the nineteenth century the ruined martello tower on Tower Hill, then used as a store, was supposed to have been built by the Dutch.[14]

About 1658 two more Spanish Capuchins came out; the elder, Augustin de Ronda, lived at Tombo and was buried there after a stay of ten or twelve years. The younger, John de Peralta, worked first at Port Loko—which by now had no resident Portuguese and consequently insufficient capital to engage in extensive trading—and then for two years in the river Nunez. These were succeeded by Brothers Salvador and André de Faro; the former worked on the river Nunez and the latter on the Sierra Leone river before returning to Lisbon some six months later. Brother Salvador was still here, however, in 1669 although much debilitated by some form of chronic anaemia. At that time an English ship brought out four more priests of the same order to the Gambia who made their way to Sierra Leone. Two soon returned to Europe, either because they were ill or because they found the work too much for them, but one, Father Ignacio, falling ill in Sierra Leone, was buried on the island of Tombo. This mission met people in Susu country who still remembered Father Barreira and, in particular, an image of the Infant Jesus which he had carried with him.[15]

After this there were no more resident missions—though ships' chaplains continued to use Tombo and Port Loko churches—until about 1715 when Signor Joseph, traditionally the first African missionary, arrived in Sierra Leone. He had lived originally in America, but went to school in England. Afterwards he travelled to Portugal, where he became a Catholic and took the name of Signor Joseph.[16] He built a village in what we now call Granville Town but, quarrelling with his neighbours—particularly the English pirate Captain Cocklyn who in 1718 seized his sloop and held him to ransom—he moved to Kissy where on 7 April 1721 Surgeon John Atkins, R.N., called on him. He says that he was 'a generous and good natured Christian Negro, who had lately removed with his people some miles up the River. With his old buildings we wooded our ship.' After a long life, tradition says, he died on the Banana Islands and was buried in Dublin village.* He was the last Portuguese missionary; not only was Portuguese influence at an end in this country, but also the Islamic invasion of Sierra Leone had begun, making residence for foreigners dangerous.

Commerce was now in the hands of the English and Dutch

* Sierra Leone's oldest monument (dated) is a marble tombstone to Captain Reed, R.N., who died of fever and was buried on the Bananas in 1712.

(although the latter soon abandoned this area), of local traders and of the interloping ships' captains in general. Of Port Loko Coelho[17] said in 1669: 'Further up is the Port of the Logos where many white people once dwelt and carried on a thriving trade. Today these people have left and the trade is in the hands of the indigenous population and of some of these white people, but the trade has diminished. Here also was another very beautiful church of St Anthony.'* Because the French were more interested in the trade to the north of Sierra Leone and the Dutch had concentrated their forces in the south, primarily in Angola, whilst Portuguese trade in this country was confined mainly to the river Great Scarcies, Sierra Leone now lay open to the English Royal African Company; they began to build fortifications and to import carpenters, masons and shipwrights. Nonetheless, fear of the Englishman's traditional enemy in West Africa lingered on and in August 1673 Edward Pierce, the company's agent, wrote from Bunce to his directors in London complaining that he was still under strength. He added: 'I am perswaded that if Your Honours would send us 40 or 50 negroes from Barbadoes that have been bred up their and speake only the English Tongue, we shall soone be more formable [i.e. formidable] then all ye Portuguezes in the Country.'[18] Soon, however, events in Europe were to send the French navy prowling down the coast to seek out and destroy English merchantmen and to plunder the Royal African Company's settlements. In 1688 the Dutch William of Orange became King William III of England; he had already struggled long and tenaciously to preserve his own country from the domination of the French King Louis XIV and in 1689 he brought England into the war as well. There now began a series of Anglo-French conflicts which were to last intermittently for one hundred and twenty-five years. The War of the League of Augsburg (1689–97), after an uneasy truce lasting four years, ran on into the War of the Spanish Succession (1701–13), fought to preserve the balance of power in Europe by preventing the French royal house of Bourbon from occupying, in the persons of Louis XIV and his grandson, the thrones both of France and Spain. The War of the Austrian Succession (1743–8) was an attempt to repeat the work of William III and to smash Bourbon ascendancy on the continent of Europe. The

---

* Similarly in 1666 Villault, Comptroller of a French West India Company expedition to Sierra Leone, bemoaned the loss of French influence here.[19]

Seven Years War (1756–63) was fought to settle the future of British power outside Europe, now in conflict with France in India, Canada, along the Mississippi river, in the West Indies and the Gulf of Mexico. The war which began in 1793 dragged on until Napoleon was defeated in 1815.

One result of this long struggle which made European waters so dangerous to English shipping was the development by the Royal African Company of the rum trade.* It was a cargo suitable for West Africa and could be obtained in the West Indies and brought direct to the coast, thereby avoiding the North Atlantic where the French fleet was most in evidence. Earlier, private interlopers had found it a useful cargo when they wished to dodge the British Navy which protected the company's monopoly but, before 1688, the company carried very little rum; between 1703 and 1709 alone thirty-one ships were despatched from the West Indies by the company in this manner.

During these wars Sierra Leone was attacked five times by the enemy. In 1695 Bunce Island was set upon; in 1704 it was again raided by eleven French vessels when it surrendered at once; in 1799 it surrendered again to the first broadside of M. de Pont-devèze. In 1705 the French pillaged the company's factory at Sherbro and in 1794 they attacked the new settlement of Freetown, surprised the settlers in the open and looted the houses. We have seen elsewhere how the Seven Years War ruined Nicholas Owen and other private traders here. Merchantmen sailed in constant fear of ambush from enemy ships, and this fear is reflected in the Royal African Company's instructions to Captain William Chantrell of the *Guynie Friggott* in January 1690:

As soone as you can gett dispatched at James Island [i.e. the Gambi a steere a Course for the River of Sereleon and as you come neere the same you must be cautious of the French and either call at Scarceras [i.e. the river Scarcies] to Windward of the said river for your Infor-macion or else to Leward thereof, if at the former you must be carefull that you are truely informed by sending up to our Factorie at Bence Island under Agent Case, if you may with safety come to deliver what [is] consigned thither, and if you have informacion there is hazard then call at Senior Tom's Towne and there you will heare, how it is with our Factors in Sherbrow River in Yorke Island as well as at Sereleon and

* In 1690 the company were shipping home their cargoes of wood from Sierra Leone by way of Flushing, a Dutch port.[20]

deliver what [is] consigned to Bence Island at Yorke Island to our Cheife
Agent Gibson and it shalbe as delivered according to the bill of lading
at Sereleon....[21]

A year before, the directors had sent similar instructions to the
chief agent at Sierra Leone:

...we not being able to goe on with our Trade as in time of peace by
reason seamen are all taken up to supply the King's Fleet...if you take
Yorke Island to be more secure than Bence Island carry to the former
the bulke of our Goods and have our shipping as much under your
command as they can lie and send them out to seeke trade onely when
you apprehend the French may be gone from those parts....Wee here
send you by the powers we have granted to us by King William and
Queen Mary a Comission against the Subjects of France and their
Estates and doe you Act hereby if you have oppertunity.[22]

Of the attack on Bunce in 1704 we are told:

...on the seventeenth of July, that same Year, two small French Men
of War, under Sieur Guerin, attended by nine other Sail of Ships, took
the Fort, without any Resistance; the Commanding Officer, with about
an hundred Men, fled, on the Fleet's Approach, leaving in it only a
Gunner, and eleven or twelve Men, who fired forty or fifty Shot before
they surrendered.
The French pillaged and levelled it....[23]

This was a very unfortunate start for the garrison which in 1690
had been evacuated to James Island in the Gambia because Bunce
was thought to be undefendable. A skeleton staff remained as care-
takers until the island was resettled in 1700. In 1704 there were
forty-six white men on the establishment. At York Island in 1688
there were forty-five and about thirty in 1708.

Europeans employed by the Royal African Company were
usually recruited in England. For the junior servants advertisements were put out and the applicants interviewed in Leadenhall
Street at the company's London office. Here is an advertisement
circulated about 1700:

ALL SUCH PERSONS
*That are desirous to serve*
THE
ROYAL AFRICAN COMPANY

As Souldiers in GUYNE upon the following Terms, may repair to the
*African* House in *Leaden-Hall-street London*, & find entertainment,

VIZ EACH Souldier shall receive as a free Gift (before he proceeds the Voyage) Forty Shillings, also a Bed, Rugg, & Pillows the Company pay his Passage over to *Guyne*, upon his arrival there to enter into pay, at Twenty Shillings *per Month*, the Company finding Diet and Lodging. His wages* to be duly paid every Month.[24]

If the applicant was suitable, he was given an advance of salary and an allowance for the voyage which was called 'Head Money'. This probably allowed him to purchase a few amenities such as a comfortable place to sling his hammock. In November 1687 'Head Money' for six passengers came to 15s. Even so, there was no quick response to these advertisements. In September 1679 Zachary Rogers, agent in Sherbro, wrote to his directors: 'I wrote to your Honours for Factors as well as Seamen for there is much want of them, for as ye Factory's one Factor to be alone is very bad... and in case of mortality the goods would lay at the mercy of the Negroes.'[25] It was only in the middle of 1688 that the company began to make cash payments as a free gift so as to encourage recruitment. In August of that year there is an entry in the company receipt book: 'Received the summ of Two pounds seven shillings and six pence videlicet Two pounds being a Free Gift and seven shillings and sixpence towards a bed I goeing souldier to Gambia.'[26] More senior officers were provided with an extra allowance for provisions: 'Received...Two pounds tenn shillings being soe much given me to furnish my self with fresh Provisions I goeing to reside as a Writer at Sherbro.'[27] Thus wrote J. Skrine in February 1696.

But many servants were drawn from among the unfortunate and the social misfits. The following letter from London to the agent in Sierra Leone which travelled with the new recruits in 1713 tells its own story:

Whitingham's Letter to Agent John Clark Informing What persons is sent over by Captain Barry in the Dorothy.

Mr John Clerke

You will receive by the Dorothy, Captain Benjamin Barry, the following Persons for the Service of the Company's Fort under your Comand.

1. John Wallace Second at £60 per annum less £20 per annum pay'd in England to Ann Little.

* These wages compare favourably with others of the time; from 1651 to 1797 the pay of an able seaman in the Royal Navy was 22s. 6d. a month. A merchant seaman, then as now, was better off with about 50s. a month.

2. Ebenezer Ware Soldier at £12 per annum and Ackey mony.*
3. Thomas Fipping Ditto at £12 Ditto.
4. Archer Willet ye Company's Apprentice for five years the Company to find him Cloths etc.

By Order of the Committee of Shiping

(signed) SAM. WHITTINGHAM

African House
ye 13 November 1714.[28]

If, whilst on service in Africa, an employee was wounded a subsistence allowance was sometimes paid both to the casualty and to those who nursed him. Outstanding service also occasionally brought its reward, as, for instance, in 1691 when £5 was paid to a wounded man for helping to 'save ye Gold in the Guyne Frigat' which was wrecked near Portsmouth.[29] At this time all gold coins minted in England were made from ore brought from Guinea; hence the name still used today.

Often, far from being outstanding, the company's servants proved most unsuitable. The collection of misfits assembled in Sierra Leone in 1707 shows that the directors were still having trouble with recruiting: 'Serraleon 12 September 1707. Robert Gold† writes that severall of the Company's servants are unfit for their respective imployments viz: William Legg a Factor that cannot read or write, Thomas Arndle now Sergeant who came over Carpenter and is not and Robert Davis a Smith that understands nothing of his pretended Trade.'[30] This state of affairs is perhaps not surprising in view of the small salaries offered and of the unhealthy climate in which only the slightest medical attention was given. In the 1690's the French merchant Barbot spoke at length of 'many sorts of distempers which are not known in Europe'. He mentions measles which near Cape Mount once carried off most of the local inhabitants, having been brought from the Sierra Leone river by Europeans about 1600; smallpox too was a potent killer amongst the African population. Yaws, known as cankers, and a form of elephantiasis were also frequent, together with worms, colic, and venereal disease. The *bloody-flux*—dysentery—was common, being introduced into the Cape Mount area from the Sierra Leone river in 1626 'eight months after the Dutch Admiral

---

* Cf. Atkins's voyage 1721: 'They all keep Gromettas...at two Acys, or Bars, a Month.'[31]
† Gold deserted within a few months.

de Laun had left that place'. Venereal disease was cured by sarsaparilla boiled in brandy and sold by the Dutch; headaches by herb poultices which drew up pimples which were then dried off by a 'certain white mould'. Colic and the *bloody-flux*, said Barbot:

is not so common amongst the natives as the Europeans; many of whom are snatched away before they can become naturalised to that unwholesome air; who generally, before they die, grow so benumbed in their limbs, and so lean, that they are frightful to behold....

The European remedies against cholicks there, are to keep warm, not to lie down to sleep on the ground; to avoid the dew of the evening and the rain; not to use spring water nor lemon juice, nor any other acids: which refutes the too common use of punch, so much in vogue amongst the English Guineans; and which undoubtedly kills many of them, by causing violent cholicks.

Pains in the stomach are cured by taking four or five drops of balsam of sulphur in a little quantity of brandy...the day after this, to be let blood; and two days after, a gentle purge....

I cannot omit,...how I used to live whilst I was at the coast of Guinea, and during the voyage....I wore continually day and night, a hare's skin well dressed, on my bare stomach, the hair next my body; which kept it always in good order and activity; though I must own it made me often sweat wonderfully...I observed very exactly not to drink wine or brandy in the morning, as most seafaring men of all nations do...neither would I drink any strong liquor till a quarter of an hour after meals; much more did I shun to drink hard of any corrupted liquors of Europe, and of the Guinea beer called *Petaw*, all of which so much abounds in the European forts at the Gold Coast.[32]

In 1722 Doctor James Houston, Chief Surgeon for the Royal African Company at Cape Coast Castle, visited Sierra Leone and his report agrees with what Barbot had said:[33] 'Two third parts and more of the Diseases so fatal to your Servants are Diarrhoeas and Dysenteries, either as the Disease itself, or Symptomatical of a Fever, which sweeps off Patients without Mercy; which proceeds entirely from their drinking Palm Wine or Potoe, and eating Bread called Cankee.'*

It is of course only within the last few years that Europeans have given up wearing pith-helmets and spine pads in Sierra Leone, but the first Europeans must have made the climate very hard

* *Cankee* was made from millet in the Gold Coast and from maize in the Slave Coast, being fermented with palm wine.

to bear if they dressed at all like Barbot. Early pictures show soldiers wearing steel breast-plates and helmets, whilst in 1726 William Smith, the Royal African Company's surveyor, when York Island was attacked directed operations running to and fro on the beach in a full-bottomed wig at midday. It has been estimated that on the average a European died on the coast every ten days, so it is not perhaps surprising that, apart from medical cures, the more ignorant sometimes turned to the local charms and magics, a practice which horrified Barbot: 'But what is more detestable, as well as deplorable, is, that even some Europeans... not only believe this idolatrous worship effectual, but encourage their servants in it; and are very fond of wearing about their bodies, some...consecrated toys or spells of the heathen priests.' Since the diseases on the coast were often unknown in Europe there was no known cure in the medical pharmacy and doctors used as far as possible local herbs which experience showed to be at least of some use either because it was the traditional medicine of the inhabitants or because it was the nearest they could get to some known European drug which was not obtainable in Africa. Houston said:

What Dispensary Herbs came under my Cognizance in this Place, are *Calamus Aromaticus, Serpentana*, but much inferior to the *Virginian*; the Roots of which Herbs I infus'd in Brandy, of which I took a Drachm now and then...and gave it as a Cordial to the Sick...a pleasant Bitter and good Stomatick, by restricting the relaxed Fibres of the Stomach. I likewise found some Herbs of the Emollient kind, resembling *Mallows*★ and *Marsh-mallows*, and the flower of an Herb much resembling our *Camomil*, which I made use of for emollient Fomentations and Cataplasms [i.e. poultices and plasters, as we should say more simply nowadays]. There is a Leaf of a Dwarf Tree or Shrub much resembling our *Bay* Leaf, made use of by the Natives and our White People in the hot Bath with wonderful good Success....[34]

Dr Houston's visit to Sierra Leone in 1722 may have been the result of a complaint from Robert Plunkett, agent in Bunce, to the directors in that year.

We want a good skilfull Surgeon and not such a morose, ignorant fellow as we have here at present, to whose ignorance and neglect a great part of the mortality we had last year may be imputed and [whose] threatening temper and nature is such that very few that then was sick cared for

★ Mallow here means okra.

taking anything at his hands, nor those now living...his greedy and covetous temper is so that though he has a sufficient salary*...yet will take no care for his patients without first having had a note from under their hands for paying so much to him out of their Wages...and as farr as I understand by those who were then pretty well, I being desperately ill my self for the space of above three months, took more care of robbing their Chests when dead then he did of their bodies when alive....[35]

Sometimes the accounts were badly kept and the company's servants' wages in arrears. These were normally paid monthly, but in 1711 the agent in Sherbro wrote that they were much behind and that this especially made for bad feeling.[36] Even for the chief agent life was spartan, as the following inventory shows. It was taken in January 1713 of the furniture in the house of the agent at York Island, Sherbro:

1 large looking glass
2 elbow cane chairs (at 13 bars for both)
5 ditto at 20s. each = 16 bars 4s.
1 oval table half damaged
1 small ditto one third damaged
1 cane couch
1 fender half damaged
1 quart pewter pot
1 pottle [i.e. 2 quart] ditto
1 quart pewter tankard
1 desk
1 bedstead curtains and vallences.[37]

The chief agent, flying the blue and red company flag, as well as the Union Jack, which by charter he was permitted to use in his own district, was entitled to a five-gun salute from all English vessels, but often his authority was completely ignored by ships' captains. In 1728 the agent complained of Captain Parker of Liverpool who had arrived from Barbados:

...this is the Gentleman who in March last was Twelvemonths come in here without coming to the Fort, and afterwards at the Bananoes intercepted the George Sloop from coming here and perswaded the new

---

* It should be remembered that a surgeon in those days was not an educated man as he is today; at the end of the seventeenth century the surgeon in Sierra Leone received £2. 10s. a month—the same as a contemporary bricklayer, carpenter and smith.

Master to Charter her for the West Indies...and this is the Captain with whom Kirkham had such Clandestine Dealings to the Southward....When he got to Berbadoes he [i.e. Parker] Discharged all his Hands...he was resolved to prevent telling tales of his last year's Conduct.[38]

This kind of treatment was a deliberate insult, because ships usually left a note recording their arrival at any factory as a matter of courtesy. This was not strictly necessary because since 1713 trade on the coast had been thrown open to all Englishmen on equal terms. Nonetheless, Captain Parker's interference with the *George* may have caused the company's agent to lose money. In 1680 the company had banned absolutely all private trading by its servants but from 1700, to encourage efficiency, part of an agent's salary was earned on commission. In 1702 the directors wrote to the new agent in Sherbro that they had decided to:

...allow you the Salary of £60 per annum and Commission the same as Mr Richardson and his Second and Third was to have had, videlicet:
Twenty shillings per Tunn on Redwood
Five shillings per Cent on Elephants Teeth
Five shillings per head on Negroes and proportionably on other Goods, to be paid after the said Goods and Merchandizes are arrived and sold in England or Plantacions in manner following:
One moyety to the Chief* or his order. The other moyety to be equally divided betwixt the Second and Third or their order and that they be excluded all Trade whatsoever.[39]

But all too often an agent had not sufficient goods in stock to continue in trade all the year round, or if he had they were sometimes spoiled by being stored too long. Thus in 1679, agent Pierce wrote despairingly to his directors complaining of Thomas Thurloe, agent in the Gambia, who had kept all the best goods sent out from London and 'hath sent us a percell of old refuse in their steed, as old small Bells with out Clappers, Pistolls and Fowling peices old and damnified...'.[40]

Altogether, an agent's life, as depicted in the company's records, was one of constant improvisation; without masons in the early days the forts could not be built, without coopers casks for the slaves' drinking water could not be made. Yet, even in the heyday of the company, from 1672 to 1689, when their monopoly was

* 'The Chief' means the chief agent.

strongly upheld by their royal patrons at home and the Royal Navy abroad, the tale is still a muddle. In 1673 Edward Pierce wrote from Bunce: '...the great stone house and Fortification I could not goe forward with here for that our Cheife Mason dyed, but one that formerly was a Mason's Labourer hath built us a small stone house which though not so regular...is a good security for our Goods and Lives.'[41] Ten years later Richard Case, agent on Bunce, complained: 'I shalbe in greate want of a Cooper for the raiseing of Caskes for I could not produce Caskes for the bringing the Negroes from Scasseros [i.e. the Scarcies] had not Captain Smith supplyed me.'[42]

When the Royal African Company had received its royal charter on 27 September 1672 its monopoly of trade along the coast resembled those which had been granted to earlier companies of this kind. It was permitted to traffic exclusively for one thousand years between Cape Blanco and the Cape of Good Hope; no Englishman was to visit this area without the company's permission and certain goods might be carried to or from Africa only with the company's special licence. These goods included iron, copper, brass, pewter, *manilloes* (i.e. slave bracelets made from brass, copper or iron), cowrie shells, cloths, gunpowder, ivory, beads, knives, redwood, hides, pepper, beeswax, slaves, passengers. A licence for gunpowder cost £10 a barrel;[43] the same charge was made for every hundredweight of ivory, and for each passenger carried the company took £20.* Curiously little cola was handled, yet the Portuguese trading at this time with settlements in Balansera, Mambolo, Rokupr, Katimpi, Rotun, Tauyia and other places in the river Great Scarcies bought huge quantities, considered the best on the coast, with which they purchased slaves elsewhere.

It was felt that the company of the Royal Adventurers had failed earlier because it had not been granted sufficient privileges and therefore the Royal African Company's charter contained three special provisions. One clause stipulated that any twelve shareholders could summon a General Court and remove the Governor,

---

* For example, in April 1687 Captain George Parris, Barbados, wrote to the Court of the East India Company complaining that in 1685 two of the company's ships at Cape Mount had seized his goods as an interloper; he said rightly that they were just as much interlopers as he was; yet his own cargo of 700 tusks was hardly come by honestly, being bought locally after a pirate ship had chased another vessel, the original owner, ashore there.[44]

Sub-Governor, Deputy Governor, or any of the twenty-four members of the Court of Assistants if they were found guilty of misdemeanours. Another clause forbade Customs officers to accept entries of goods consigned to or from Africa unless they were those which the company permitted private traders to carry. The third and most important innovation set up a court of judicature to hear and determine causes of seizure of interlopers by the company and also other mercantile suits. No doubt, if King Charles II had had at his command the special department of the Council known as the Star Chamber, he would have used it instead, but the Restoration settlement of 1660 had not included this prerogative court, which had been abolished in 1641 at the beginning of the Civil War. On the other hand the restored Privy Council itself, with its restricted judicial functions, was quite inadequate. Yet many of the complaints brought by the company against separate traders on the coast were not punishable at Common Law; therefore, because the duke of York, later James II, and a big shareholder in the company, was Lord High Admiral at this time, the company tried as often as possible to have their cases tried in the Admiralty Court which was closely associated with the Council and which was guided by principles more akin to those of our modern international law. The interlopers, of course, wished to have their cases heard in the Common Law Courts, where they might expect to be found not guilty and where they could join the common lawyers in their long fight against prerogative courts in particular and all other rival systems of law in general.

Monopolies had been criticised in the last Parliaments of Queen Elizabeth I, not only because they seemed a manifestation of an overbearing royal authority or prerogative, but also because they restricted trade. A monopoly meant that only one market was open to a manufacturer; free trade meant many markets, and the new class of industrialists just emerging at the end of the seventeenth century added its weight of criticism, which became heavier as the industrial revolution progressed. Actually, the Royal African Company was careful to place its orders for goods in England as far as possible, but the previous company had outraged an already hostile body of criticism by ordering some of its cloths and carpets for export from Holland.[45]

In the face of such opposition the company in 1672 had to rely almost entirely upon the support of the royal house of Stuart, upholders *par excellence* of the royal prerogative. When the Stuarts failed so did the company; eventually, after 1713—the year which saw the death of Queen Anne, the last Stuart sovereign—free trade won the day.

However, from 1672 to 1689 the company was in its full glory. The monopoly was in force and the Lord High Admiral saw to it that ships of the Royal Navy were sent to protect the company's ships in Africa and to arrest interlopers. In those years five ships were ordered to the coast: *Phoenix* (1674), *Hunter* (1676), *Norwich* (1678), *Orange Tree*\* and *Mordaunt* (1684). Nonetheless, many interlopers succeeded in running the blockade and by 1680 interested parties were already making attempts in Parliament to have the monopoly abolished. Within days of the flight of King James II in December 1688, the Company tacitly abandoned its claim to seize interloping ships, and from 1689 to 1698 their charter was almost entirely disregarded whilst no fresh basis for African trade was devised.

In 1698 an Act of Parliament opened the trade to all private traders upon a payment of 10 per cent of the value of goods exported from England to be paid to the company. Between Cape Blanco in the modern Rio de Oro and the southern boundary of modern Sierra Leone a further 10 per cent duty was payable on all goods carried from that area except redwood, which paid only 5 per cent. This, of course, automatically abolished the previous rates for the period of the company's monopolistic days. Gold, silver and slaves paid no duty. This act satisfied nobody; the company had wanted a duty of 15 per cent and trade opened to the public only to the south of Sierra Leone; the private traders said that they now had to pay for what once had been free, that they could no longer compete with foreigners who paid no duty, and that they did not want the dubious privilege of protection by the company's forts and guns which their duties were intended to keep in repair.

There now began a struggle between the private traders and the company fought until 1706 mainly on the coast and thereafter, until 1712, when the Act was due to come to an end, principally before the Lords Commissioners of Trade and Plantations, in Parliament and in the Press. The traders hoped to have the 10 per cent and other duties abolished altogether; the company, anxious to retain its percentage in the early phase of the struggle, as time

---

\* The *Orange Tree* was lent, 28 May 1684, to the company for twelve months.[46]

went by and the Act ran out, lobbied for a return of its monopoly. In fact, for a short while in 1713 the directors were writing to their agents on the coast informing them that, because the Act had come to an end, they had regained their privileges. But this was only wishful thinking; after 1713 trade was free to all. This meant that the company was doomed, but it managed to struggle on with financial help from the Government until finally wound up in 1752.\* Obviously, with forts to keep under repair and a large shore establishment in Africa, it could not hope to compete with other competitors who traded directly from their ships and whose overhead expenses were so much smaller.

In its early days the monopoly was so frequently ignored—in 1682 the agent in Sherbro said that the ivory trade there was ruined by interlopers who paid twice the company's price—that the directors employed informers to tell them of unlicensed trading:

Received the summ of Twenty fower shillings in full for our share of unlicensed Goods discovered on board the Bonaventure, Captain Doegood.

(signed) JAMES WESTTEN
HUGH JONES        17th March 1686.[47]

On the other hand, the company did sometimes permit official trading by ships' captains. On 6 September 1700 there is an entry in their books: 'Elephants Teeth and Beeswax Account of Captain Williams and ye seamen of ye Pagett Frigatt Brought home in said shipp and sold at ye Company's sale ye 8 August 1700.'[48] Since the company's 10 per cent duty was levied on this cargo it must have been loaded to the north of Cape Mount. The sale realised £230. 11s., but the company, who handled the goods from the frigate to the sale rooms, charged Williams a total of £44. 13s. made up as follows:

|   |   | s. | d. |
|---|---|---|---|
| 1. | Customs duty paid on 1¾ cwt. of beeswax | 10 | |
| 2. | Company's 10% duty on the wax, which they valued at £8. 15s. | 17 | 6 |
| 3. | Customs duty on 5 leopard skins | 17 | 9 |
| 4. | Company's 10% duty on the skins which they valued at £1. 5s. | 2 | 6 |
| | Total        £2 | 7 | 9 |

\* An act of 1713 relieved the company of its creditors. It later received an annual subsidy of £10,000, subsequently increased but stopped altogether in 1746. See Davies, *Royal African Company, passim.*

The Ivory Account was made up as follows:

| | | £ | s. | d. |
|---|---|---|---|---|
| 1. | Customs duty paid on 25½ cwt. of ivory | 19 | 8 | 6 |
| 2. | Company's 10% duty on the ivory* | 20 | 8 | |
| 3. | Paid to Customs House porters & weighers | | 5 | |
| 4. | Charges for landing and loading on a cart and for 'a man following ye Cart' | | 2 | 6 |
| 5. | Charges for the cart from the Customs House to the Head Office, Leadenhall Street, London | | 2 | 6 |
| 6. | To a later entry of 80 lbs. of ivory | | 10 | 6 |
| 7. | Company's 10% duty on the 80 lbs | | 10 | |
| 8. | For storing, weighing and preparing for sale at 3s. 4d. a ton | | 4 | |
| 9. | Lighter and wharf charges at 3s. a ton | | 3 | 10 |
| 10. | Warehouse charges | | 8 | |
| 11. | Expenses | | 2 | 6 |
| | Total | £42 | 5 | 4 |
| | | £2 | 7 | 9 |
| | Ivory and Beeswax Account | £44 | 13 | 1 |

The crew and captain, therefore, received the balance of £185. 18s. However, by 1721 this practice of permitting ships' captains to trade on their own account had been stopped; instead they were given a special allowance 'as an equivalent to their not trading on their own Account'.[49]

The battle between the separate traders, or Ten Per Cent Men as they were now called, and the company is reflected in the latter's minute and account books. Two days after the Royal Assent was given to the Bill in 1698 the directors wrote to their agents about these traders saying: 'it is our desire that they be protected and treated civilly, but we positively expect you should not assist them in buying or selling goods'. Later they said that separate traders should be given protection only in time of war, either tribal or European, and that ''tis conceived that it is not the meaning of that clause of the Act that the company's forts and castles are to be the common habitations of or warehouses for the separate traders except in the cases aforesaid'.[50]

* Ivory was, therefore, fetching about £140 to £160 a ton at this time according to quality; in 1687 a large tusk could be bought for 18 bars a cwt. (about £5) a small tusk for 9 bars.

But Leadenhall Street was a far cry from Bunce or Sherbro in those days and do what they might the directors had little control over their servants in Africa. Although the company increased the salaries after they had forbidden all private trading by their employees, this practice still continued; if an agent could get a good price from a private interloper which he could put in his own pocket he frequently did so. This meant, of course, that when a company ship arrived there was often a delay whilst a cargo was hastily collected; in 1699 the directors wrote caustically to the agent in Sherbro:

Pray take notice we buy the best of Goods and many of the 10 per Cent men (because they will have cheaper Goods on purpose to undersell us at the Market) buy trash goods and such as are refused by us, which by your taking notice of to the Natives, will soon be discovered.

It has been usual for our ships to receive quick dispatches with 20 or 30 tons of Bees Wax and 20 to 30 tons of elephants teeth per each ship, but of late we have found the contrary practice, that for some humour of our Factory our ships have been detained without reason untill their bottoms are eaten with worms. . . . It can be no inducement to us to maintain Garisons and Factories abroad at so vast expense, except we can find the benefit by it to receive large and quick return, which we pray use your uttmost endeavours to perfect.

We have account of some 10 per Cent men designed for your river for Wood, but wee hope you will endeavour to provide for us all that can be gott of that Commodity.[51]

It is rare to find an agent such as he who laid his ship across a river-mouth so as to prevent an interloper from sailing upstream or he who was agent in Sherbro in 1711 and who, with at least three ships already under his command, wrote home:

I have bought a Sloop. . .Burthen 7 tuns or thereabouts. I had not so much necessity of her at present but to prevent other Whitemen buying her, which would have been prejudicial to your Trade if they had, the Starr Sloop and Flower barge being both in good order. I have paid George Yates 20 bars. . .for piloting the Broughton and Dorothy from the Gold Coast.[52]

Unfortunately, when the company's affairs declined and a strong character was needed if a final collapse of authority in Sierra Leone was to be avoided, the directors, in 1726, appointed a Mr Walter Charles as their chief agent in this country, to succeed a Marmaduke

Penwell. The 'Minutes of the Proceedings of the Royal African Company in Sierra Leone District' kept by him for the years 1728 and 1729 reveal a character both fussy and ineffective. He had little control over his own officers and was quite incapable of formulating any plan to defend the company's rights from attacks either by other European residents or by his African neighbours, who were, of course, egged on by the private traders. In the end he was driven from Bunce Island, after an ignominious retreat over the walls at night, by a band of Africans led by three descendants of earlier Portuguese traders called Lopez, Jerome and Thomâ. Returning a few weeks later to the island to collect his papers and certain other company property, he learnt that Lopez had put up a notice on a tree by the watering-place which proclaimed 'that ships of all Nations, English, French, Dutch, etc. shall have free Liberty of trade in the river and the utmost safety, Except those belonging to the Royal African Company of England'.* The company's affairs in Sierra Leone never recovered from this defeat.[53]

In its early days, although small boats for local trade were built at Bunce and Sherbro, the company rented the larger ships which plied between England and Africa and Africa and the West Indies. At this time they were not short of money and the hiring of ships was part of a deliberate policy; if the company had owned the ships they would have had to find a cargo for them on the third stage of the round trip—from the West Indies to London. But between 1670 and 1690 West Indian products fetched low prices in Europe and it was not profitable to carry cargo in that direction after one had waited perhaps two months in the West Indies before gathering a full load. Therefore the company preferred to accept cash or bills from the planters; for the transport of these to London no special vessel was needed. In any case slaves formed such a small part of the Sierra Leone trade that many ships calling at Bunce or Sherbro, whether hired or not, made the journey directly to and from London. To call at Sierra Leone for slaves would mean

* Some idea of the volume of trade at this time may be had from the number of ships recorded by William Smith, who sailed with Charles in the *Bonetta*. In the Gambia they were joined by the *Byam* of Antigua, a slaver; at Bunce lay the *Jacqueen* sloop and the *Sierra Leone* sloop. In the latter Smith sailed to Gallinas where he met the *Queen Elizabeth* and the *Friendship* brig of Bristol; at King Jimmy lay one small trading sloop and the *Friendship* sloop of Barbadoes. All these were met in the space of a month.[54]

calling at other places on the coast in order to make up a full cargo, and this would have added further to the cost of the trip.

These hired ships belonged usually to syndicates of eight, sixteen or more owners, many of them holding shares in the Royal African Company. The company paid demurrage of between £2. 10s. and £6 a day whilst a vessel was in an African port; on the other hand, if the ship was loaded quickly the company charged the owners for a quick despatch. In April 1698 the directors wrote to agent Thomas Corker in Sherbro:

This goeth by the Hannah and Elizabeth, Captain Roger Kirby Commander, on whom we have laden severall goods for the Trade of those parts...as by Invoice and Bill of Lading inclosed with a Copie of her Charterparty, to which you must have regard to give her dispatch in due time, it being agreed that [she] shall be Laden in Eighty dayes, otherwise to be allowed Demorage, for what time she shall be detained longer so far as Twenty dayes, but if Laden before that time the Master is to pay us for his dispatch.[55]

Peacetime rates for transport varied from £5. 10s. a ton to £6; in wartime they were about twice that so that enormous profits were earned by the owners. For example, in 1701 the *Thomas and Elizabeth* carried a cargo worth £1768 from London to Sherbro and returned directly with another of ivory and redwood, thereby earning £867 in freight charges. She was a ship of only one hundred and twenty tons and this one voyage probably paid for the cost of her building. On the other hand, later eighteenth-century ships, though cheap to build, were costly to maintain afloat, especially in the tropics. We have seen already how the company complained of ships 'detained without reason untill their bottoms are eaten with worms'. Consequently, even between 1700 and 1709, when one hundred and eleven ships were sent out on the company's business, only sixty-four of them were owned by the company itself. In 1713 a clause in the peace treaty gave to England the *Asiento*, or contract for supplying slaves to the Spanish possessions in the New World. This contract the Government gave to the South Sea Company and although the Royal African Company undertook to supply a certain number of slaves every year, yet the slaves were to be carried in the South Sea Company's vessels.[56]

The settlements in Sierra Leone depended entirely for trade

goods and building materials, and to a great extent for food also, upon what was shipped out to them from England. In June 1680 there was drawn up on Bunce Island an 'Inventory of Goods that will be wanting For next yeares Cargo'; warehouses, fortifications, living quarters and a safe anchorage were still not completed and these wants are all reflected in the inventory:

Salt 50 hogsheads*
Pitch 20 barrells
Tarr 10 barrells
Rezin 10 barrells

Factors Seamen and Soldiers
two Bricklayers or Masons
A Smith
Smith's Tooles and Bellowes
two smacks or sloopes†
A large Wherry‡
two Chaldron§ of Coales
    Provisions videlicet:
two Barrells Pickle herrings
1 Cwt. Poore Jack||
200 stockfish
4 firkins hard Tallow
Muster [i.e. mustard] seed
new Garden seeds
Garlick and oynions
a Quarter Cask Vinegar
Hambrogh Lines¶
20 white ⎫
20 tard [i.e. tarred]⎬ deale boards
Pan Tiles**
a Chirurgion [i.e. surgeon]⁵⁷

It was usual for all traders on the coast to pay a toll to the local kings and, although we do not know upon what system the percentage was based in any one district, the list of goods given up at York Island for the month of mid-November to mid-December 1698

* A large barrel of about 54 gallons capacity.
† A smack is a light single-masted sailing vessel.
‡ Wherry: a light rowing-boat.
§ Chaldron: a dry measure; of coal it is 36 bushels.
|| Like stockfish, it is a kind of salted fish.
¶ Presumably cord used for fishing- and sailing-tackle.
** A curved tile used for roofing houses.

suggests a flourishing trade; it also indicates what were the favourite imports at this time:

...26 Brasse basons
12 lbs wyer bound kettles
Bastes [i.e. a coarse cloth] 4 yards narrow ditto
Spirits 2 Whole Cases
      1 Half ditto
Country Cloths 1 Cape Mount Shirt [i.e. blue and white striped cotton like a modern Mende *Barri* cloth]
Gunn Powder 2 lbs ditto.
Shott 4 lbs ditto.
Brandy 6 gallons ½ ditto.
Plaines [i.e. plain cloth, of flannel] 8 Yards redd
Pewter 4 lbs Pewter basons
Christoll 250 Stones no. 18
      100 ditto no. 24
Knives 4 dozen and 8 ditto.
Iron Barrs 1 ditto.

Total 71 bars* 5s. 3½d.[58]

If a vessel was not bound for the West Indies, she would be loaded with local produce and sent back to England; such a one was the *Camwood Merchant*, which arrived at York Island on 1 October 1709 and left on the 24th with a cargo of:

78 tons Camwood
34 large Tusks weight 1300 lbs.
220 small Tusks weight 1206 lbs.
2 boxes of 102 lbs. aggrey beads†

* A *bar* was a recognised medium of exchange like the pound sterling, but it was very imprecise; the value of any article in bars varied often from river to river; for example, a gun valued at 20s. might sell for 6 bars, but 6 bars of tobacco might be worth only 4s.; in one place a piece of cloth would fetch 6 bars, in another 8; generally a bar varied from 1s. 6d. to 5s. 6d.

† These beads are first mentioned at the end of the sixteenth century; Pereira mentions blue beads with red streaks which the Africans call 'Coris' and which were used by the Portuguese to buy gold, especially at Elmina, but also on the coast between the rivers Rio Grande and Sierra Leone.[59] Their origin is obscure; they are said to have been made from a stone called chalcedony in the north of Africa by a people living in the Fezzan district in pre-Christian times called Garamantes.[61] It has also been suggested that one species was a coral-like substance *Allopora subviolacea*. Generally speaking all the peoples living west of the Niger were importers of this substance by the time the Europeans arrived on the coast and then it was said to come from the mouth of the Congo and in Guinea to have been literally worth its weight in gold. Soon the Europeans,

5 damaged Bucaneer guns
16 damaged muskets
12 damaged fusils
4 men slaves
60 gallons palm oil
5 hundredweight clean rice.[60]

The guns were being sent back for repair; the Aggrey beads, once common currency along this coast, but now found only very rarely by archaeologists, were perhaps destined for the Gambia where they would be used to buy slaves. But it is more likely that they were being shipped to England for re-export to Cape Coast Castle, for it was there that these beads were especially prized and the castle was the company's administrative headquarters for all their factories on the coast. The four men slaves may have been sent to England to learn a trade; this was not uncommon at this time as we shall see.

In the Royal African Company's early days the number of slaves kept for sale in the Sierra Leone factories was not a large one; but others, not for sale, were employed permanently as servants in the various settlements. The two classes were distinguished usually by the terms 'sale' slaves and 'factory' slaves or *gromettoes*.* Some of the *gromettoes* were, or could become free men, but there were others again who worked in the company's service only for a short time, like apprentices, before returning to their homes. Often, like Sephalo—son of a Bullom chief called King Harry whom he succeeded about 1730—these were members of royal houses who had been sent to learn something of the company's administrative affairs which might be useful to their families in running their country.† Often the *gromettoes* were put in charge of the chained batches of sale slaves.

In August 1683, when Henry Ballard and John Craford were

but especially the famous Italian glass-makers, found a way of counterfeiting it, so that by 1550 it was necessary to test the beads for purity in a flame.[62] As the eighteenth century progresses Aggrey beads are mentioned less and less, and it is interesting to see that they were exported from Sierra Leone as late as 1709. From the nineteenth century on, there has been a tendency to call all old beads, whether of stone, glass, or anything else, Aggrey beads, but the term is especially used for the blue glass beads found in Dahomey and the Ivory Coast. Significantly, 'old' King Aggery, a man of eighty-two in 1848 and then king of the Gold Coast, had served as a boy on board a coastal trading vessel.[63]

* Cf. the French *grommet:* a ship's boy.
† In the same way Bo School was opened in 1906 for the sons of chiefs.

discharged from command of a factory at Jassily,* the inventory taken there included: four *gromettoes* called Christopher, Bettow, Saggy and Anthony; one woman called Yamboy; one boy and one girl.[64] In November that year—because of the dry season usually a busy month for trade—Jassily and Bunce together contained thirty-nine *gromettoes*, fifteen young women, one old and one 'decriped' woman, four children—three of them girls—and only thirty slaves.[65] Yet, from 1683 to 1686 the company was supplying slaves to agents of the Spanish *Asiento*, on contract to provide the Spanish colonists with labour for their plantations. Wherever these slaves came from, it is pleasant to know that they did not come from Bunce. It is possible that some were sent from the Bonthe area because at this time the company mostly sold its *Asiento* slaves in Jamaica and it is about this time that one first hears of Jamaica town in the Sherbro district, a name derived from the West Indies.†

In 1721 the company's African servants in Sierra Leone numbered forty-seven,‡ but in December of the same year the directors wrote to Bunce: 'very soon you may expect Captain Barry in the Sarah for 250 slaves.'[66] Yet it is very doubtful whether Barry received all these because, seven years later, when two captains called there for food and water the agent reported home that they were 'bound down the Coast for 300 Slaves'.[67] That is to say, there was no question of asking for, or being offered slaves from Bunce. But, as the eighteenth century advanced, slavery in this area increased and Captain Baird, who inspected Bunce—at that time referred to as 'George Island'—on 18 November 1750, reported: 'At Sierra Leone is a prodigious Trade for Slaves, and some teeth, Carried by different Nations, of which he believes the Trading ships of England have their share.'[68]

By now the company had abandoned Sierra Leone in all but theory and the main slave-dealers on shore were the Fulahs. At the end of this century as many as fifteen hundred slaves were

---

* I.e. Jatt's Island.[69]

† From 1663 to 1671 the Royal Adventurers had held part of the *Asiento* contract, but had been unable to fulfil it. Another contract was signed in 1689, but the outbreak of war put an end to it. In 1713 when the company agreed to provide the South Sea Company with slaves, six ships were sent out, but the effort was short-lived; between 1715 and 1721 only 1743 slaves in all were delivered across the Atlantic by the company.

‡ In that year there were also at least three European wives in Sierra Leone.

brought down in one season to the estuary of the Sierra Leone river and there they were sold to visiting ships of all nations. For instance, in January 1794 Captain Samuel Gamble of the ship *Sandown*, himself a slaver, saw about twelve craft in the river, most of which were also slave ships; in his log-book he wrote:

Representation of a Lott of Fullows [i.e. Fulahs] bringing their Slaves for a Sale to the Europeans which generaly commences anually in December, or early in January, being prevented from coming down sooner by the rivers being overflow'd....* They sometimes come upwards of one Thousand Miles out of the interior part of the Country.... Their Principal Places of trade are Gambia, Rio Nunez and the Mandingo Country. Fifteen hundred of them have been brought here in one Season. They are of [i.e. off] in May as the rains set in in June.... Their darling Comodity that they get from the Whites is salt which they feed their Cattle with to prevent them from certain disorders.——Tobacco and Beads are next in demand. Guns, Powder and Cloth not so great.[70]

During the night the Royal African Company kept its slaves on Bunce in slave 'holes' and it also branded them so as to distinguish those purchased elsewhere. In 1702 the directors' instructions to John Freeman, agent at Bunce, were:

You are in buying Negroes for Exportation to the West Indies to take care that none sickly diseased or maimed nor above Thirty Six or under Fourteen Yeares of Age be purchased or put on board the Company's ships sent for that purpose, and that during your having them by you, you are to see they be well fed, well Lodged and well secured, and if it can be done safely without much hazard of their running away, they or some of them be daily gently employed in clearing the Island of Torsus [i.e. Tasso] or such other Service as you may in the Company's Service have Occasion to employ them in and that such may be known in Case of deserting Let them be markt on their being purchased or arrivall at Serelion as† the Company's Slaves for continuance on the place are to be marked, and upon their Shipping off let them have for an additionall mark the Letter S to distinguish them purchased by You and those under you from such as may be purchased by the Masters of the Ships

---

* Gray's *Letter on the W. Coast of Africa* (MS. from the Colonial Secretary's Library, now at Fourah Bay College, Freetown) says of the Fulahs and slavery: 'they deal pretty largely in that Traffic', but adds that they did not like the trade and undertook it as the only way to obtain European goods. Similarly early nineteenth-century European slave-traders used the money made from slaving to come to Freetown and buy condemned slave ships.

† As: that is, in the same way as.

or put on board by the Company's Factors at Gambia or other places not within your district or persons not under your Cognizance.

...You are to cause the Companies Negroe Slaves to be Instructed... in such arts and trades as may be most Serviceable to the Company as House Carpenters Ship Carpenters Bricklayers Spinners Weavers Dyers Seamen etc.

...You are to marke them that the Company now have and shall hereafter buy on the Right Breast $\begin{cases} \text{RA} \\ \text{CE} \end{cases}$ and the Children of them at Three Years of age.*

You are to give names of Distinction to all the Negroe Slaves of the Company that are kept for the use of Serelion or Sherbrow and Ships sailing in and to those parts.[71]

Whilst in a factory the 'sale' slaves were fed mostly on rice, often brought in from Port Loko, where it was exchanged for salt. The usual ration was one pound a day. The *gromettoes*, however, received an extra ration of half a pound of rice and sometimes, on such occasions as Christmas, an allowance of brandy. Some agents dressed their factory *gromettoes* in a livery.[72] Extra provisions—very often beans—specially for the voyage to the West Indies, might be exported from England to the coast free of duty, although a report of 1698 upon the Royal African Company's undertaking to do this without selling the cargo contained a rider: 'But whether all private Merchants will Comply therewith, is to us Doubtfull.'[73] The instructions of 1702 to Bunce, quoted above, have a paragraph:

You are always to have sufficient of Provisions for such Slaves that they may have daily their Bellys filled with that which is most likely to give them the best Nourishment and sufficient to putt on board ship to support them on for six or eight weeks voyage. You are for these purposes to produce what Beans, Carravances† and Rice if you can and feed [them] therewith that they may be enured to the same diet they must eat on board ship. If wheat can be made to grow with you then you are to grind it and make Bisket thereof, and if Flesh and Fish can be preserved you are to putt a suitable proportion each, that they may have plenty of each during their Voyage.

If the slaves were shipped in the smaller boats which sailed the Atlantic their destination was likely to be the Caribbean because

---

* R.A.C.E., that is, Royal African Company of England. In 1720 a new branding-iron of silver—probably silver wire—was sent out bearing the design ⅅ.[74]

† Caravance: a kind of bean, probably a kidney bean.

it was a shorter voyage than that to Jamaica; in any case, the Barbados planters did not favour the slaves from this part of the coast so much as those from elsewhere.[75] In 1702 a captain's instructions allowed him a commission of four slaves for himself out of every one hundred and four delivered safely to Montserrat and ordered him: 'To prevent the mortality of your negroes you must observe frequently to wash your decks with vinegar...and divert them with some sort of Musick and Play, you must also take care...no Salt Water be mixed with the Fresh wee have suffered very much by Carelessness in that respect.'[76]

Besides the factory slaves, apprentices and *gromettoes* there was yet another class of servant which led an independent life whilst working full-time for the company, or for the interloping ships' captains. For instance, there soon grew up a professional band of interpreters who would keep a sharp look-out for approaching ships and, meeting them in their canoes, offer their services for the ensuing palavers; often they carried credentials in the form of certificates issued by previous captains.[77] Others again helped the company in their local projects, such as the fisherman who was employed daily at Bunce Island to catch fish for the settlement.

Generally speaking, local enterprises do not seem to have formed part of the activities of the Portuguese settlers who traded mainly in gold, spices, ivory, wax, hides and slaves. They did, however, plant citrus fruits at the end of the Sierra Leone peninsula though this cannot be said to have been for commercial purposes since it was merely to provide their sailors who called in here with fresh fruit. Later, when they had discovered the Far East, they concentrated their endeavours in that part of the world or in South America, since the returns were so much greater than anything the coast of West Africa could produce.

The Dutch and French, as we have seen, did not settle in Sierra Leone for more than a few years, and any long-term industry was obviously out of the question.

However, the English, from the earliest days of the Royal African Company, tried their hand at local industry, although they had little success. Many of the schemes suggested by merchants in London who had never seen the coast were unpractical; for instance, an order to plant vines on the Islands of Bunce and Tasso. Other schemes, feasible at least in theory, covered the production of lime for building, quicksilver, potash, indigo, rum, sugar, spirits made from rice or local corn, iron ore, cattle, silver, ginger, soap made from potash and palm-oil, isinglass and Sherbro mats. The latter, well known to the Portuguese in the sixteenth century, were still in great demand, as the directors' orders to Sherbro in 1721 make quite plain; but the quantities asked for show a most unrealistic approach to the potentialities of any local labour force: 'Notwithstanding the Letter from the Court of the 31st of October...you are desired to send over some of the Sherbro matts, tho' they should amount to Ten Thousand.* I am directed by the Court to let you know that the larger the Number you send is the better, even to a million or more, if to be got.'[78]

Cattle-breeding was also tried by the Royal African Company, although the Portuguese and Dutch had brought out bulls in their ships previously.† In 1673 the agent in Sherbro asked to be allowed to produce a new strain from stock which he suggested should be shipped from St Iago in the Cape Verde Islands; this stock would, of course, be descended from an earlier strain shipped out probably in the early sixteenth century.[79]

Experiments were constantly made with indigo; in 1687 a trial consignment was sent to the West Indies and in 1688 it was reported from the Rio Nunez: 'That River produceth nothing but the Indico weed.' Usually this plant rotted before it arrived in Europe; this may have been due to carelessness or to ignorance at the time of harvesting; for example, the Royal African Company directors wrote to Bunce in 1703: 'You must send another Barrell of wild Indico Weed to be tryed here, in the gathering of it observe that it be gott at the proper time, which must be before it run to seed, and just before the Leaves runn in to Blisters, when the Leaves are all Blistered and the weed runn to seed 'tis good for nothing.'[80]

The first controlled experiments with indigo in Sierra Leone seem to have been made at Sherbro, because in April 1692 agent Henry Gibson wrote home that he had sent Richard Bridgman, his gardener, to Bunce to sow indigo seed. Bridgman immediately reported that he 'Feares the goodness of the Indico Seeds. If the Company will send a Still etc. he will supply their Factories with Rum and Suger.'[81]

---

* Pereira[82] said the Africans called them *bicas*.

† Fenton at Elmina, 1582, met a Dutch ship which had brought out a bull and a hog.[83]

In May 1694 seed, presumably grown in the West Indies, was therefore sent from England and it was planted in Sherbro where it was then said to be growing successfully. But in the following January the agent expressed his doubts of the 'Indico design'.[84]

Nonetheless, undaunted by failure, in 1703 the directors were instructing Freeman, agent at Bunce:

You are in the Garden on the Island of Bence or at the Island of Torsus [i.e. Tasso] as a Nursery to Sett Sow and Plant all things that may be found out in those Parts that may be improvable for Trade, as Cotton Indico Ginger Sugar Canes Pepper Spice Gumm Trees Druggs, etc.

You are to put a Stock of Cattle on the Island of Torsus, clear the Island of Wood Trees and make Plantacions thereon and to consider how the Island may be made most defensible, and you are to direct what is proper to be done as soon as possible with all good Husbandry and to carry on the Indico and Pottash Works.

Memorandum. There was the seed of the Barbadoes Prickle sent over which may be sowed and planted for defence and increased untill planted round the Island allowing but a few entring Places (if more then one). There is one point of the Island if Fortified will hinder any Shipp coming up the River.[85]

The Barbados Prickle was quite a new plant, recently seen in England and imported from the West Indies. Similarly 'Cardomum', that is a species of ginger (probably *Elettaria cardamomum*), was a newcomer from the same part of the world and in 1721 the directors, knowing that it was a native of moist forests, asked the agent at Sherbro to show some to his neighbours so that they could say whether it grew in Africa or not; actually it is not indigenous to West Africa.[86]

The potash too was a failure; in 1722 Doctor Houston, the company's surgeon at their coast headquarters in Cape Coast Castle, visited Sierra Leone. Later, speaking of Bunce, in his *Memoirs of his Own Life-time*, published in 1747, he recalled how 'our first Project was making of Pot-ash', but that it failed because the water, though used for drinking, was too brackish to produce the necessary alkali.[87]

Cotton was planted on Bunce and Tasso as early as 1681; the seed came from Barbados and in that year Pierce, the agent, wrote to the West Indies asking them 'to send him a Negroe from hence

---

\* In 1726 indigo was still grown on Bunce.[88]

that was a good Ginner of Cotton with a Ginn, etc.... which we sent accordingly which cost £35'.[89]

The gin was used to clear cotton of its seeds but, in spite of this expert technical assistance, some time later the agent wrote despairingly that the cotton could never be made anything of unless trained men were sent from amongst the African staff at Cape Coast Castle. In 1702 the directors complained: '...this last Cotton you sent some of, it was not cleaned from the seed which quite spoils it. You must take care to have it cleane and the seed taken out.... Improve the Plantations of Cotton all you can, you cannot send too much of it.'[90] About this time quicksilver may have been reported from Sierra Leone because in January 1712/13 the directors wrote to agent John Clark in Sherbro: 'We have sent you some Dog skins which is proper to pack up the quicksilver which must be in Bulses*...the Grainside inwards and double skin'd and tied very close, and if it break out it will be all lost.'[91] Perhaps the best selection of samples ever sent back to England was that of 1722, despatched by an enterprising agent, either Robert Plunkett† or Abraham Knox, from Bunce:

1 cask of Potash
1 cask of long round Guinea Grains [i.e. a pepper]
1 cask of paint [i.e. presumably a vegetable dye]
1 Bundle of Rattans [i.e. palm fibres]
4 Bundles of Rattans for Matts and 1 Cleane with black white and red
    stuff fitt for weaving.
1 small Bag of silk Cotton
1 paper of Country poison
1 small parcel of Mettle extracted here supposed to be silver.[92]

In July of that year other samples sent to London included soap made from potash and palm-oil, sand full of 'Ising glass', and stone said to contain enough iron for smelting, which some tribes made into shot for their guns.[93]

In that year there was a noticeable briskness and efficiency about the conduct of the company's business in Sierra Leone and this, though the calibre of the agents in the country at that time must have had something to do with it, was no doubt partly due to

---

* A bulse, like a purse, was a bag of money or precious stones; originally both were made of animal skin. There is no quicksilver in Sierra Leone today.

† Plunkett, in 1725, when chief agent at James Island, the Gambia, was killed when the powder magazine blew up destroying the fort.[94]

the prosperity of the company which, for the only time in its eighty years of existence, in 1723 exported more than £100,000 worth of goods. This fact is all the more surprising when it is remembered that in 1721 there occurred the disastrous smash of the South Sea Company which ruined so many shareholders, brought down the Government of the day and for many years made people chary of investing in such joint-stock companies; also in 1726 and 1728 respectively the settlements at York Island and Bunce were abandoned.

The first English settlement in Sierra Leone was in the Sherbro area. As we have seen, it had been established before 1651; probably it was built by the Company of Merchants trading to Guinea who received their charter in 1630 and who developed there and in the Sierra Leone river a trade in redwood. At any rate in 1631 they built the only other English factory then on the coast, at Kormantin in modern Ghana.[95] In 1651 these two were still the only English strongholds in this area.* In 1631 this company was already in debt and in 1657 it was decided that the East India Company should take over the forts on the coast for five years to be used as harbours on the way to India. It is therefore unlikely that any English settlement was built in the Sierra Leone river in the years immediately after 1651 because the company's affairs went from bad to worse. In 1662 the Royal Adventurers were incorporated and they immediately erected a fort on the Island of Tasso. This was attacked and destroyed by de Ruyter in September 1664, so that the settlement was moved to another island called Cogu—the modern Konkaw. In December 1666 Abraham, the factor there, was living on good terms with the king of Bullom in what Villault, a Frenchman, at that time described as a 'handsome house'.[96] The factory was built of brick and free stone, and was defended by four 4-pounder cannon, being surrounded by palm trees. On one side lay a spring of fresh water and on the other a village of some twenty houses. On New Year's Eve Abraham was invited on board the Dutch ship *Europa*, which Villault had chartered, for the usual end-of-the-year celebrations. He arrived only to be kidnapped and held to ransom; on the following

* Coelho,[97] in 1669 said the English had had a factory on Tasso for 'more than 60 years', but the English Captain Keeling who called here in distress in 1607 makes no mention of a settlement and Coelho admits that he had never been there himself.

morning the French attacked his settlement. There they found some two hundred armed Africans, who, seeing a French sloop row up-river so as to take advantage of the wind, imagined that the expedition was aimed at Burré, a king's town on the south shore, and sent a canoe to give the alarm. It was captured and upon inquiry the French discovered that it belonged to a Portuguese who was a prisoner in the English factory. Meanwhile, shot from the guns on Cogu were falling close to the small French boat and, as soon as the tide began to ebb in their favour, they fell downstream leaving the settlement unharmed. When they reached their flag-ship they found Bombo, the king of Bullom's son, who had bravely sailed under the enemy's guns to ransom his friend Abraham for nine hundredweight of ivory and two civet cats. And so, the following day, the English factor was released with a present from the French captain of a barrel of spirits, a roll of tobacco, a cheese and a salvo of three guns as he departed. In February Abraham, helped by the Portuguese, seized a visiting ship's longboat and nine of the crew and held them to ransom; in revenge the captain destroyed the settlement and so a third move was made, to Rotumba on the south bank of the river. Only later, probably about 1672, was a fort built on Bunce Island—sometimes called Bance, Bence or Brent Island. In 1673 a small stone warehouse was put up with a counter fitted by a ship's carpenter; the large stone warehouse and fortifications which had already been planned were being held up for want of a skilled mason.[98]

Basic equipment was taken over by the Royal African Company from its predecessors and this included: fourteen iron and two brass guns, nails, smith's and carpenter's tools, seals and weights, paper, fowling-pieces, muskets, beads, old hats, blue jugs, wool cards (i.e. for combing or 'carding' wool; still sometimes used today), pewter basins, kettles, swords, brass candlesticks, horse and hawk bells, canvas, 'pintadoes' (i.e. cotton cloth from the Far East printed in colours), calico, buttons, ribbons, worsted and silk stockings, shirts, coral, amber, English brandy, fifty-seven pairs of large and six pairs of small shackles, slippers, powder and shot, padlocks, staples, anchors, canoes, twelve men, two women *gromettoes* and the *Hope* sloop.[99] This inventory was made by Edward Pierce, chief agent, and his second, Philip Heron. In the same month Pierce wrote home again to say that he would prefer to have his headquarters in the Iles de Los because there, in his opinion, lay the heart of the trade and if the Dutch or French were to settle there Sierra Leone would get nothing.[100] He continues:

...I have entertained one John Maddyson att £24 per annum who being a Stone Mason, hath promised to finish a Stone house and fortifycation that I formerly began upon this Island....With the old Sloope that wee have now left I shall with all expedition by the helpe of God goe atradeing to Rio Noones; and to Resettle that Factory now vacant; I hope you will send us a factor fitt for such imployes as also a Carefull man to be a Store house keeper...to place at Rio D'Punga.

At this time there were at least five other Englishmen on Bunce including Henry Heath, a surgeon, but he died on 5 December 1678. His clothes were auctioned on the 31st amongst his colleagues, as was the usual custom. There was a heavy mortality rate in the garrison at this time and it was not confined to Europeans. In January 1679 we read 'I man dyed att Tasso sent thither to cure and...one dead here on ye Island'.* In August 1680 a leopard killed another African on Tasso.[101]

In 1681 we hear of a factory established on the Rio Nunez 'where Mr Pierce settled a Factory and left it in the Hands of Mr Porter'.[102] Very shortly, however, Porter was trading illegally on his own account, selling ivory and other goods worth £44 'to Flemish and other Interlopers'.[103] Other stations operated from Bunce at this time were *Jassily*, *Samoes* and the factory at *Logoe*. Jassily is probably Jatts Isle, in Portuguese Guinea; Samo is reached by the river Mellacourie; Logo is a common name derived from the Portuguese for a swampy place, but in this instance stands for Port Loko.

Meanwhile, building was resumed on Bunce Island and in 1680 Pierce reported that he had built a church on the island;† in January 1681 a stone house was complete except for the tiles, which were not available.[104] In May 1682, when Pierce died, the inventory made by John Case and Henry Clark, his successors, included coats and breeches for the *gromettoes'* uniforms, twenty-nine snuff boxes, forty-eight jews-harps, 467 swords, four 'good' trumpets and the *Charles* frigate,‡ the *Francis* smack, a ship of fourteen tons unfinished and still on the stocks, one longboat,‡ one hooker,‡ one wherry,

---

* In 1679 two Africans were sent from Bunce to England to learn a trade.[105]

† In 1728 domestic water was still being brought to Bunce from Tasso.

‡ *Frigate*: a ship of some thirty guns; *longboat*: a ship's large boat; *hooker*: a two-masted ship.

one large canoe, five other canoes, a stone storehouse pallisaded at the top, another stone storehouse thatched, and the stone foundations of some other building at that date six feet high.[106] About this time Barbot wrote of Bunce:

The fort is of lime and stone, the walls low, has a round flanker with five guns, and a platform just before it with six guns, all of them well mounted. But there are no considerable buildings in it, the slave booth being the best. The garrison generally consists of twenty white men, and thirty Gromettoes, who are free Blacks, and have a small village under the shelter of the fort. The island is of little compass, and the soil barren.[107]

Sixteen years later these foundations were still unfinished; an inventory taken on 22 October 1698 mentions:

A Fungo or Granary with 15 Arches and 13 Pillars covered with Thatch, a house or cover over the well center work. A stone foundation six Foot high. A Stone Wall standing but damnified per Fire. A Pidgeon house and Pidgeons. 4 Pillars and 4 Arches covered with Thatch. A Fortification or Closure covered, with 3 close Towers Flankers etc. with a Cookroom house within covered with Thatch.[108]

In 1700, because war seemed likely to break out again at any moment, a considerable quantity of artillery was sent out for Bunce:[109]

5 February 1699. The Duty Arising By Act of Parlement To the Royall African Company £47 6s. for ye following Stores shipt on board ye Amity Captain John Miller Bound for Serralion for ye Use of that Fort Videlicet:

2 Minnion Gunns
2 Ditto 3 Pounders
30 Minnion and 30 threepound Shott
6 Spunge Staves...24 Rammes heads...and 4 Sheepskins
2 Copper Ladles...2 Wormes...1,000 Spunge Nayles...2 Formers
4 Powder cases...1 hammer...1 pr. Sheeres...2 quire paper
¼ lb. thred & 12 needles...Starch & Starch Pann...2 steele bitts
4 powder Hornes with Priming Irons...6 shod Handspykes
1 Budge Barrel...12 Tomkins...4 lead Aprons
¼ cwt. Match...½ lb. Brasse Wire & 1 Mallet
4 Carridges with beds and quoines
Iron Worke for ditto...*

* *Minion*: a small gun of some three inches calibre; *sponge staves and sheepskins*: used for sponging out a gun after firing—guns in those days were muzzle-loading; *rams*: used for ramming home the powder and wads—there were no

In spite of these warlike preparations the French attacked Bunce in 1704 and handled it so severely that a report of 1705 speaks of the site as being 'demolished' and suggests plans for its re-establishment with twenty-four men and sixteen guns.[110] Presumably the enemy had removed all they could from the island. The Act of Parliament referred to in the list of goods sent to Bunce in 1699 is that of the previous year which opened trade on the coast to all, providing that the private traders paid a 10 per cent duty to the company on all their exports. This duty was intended for the upkeep of the forts, but it sparked off a pamphlet war in England and a commercial one upon the coast between the company and the private traders. This was because the latter objected to being charged for the use of the forts which hitherto they had done very well without. One broadsheet came out bitterly with the remark that 'nothing can ruin or cramp this Trade but* Pyrates abroad and Projects at home'.[111] There was a great deal of sense in this; apart from war, interloping and lack of governmental support—particularly financial support—proved to be the undoing of the company. After 1713, when the Act of 1698 came to an end, neither Bunce nor the fort at York Island received much attention.

Originally, besides the stock, some of the previous company's servants were also taken over by the Royal African Company, as, for instance, Zachary Rogers in Sherbro. In August 1678 he wrote home: 'Now to give your Honours notice of the Great Guns and all other materialls I found and received at my coming in to this River which was on ye account of Gambia Adventurers being in June 1668....'[112] In 1680 there was a tribal war in the Kittam country which hindered the cutting of redwood and forced Rogers to move his factory. At this time the chief shortage at Sherbro

gun-cartridges then; *worm*: a screw fixed on the end of a rod for withdrawing the wad; *former*: a small wooden cylinder on which musket or pistol cartridges were rolled or 'formed' to the required size; *handspike*: a wooden bar shod at one end with iron for levering heavy guns into position; *budge-barrel*: a small powder barrel with a long-necked leather cover; *tampion* or *tomkin*: a wood block used as a disk and placed between the charge of powder and the shot, used especially with grapeshot which is small shot used in large numbers and which scatter when fired; *lead aprons*: square pieces of lead laid over the touch-hole or small hole at the near end or breech of the gun through which the main charge is ignited; *match*: wick of hemp, cotton, etc., used as a fuse in the touch-hole; *carriage, bed, quoin*: the carriage was a gun's main support, a bed was a movable block of wood laid under the breech to give elevation, quoins were wedges for fixing the gun when elevated.

* But, i.e. except.

seems to have been in boat-building equipment; in July he ordered nails, two small pumps, resin, tar, cordage, blocks for a sloop, one dozen small boat oars, two pairs of wooden hand-screws, fifty foot of oak planking, a pair of weighing scales and pens and ink.[113] By March 1681 Rogers was dead and was succeeded by Joshua Platt, but before he died he had established depots at Kittam, Boom, Sherbro and Gallinas. In 1684 negotiations were completed for building a house on an island near Cape Mount, possibly on the site of the Dutch fort occupied for about a year at the beginning of the century. The clerk in the London office noted these facts briefly: 'The king there is absolute. Grants leave to build an house on ye Isle. Given him a present for it, but not to remove the factory.... When the house is built the Factors intend to remove all at once. The king to have his Costoms paid as formerly.... Noe water but brackish though hopes to find some. A ship may lye within 50 yards of ye Factory.'[114] By the end of the century other depots had been established from Sherbro at *Marry, Ham, Tibball* and *Yonni*[115] (modern Mai, Tiboe, Yonni, and probably Hahun). The Plantain Islands are situated so conveniently for ships that do not wish to negotiate the shallow waters around Sherbro no doubt goods were landed there from early days and taken up-river in smaller vessels.* In 1713 they certainly were.[116]

In March 1685 the company suffered a considerable loss of stores and also the destruction of a warehouse at Bunce valued in all at £300. Agent John Case having paid a visit to Sherbro was saluted upon his return to Bunce with the customary gunfire. Unfortunately, some of the wads set fire to the thatched roofs and soon the blaze was out of control.[117] This kind of accident was not uncommon, probably because the gunpowder, becoming damp, often misfired and so no doubt the gunners tended to ram home too big a charge. In 1710 another fire at York destroyed the sails of a sloop and a barge as well as other nautical equipment and seven tons of clean rice which represented their entire stock.[118]

In July 1687 a factory was settled in the Rio Nunez—north of modern Sierra Leone—and in the following year a dry dock was completed on the east end of Bunce; the remains of this may be seen still. Having learnt their lesson by now, the company's ware-

---

* In the 1740's the Plantains were used as the headquarters of a private slaver who had previously been at Cape Mount; John Newton, slaver, later in Holy Orders, worked there.

houses were no longer thatched with palm fibre.[119] Inquiries were also made at this time about obtaining the king's permission to build a house on Bob's Island in the Sierra Leone river.[120]

By June 1688 the factory at Sherbro had moved at last from the river bank to York Island, named originally after their most exalted shareholder, the duke of York, who was now king of England, having succeeded his brother Charles II. The earlier fort had been opposite the 'King's Town', so we are told; probably near the modern Bendu. In the following year the foundations of the fort were laid and in 1690, to supplement their diet, a pigeon-house was built.[121] Barbot described the fort in his time as 'built square; having three round flankers and a square one, with eleven guns; and about twenty paces from the fort on the sea-beach two large round flankers with five good guns in each, all built with stone and lime, and defended by about twenty-five white men and between fifty and sixty Gromettos, all in the Company's pay'.[122]

As a Frenchman and therefore a rival, Barbot was not, of course, invited inside, and we have to wait until almost the end of the century for a description of the interior: 'A Dwelling house and store with a Fortification or Closure (with 4 Flankers, 3 of which Storehouses) with a Cookroom adjacent covered with Stone. Two new Forts built since Mr Gibson's Agency. One Fungo or Grainery (with many Arches on Pillers) covered with Stone. One pidgeon house with 4 Arches on 4 Pillers.'[123] During the pamphlet war which followed the Act of 1698 both sides began to lobby ruthlessly and inaccurately for their ends and it is difficult now to sift the truth from the mud that was thrown by both sides at the time. One pamphlet, headed 'Forts and Castles which the African Company pretend to have',[124] said that York, in spite of the company's reports, possessed only ten men and 'Two Guns 6 Pounders, 14 Guns of two pound Shot, all old and unserviceable, very large Vents and no Carriages'. The buildings were dismissed as 'a large House very much out of repair, incompassed with a Mud Wall'. This was certainly inaccurate; Barbot, who had no reason to lie, said that the walls were of stone. But there is no doubt that the fort at York was not so well prepared for defence as the company made out; it was attacked by the French in 1705 and soon after went into a decline. From 1713 to 1730—when the Government granted a subsidy—the company had to keep up their forts unaided. By this time, as far as Sierra Leone was concerned, it was too late; reports of 1729 and 1749 make no mention of either Bunce or York Islands.[125]

However, the company replied to the report of their pretended forts and castles by 'A true Account of the Forts and Castles...on the North Part of Guinea' and this credited York with: 'a Fort of 2 Palankers very strong, built of Stone and Lime, in a Half-Moon, very high, the Water beating upon the Walls in some places; the Factory adjoyning to it is a strong large House built of Lime and Stone, covered with Lead, and in very good Repair, besides several Outhouses for Conveniences of the Trade.'[126] There were also, according to this account, twenty guns and one hundred and fifty men on the island; this certainly bears out Barbot's description— in fact he credits the factory with twenty-one guns—although it is difficult to believe that almost twice the number of servants had been suddenly squeezed in. Probably the total included slaves as well.

Until 1700, when agent Platt was succeeded by Henry Gibson, it seems that Sherbro and its factories were under the general supervision of the chief agent at Bunce, but in that year the directors decided to separate them. Trade in the Rio Nunez and Scarcies areas had declined in recent years and the directors felt that this was because of the difficulty of supplying factories lying to the windward from sailing ships whose main depots were so placed that every journey meant a long haul against the prevailing winds. There seemed to be no point in having cargoes brought up from Sherbro and unloaded at Bunce, to be loaded again when a ship from England called. The company's ships could perfectly well put in at Sherbro in the course of their normal south-bound trip.[127]

And so, in 1709 we hear that John Clark in Sherbro is again fortifying the island of York, presumably after the French sack of 1705. Yet, only eleven years later the directors wrote to Plunkett, chief agent at Bunce, to say that they considered the fort at Bunce, recently attacked by pirates, as well as that on York Island, was too dilapidated to be worth repairing.[128] Consequently, an idea was revived which had first been suggested in 1714. In that year they had written to Clark:[129]

...we understand the distemper of the Country has been fatal to most of the Servants we have sent which We imagine must proceed from the rainy season. To prevent the like misfortune for time to come We recommend to You the fixing a settlement at Cape Serraleon which We are advised is the most Convenient place for Command of that River and Trade and a very good Air. We would have this so accomodated [*sic*] that all Our White Servants not accustomed to Sherbrow may in the rain time especially be at that Settlement.*

Plunkett, however, was not in favour of this plan and the directors had to write ordering him to stop the rebuilding he was undertaking on Bunce. 'We desire you will... be ordering your Negroes to clear a peice of Ground on the pitch of the Cape and be gathering stones for the building and proper Shells for making Mortar.'[130] In May 1721 they changed their minds and asked whether a fort could not be built at the watering-place, or even at both places so long as they could be mutually supporting. The reason for this vacillating attitude was that the directors had heard a rumour of an intended French settlement on the river. However, the French did not come and Plunkett got his own way, but not before the company in November 1721 had sent out Captain Samuel Heartsease to confer with him. In this year they were short of money and Heartsease' instructions commanded moderation:[131] 'You are to consider whether instead of erecting a Fort, a proper Platform, with a convenient Logement for the Men, may not be of more use, as We know it will be of less expense, to be made in any place you shall think proper for securing the Command of the River.'† The directors also asked him to confer with Plunkett about making a settlement at Cape Mount and at Cape Mesurado. Cape Mount had been settled once before in 1684. York Island, at present abandoned, they suggested should be given up and the factory moved to the north shore by Zachary Cumberbuss's town. The relations of the York settlement with their neighbours were seldom amicable for very long. Some idea of this embittered struggle may be had from a remark of William Smith who visited York Island in 1726. He heard, he said, of 'there being a Law at *Sherbro* that whosoever struck a White Man, should, if he was merchantable, be sold for a Slave, but if old, or unmerchantable, that he should be put to Death'.[132]

---

* Clark died 3 October 1714, 'he having no Will but Verball which was to his Woman and her Friends. They together rifled all his Effects.'[133]

† The state of the company's ships in Sierra Leone reflects a similar poverty: the *Sierra Leone* and *Bense* sloops laid up for want of repair, the *Africa* sloop, *Sherbro* shallop, *Queen Elizabeth* longboat and two canoes 'almost wore out'.[134]

In 1714 agent Richard Smith had written from Sherbro:

...The River is not settled as yet, neither have they made any King of Sherbrow but every Town demanding a Cole [i.e. a toll] as we pass up the River, so that they make themselves all Kings. Some time after Mr Clark's death the King of the Bulloms seized of your Honours Effects to the Vallue of 536 Barrs and refuses to return it, his Palaver is per reason he was not called in to ye Cry [i.e. burial] of Mr Clark with all other Kings....Also he hinders us from bringing our Camwood down the River which is at Cooley Factory and John's Factory....[135]

There is no doubt that there were faults on both sides in this quarrel. In May 1720 Plunkett wrote about one of his agents named Callow that he was 'to hasty and pasionate for the temper of the Natives and the relinquishing the Factory at Sherbrow was Cheifly owing to him; as for Mr Archbold he has ye way of humouring them, but is not sharp enough to deal with so many Competitors'.[136] However, in 1721 the factory was resettled and we hear that Plunkett has been there 'accomodating matters' whilst agents were being regularly sent to the Rio Pongo, Rio Nunez and in the south to Cape Mount and Gallinas.* But in 1726 trouble occurred again at York Island and this time, after two years more of bitter wrangling, the company left it for good. The incident has been described by William Smith, who was not only an eyewitness, but who himself directed the defence of the garrison dressed most unsuitably for the climate in a full-bottomed peruke or wig.

On *Saturday*,† we got up the River as far as a small Town belonging to one Zachary Cummerbus, a Mullatoe, who was the Son of a late *English* Agent upon *York* Island. Here I was very kindly entertain'd, but being impatient to see in what Posture the Company's Affairs were upon *York* Island, I made no stay here, but immediately proceeded up the River, and arriv'd at the said Island next Day. When I went ashore, I found no white Man but one Mr *Holditch*, a Factor, who was destitute of all Manner of Defence against the Natives. He told me, he had receiv'd several Visits from them, and that they always took care to carry away whatsoever they fancied of the Company's Effects. Here once stood a very good Fort, which is now a dismal Heap of Ruins.[137]

* We also hear of a factory in 1721 at 'Manya...in the Sousas'[138] and in 1713 of John's factory 'Rio Mary'.[139]
† I.e. 19 November 1726.

The next day the king of Sherbro with some three hundred attendants came to see Smith, bringing with him as a present two hundredweight of rice, two goats and a wild boar. The king stayed the night and, on the following morning, Smith made an inventory of the company's goods on the island. Then, saluting the king with five guns, he left. 'It was imagin'd', he says, 'upon my Departure, by *Holditch* and *Allen*,* that his Majesty would have return'd to *Sherbro*, but they were mistaken, and the King's stay they knew would be very expensive to them.' Consequently they asked the king to return home to Sherbro Island: 'At which, the King fell into a great Rage, and swore by his Fittish [i.e. a lion's tail], that all the Country was his, that he only suffer'd the *English* to reside there upon certain Conditions; that *York* Island and all the Goods upon it were his, all which he would soon make them sensible of, since they had not paid him his COLE.' After Smith had left, the king, certain of superior strength now that the armed sloop had gone, helped himself to such of the company's goods as he fancied, and so Holditch sent a plea for help. Smith therefore returned that same evening, taking the precaution of loading his ship's guns with grapeshot. Landing with his sword drawn he arrested the king, but the latter escaped from the canoe which was carrying him to the sloop. Immediately preparations were made to prepare for a siege of the fort. Later that day, being shot at by the enemy, Smith signalled to his ship to fire two guns at a group of Africans standing by the water's edge. Eleven of these were killed and this brought resistance virtually to an end. An embassy from the king sued for peace, but, feeling unable to rely upon him, Smith decided to move the company's stores from York Island to Jamaica Town, towing them behind his sloop in canoes. Straight away the Africans realised that they would lose for ever the company's tolls and they turned upon their king, who fled, never to be seen again. In his place his Speaker, Maximo, was elected.

These events, coupled with the depredations of the private traders and pirates on the Bananas, at Sherbro and in the Sierra Leone river, were to be the end of the company's effective business in this country. Of the pirates Charles, Factor at Bunce, wrote:

...at that time, they had on the Island [i.e. the Banana Islands], in their Service, Tuft a writer, and Waring a Marriner, who before my comeing into the Country, had deserted the Service, one had pre-

* Smith had just appointed Allen as Holditch's assistant.

viously retir'd amongst them, with the Company's effects from Sherbro factory under his Care, the other had carried off some hundreds of large teeth from the Jaqueen sloop, then under his command. And besides they had also on the Island, Penwell,* whom they have entertain'd, ever since he and his gang left Bence Island, and had Pyratically plunder'd the Jaqueen sloop in the road....[140]

And so, in 1728, there was further trouble in Sherbro when the private traders and pirates combined against the company. Walter Charles did not go immediately to Sherbro when the crisis arose because there were so many sick men on Bunce Island that he could not well leave them; also, one suspects, because he was not a man of action he was not at all keen to become involved in any violence. For a month he remained at home apprehensive of: '...the difficulties I surely Expected from the endeavours of the white Banditi, upon the Bonanos; who have, as I had been lately informed, insinuated themselves with the leading Natives of Sherbro; even the Company's Freinds and also underhand encourag'd Buck and his Pyratical accomplices, whereby they then were got into the secret of the Camwood trade....'[141] However, Charles finally reached Sherbro at the end of August:

Satyrday Aug 31st...I anchor'd in Jamaica Road, in which time the Shallop lost Company with us, and getting in before us, was seiz'd by the natives, I could perceive the Banks of the River, all the length of the town pallisadoe'd, and in Sundry places several Carriage, and Swivell guns planted, I saw also a White man walking in state like an officer... amongst the people; (which and no Canoes comeing on board with Zachary Cumberbuss to visit me as I Expected, and is customary, gave me some reason of surprize). I therefore began to think that my long stay from amongst them had effectually enabled the vagabonds on the Banano's to seduce the people into their measures....I sent on shore the long boat...with a message to senior Zachary, and the headmen of the town...that I wanted to speak with them on board...all the people of the town were gather'd under the Palaver house, and amongst them, Saunders one of the Banano Gentry, as a very great man....At last the boat return'd...they sent me a most insolent and illmannerly answer,... that they were surpriz'd at my not saluting the town, and till I did that, and sent on shoar an officer to them they could not nor would not come to see me....I concluded these unhappy people were intirely deluded and influenced by the Bonano Vagabonds, who have taken for their Wenches the Daughters and Relations of the leading men in the Country and town.[142]

* 'The worthless Penwell my Predecessor...'.[143] Charles arrived in 1726.

Weakly and misguidedly Charles did as he was asked and fired a seven-gun salute, but still he received no deputation; great activity on shore, however, led him to believe that something was afoot:

...our vessels being so near, we could hear and see much of their proceedings on shore, and frequent goings and comeing between the Palaver house and that of Saunders, who keeps the Bonano Store in the same house where our factory was...Zachary by means of their freinds was very irresolute, because they made him believe I would certainly detain, if not murder him, should he go off to see me....A letter from Saunders, wherein he inclos'd one from the Bonano's signed John Bannerman and Company, that being the regulation they now go under....[144]

Of course, what Charles could see were preparations for a siege. During the night Pierce and Bannerman arrived from the Banana Islands bringing with them an iron gun; the next day there came 'some hundreds of Negroes' led by Will Cumberbuss 'the Idol of the White vagabonds'. On Friday, 6 September the iron gun and seven others in the town fired upon Charles's two ships, Zachary Cumberbuss, a company servant at Jamaica Town, being unable to stop them. The irresolute Charles thereupon sailed away having settled nothing.

However, in October the situation became more hopeful and a deputation from Sherbro arrived at Bunce:

Senior Derby who since my return from Sherbro had come...with proposals for accommodating the differences in that River, Zachary Cumberbuss and many others of the peaceable men being come to his town, and had brought with them the Expedition's boat; also the Company's Slaves and hir'd Grometoes, who were panyard [i.e. kidnapped] when I was in Sherbro...I bid him tell Zachary that I would enter into no treaty with him till all things were again on the same foot as when I left Bence Island to come at their own request amongst them...they must deliver up Buck the Pyrate.[145]

Cumberbuss actually seized Buck but a party from the Banana Islands rescued him.

But Charles's troubles, though he could not know it, had only just begun. During the night of 25/26 October 1728 he and all his staff were driven from Bunce Island by a band of Africans led by three Afro-Portuguese men called Lopez, Jerome and Thoma; Charles wrote a long account of this disaster:

Here begins account of the attack and taking the Fort by ye natives.

Friday October 25. I had no rest not a moments sleep from going to bed last night, and after 1 o'clock; I never failed to call upon the watch on the parade every half hour;...half past 2 I call upon the watch, I found them on Duty, and the sloops in the road had but just answer'd the watch forward, which was enjoyn'd by me, and justly observ'd every ½ hour, for the watch on the Parade hail'd the sloops, and they answered with the word; 2 men forwards and 2 men backwards, with an officer and another man, who were under the fungo,* were the night watch, and reliev'd every 3 hours after 8 Clock, till 6 in the morning and from thence till night. Mulatta Soldiers did Duty for the better preservation of the health of my white people....

I will also relate the Condition of the Fort....From the gate which almost faces the port the flag Bastion begins, on which are mounted 4 large Saker† and 2 large Minion Guns, the stone wall is continued from it, in a direct Line, for about 20 Yards, and ends in what formerly had been an irregular Bastion, which jetts out from the Curtain aforesaid only about 4 or 5 foot, between the Flag Bastion and the other, 8 Demy Culverin‡ lye in the Ports, and make a good appearance from the Road, but having no carriages could not be fir'd usefully above once or twice. This is all the stone fortification belonging to Bence Island, but as I propos'd to fortify the whole Factory I begun a regular ½ moon Bastion,§ from that last mention'd, and also a Curtain wall, which I intended to continue on to another design'd bastion, and in that manner by carrying on the work, quite round to the Port Gate, to compleat the Fortification of the place with 2 more Bastions, in all five, which would have made the Factory a fortress of great Consequence, and after the design'd buildings within had been compleated would have lodg'd 100 white men....The first intended ½ moon was carryed up 3 foot thick to the height of 4 foot, and the Curtain of the same thickness, about 6 foot high in the first dry season that I was here [i.e. 1726]...and ever since I could never carry on the work for want of tradesmen; however I enclosed the Factory with wooden stakes, beginning about 20 foot from without my new Bastion, and so continued them round to the Port Gate. They were some of them 10 many 12 inches through, 4 foot in the ground and 12 foot above and lash'd together towards the upper

* A fungo is a grain-store.

† A saker was a cannon firing a shot weighing about 6 lb.; it was a favourite gun with ships' captains. See p. 99 n. above.

‡ A demi-culverin was a gun slightly larger than a saker, with a bore of some 4½ inches, firing a shot weighing some 10 lb.

§ The original flag bastion (on the right as one approaches up-river), the curtain wall, irregular bastion and Charles's half-moon bastion may still be seen today.

ends...within side are Gallerys of communication all round, where 5 or 6 men can walk a breast, the tops of the stakes being about breast high above. Over the back Gate were two Swivel Guns and in other places 3 more, which intirely commanded all the landings behind the Factory. Upon platforms rais'd of equal height to the foremention'd Gallerys, behind my own apartments, were mounted a 4 pounder and 2 one pounders, on Carriages, and these commanded all approaches from the Port to the backside landings upon the Island.*...In my hall were 20 Buccaneer Guns, 10 pair of pistols, 6 Blunderbusses, 20 Brass hilted swords and 10 brass Dog headed Cuttlasses....Yesterday all the musquets were clean'd and also 5 pair of Pistols, the latter I loaded myself and put them up, but deferr'd loading the musquetts till next morning because the men had chang'd and misplac'd the Bayonets.... As to the Great Guns...for want of sheet Lead to make aprons, and Tompions, we were forc'd to make one out of Barrell staves and the other of Goat skins, which proved to be insufficient against the weather in the Rains and to a greater Expence of powder than was needful. They often disappointed me in returning salutes so that in firing 3 or 5 guns twice the number have blown, besides, before I could make a return....Nothing under God could have hurt us, and the Extravagant encouragement which I had solemnly engaged my self to promise my people, viz. $\frac{1}{8}$ of all that should fall into their hands in case of any hostile attempt...was enough to make Cowards fight....As I have a little before observ'd, I had called to the watch on the Parade...and was but just dozing when a sudden and confus'd noise yet somewhat triumphant even disturbed me....I immediately conclude the 3 Chain of Prisoners and the Sale Slaves were broke out, for I did not dream of an attempt from without....Not finding my slippers or Banian Gown [i.e. a loose gown worn in India], I run out upon the Parade in my shirt and trousers and barefooted with a highland broad sword in my hand. I am attacked by about half a dozen Blacks arm'd, against whom I defend myself as well as I can, still calling out 'my Lads, my Boys, my Bences come, come, here I am'....No person all the time comeing to my assistance, only I see one by me, but I know not who...I therefore judge it best to retire, which I do in a fighting posture, not being above 8 yards from my own back yard; but I was no sooner enter'd it than the Cowardly Rascals went backwards and durst not follow me. I find the Scotch merchant and Doctor in a great consternation, drawing on their breeches, for they lay in my appartment; they ask me what they shall do. 'Do', says I, 'go with me, we will do well enough', so I run into the hall and brought out 2 Cutlasses and 2 load'd pistols which I deliver to them.

* The wooden beams at the east end of the island, where vessels were beached for unloading, may be seen today if one wades far enough out from the shore.

'Now come along, for we are 4 white people and shall soon be more, for my own people will certainly get to me'; then away I go upon the Parade...but with no one with me, only one, though I thought all followed. I was hardly out of the yard Door when we were attacked by near a score....We both retreat backwards to my Yard and....I see Simeon Wild in it, but he is short sighted and of little Service. The person with me, whom I took to be the Scotch merchant,* tells me upon my asking for the other two white men that they did not follow, but went both over the wall....I mount the Tarrass of my new Rooms and call upon the Bomboys who answer me, and then were with me near 20 of the Castle Slaves and Grometo's....I bid them come into the Fort, but the Rascals said they had no arms. I believe now that I am betrayed but resolve upon another sally....Upon this my 3rd sally out I see them only firing briskly at the windows of the hall and when they hear my voice they attack me. I think my men to be all murther'd or prisoners, so I retreat into the yard...Mr Crawford begs me to go over the wall...when on the farther bank of the Ditch I see a number of negroes in a body ½ way to the water side...we call to them and...find them to be the Castle Slaves and Grometo's, and with them the Bomboys. We join them and I chide them very severely...but at the same time, I see a Crowd on the Beech, and being dismally dark can't distinguish whether White or Black....By the voices I soon know those at the water side to be white people and I am quickly with them, being Captain Ryvees of the Recovery, Captain Fernly of the Fortune, their 6 hands, and 4 of the Scotch' ship's boats [Barbados merchant from London] boats crews....The people shew greatest concern for me and beg me to go on board...they see me standing barefoot in the mudd [being then almost low water]...and so we all Imbarque in the two boats and go aboard the Recovery, she having her sails bent [i.e. made fast], the other sloop's mast being on shore to be fish'd [i.e. strengthened], but the Rascals at the fort fir'd some hundreds of small shot at us... without hurting any of us....When on board...I find that all the powder we have is not above 10 or 12 pounds, only one Iron shot, and 2 Cartouch boxes of musquett cartridges a very sorry provision for defence, but such a sudden surprize was little expected....However we fell down about 4 miles below the fort, and as I judg'd us without reach of the Great Guns on the flag bastion.[146]

Later, Charles discovered that the castle slaves and the *gromettoes* had been part of the conspiracy and the next morning, being unable to see Crawford, the Scots merchant, or the doctor, he learnt that they had been taken prisoner by Lopez and were held at

* It was pitch dark. Wild was a company soldier.[147]

Fourah Bay. On 4 November Charles returned to collect his papers and a few of the company's effects, but he did not dare to remain on Bunce because of the still hostile Lopez who had, of course, two of Charles's men as prisoners. Later he shipped 28 'Great Guns' to Cape Coast Castle; on 5 December he decided that it would be diplomatic to leave the river altogether and so he ordered:

the Captain to alter the course and to stand round the shoals of St Anne in order to proceed to the Southward, for having consider'd on what I had heard...so often, of Lopez' threatning not to give my white people, his Prisoners, their Liberty,...till he was assur'd of my being Gone off the Coast, I concluded it equally the same if not better to keep the Sea than to return into Sierra Leone River for there I can get no Supply of Wood or Water without the Assistance of Interlopers, which they esteem a favour, notwithstanding my paying their People for their trouble, and to go upon trade to the Northern Rivers, may be a means of my missing the Guinea Packett....I resolve therefore to proceed Southardly round the Shoals, then to call at Galinas, and from thence to trade all the way down, till I come to Cape Palmas, the most Southerly Limits of this District.[148]

Later, Charles sailed for England, and this was virtually the end of the company's effectiveness in Sierra Leone which was now left to the pirates and private traders. In 1751 the company's forts on the coast were delivered over to the Committee of Merchants Trading to Africa, and the British government promised to send warships to protect them. But it was too late because the forts had fallen into such bad repair. About this time a Captain Pye in his report said that masons were the first necessity and, until some were sent from England to teach the Africans, any money granted would be completely wasted. In 1750 a report by Captain Reed on Bunce Island—which he calls George Island—spoke of:[149]

6 men in different Employment and 2 White Boys, servants—the Fort in very indifferent Repair—a Magazine under ground, 1 extream good Store House—a Large stone built Dwelling House, a great part of the Front down—an exceeding good Harbour to clean and repair Vessels in the Tides—Factory slaves, 21 men, 4 women, 3 boys—10 guns, 9 Pounders, mounted; 3 ditto, 3 Pounders unmounted; 12 ditto, 2 Pounders for Carriages, unmounted; 1 Swivel,* 200 shot—10 Barrels

* Swivel-guns were almost the hall-mark of a slaver; unlike the ordinary ships' guns, they could be turned inboard against slaves in the holds. For the eighteenth century it is practically a rule that if a ship's documents mention a swivel-gun, but contain no Letters of Marque (which would have created her a legal privateer) then she is a slave ship.

of Gunpowder—1 Barrel of Beef and 1 of Flour—2 Sloops, 1 Schooner, 2 small boats, 2 large Canoes, 2 small ditto.*

But the Committee of Merchants seem to have been unable to get possession of Bunce because it was occupied by three London partners trading privately. These made treaties with local rulers in 1758 and 1766, mainly for supplying timber, although slaves were also bought. In 1779 the factory, still in disrepair, was again attacked by the French and surrendered to M. Pontdevèze's first broadside. In 1785 the three merchants, now fallen on hard times, decided to cut their losses by leasing the island to Ormond, a notoriously cruel slave-trader, and it was probably he who rebuilt the fort at the end of the following year to protect his garrison of seventeen men against a French settlement on Gambia Island close by. We are told that the magazines, the houses of the governor and clerks, the docks, halls and warehouses were all newly built though 'with less luxury than appear to have been employed in the former buildings'. Ormond died about 1790 leaving, amongst other children, a son Jack who committed suicide when both drunk and drugged in 1828. Although educated in England, he became a slaver on the Rio Pongo, presumably amongst his mother's people who came from that district.

Gambia Island was first occupied by the French in 1772 and in 1780 a M. Ancel settled there, entering into partnership with M. Hannibal, the first resident, who died in 1781 leaving his share to Ancel. Ancel later persuaded the French Government to build an official depot and in 1784 M. de Jaille began to put up buildings, having leased the island from the Temne King Forbana. But the factory was not well situated; it was off the main stream of the Bunce river in a muddy fever-ridden creek, with a narrow channel between it and the mainland, filled with trees which kept away the cooling breezes; also the island was not really large enough and it was not an easy place to defend.

About 1770 the Liverpool company, known in Africa as the Sierra Leone Company, had tried to make a settlement on the river, but their agent had been murdered and ships' cargoes plundered, so that the attempt was abandoned. However, in September 1785 their agent, Lieutenant John Matthews, R.N., agreed with the chief at Whiteman's Bay that he should be allowed

---

* About this time the second in command was 'Jubly' James, but in 1758 he became a private trader.[150]

to put up stores and workmen's houses there and this time the scheme prospered so that it quickly became the richest of the three settlements on the river at this time:

By continuing to coast along the South bank, about half a league from Pirate's Bay, we arrive at the anchorage or road of the English factory, formed near the village of Sierra Leona.

This little road is in fact merely a creek.... The bay is healthy and the bottom good; and the vessels anchor there in ten fathom water. This creek is capable of containing from twenty to twenty-five vessels, and its situation is extremely agreeable and favourable to commerce.

It was at the bottom of this creek, on an elevated soil forty feet above the level of the sea, which is cultivated to an extent of three hundred fathoms, covered with the finest vegetation, and the ascent to which is extremely gradual, that an English society, then known in Europe by the name of the Liverpool Company,...had in 1786, a very considerable establishment and factory, which were as well organised and well conducted as they could have been in England.

A negro village, which is also denominated Sierra Leona, consisting of upwards of 300 huts, is situated on the mountain, about 500 toises* from this English factory.

Immediately after the creek of Sierra Leona, and on the same coast, is the bay of Aiguade† (*Fresh Water Bay*) to which we‡ have given the appellation of French Bay. Vessels can anchor in seven fathoms water; and the *Emeraude*, commanded by M. de la Jaille, remained at anchor here in 1784, during the whole of his stay in the river.

At the bottom of this little bay...is the Aiguade or fountain of fresh water, formed by a rivulet which descends from the mountains....In fact the situation of this bay may be said to unite every advantage.

By still continuing to proceed southward, we arrive, about eight leagues from Cape Sierra Leona, at the entrance of the river Bunck,§ the breadth of which is a league....

After having ascended the Bunck about a league, we arrive at the island of Gambia, where M. de la Jaille formed, in 1784, what is called the French establishment.

It was composed of a few wooden huts, covered with straw, two of which were destined for the accommodation of a detachment of twenty men from the African battalion, and the commander of this detachment, while another was used as the magazine; and lastly, a sort of

* About three-quarters of a mile.
† From the Portuguese for a watering-place.
‡ The author of this passage, Golberry, who visited here in May 1786, was French.
§ I.e. Bunce.

warehouse and granery, and a bad oven for baking bread, formed in 1786 this French establishment in the river of Sierra Leona.

All the defence and security of this post consisted of two structures, each of which might mount about three twelve pounders; but these pretended batteries, without embrasures, might be overpowered in any direction by the first vessel who should attempt it, for it could not resist a single broadside. But there was neither time, means nor money to make it better; and the parsimony of the establishment of Gambia could not be retorted on the present projector, for I well know that he even exceeded the sums which were destined for this purpose....

I shall not here describe or enumerate the vessels, magazines, docks, or warehouses, which compose the establishment of the mercantile society of Liverpool, in the English creek of Sierra Leona; but I shall merely observe that nothing was forgotten which could render this factory healthy, agreeable, and commodious; and that it may be considered as a model for all establishments of this nature.

The chief or director of this factory, held situations which produced him a yearly income of eight hundred guineas; his residence was at Sierra Leona, but he occasionally visited the Island of Los Idolos, and other parts within his jurisdiction. The Liverpool Society allowed him two per cent for every black, which he may deliver healthy and in good condition into the English colonies; and the other advantages attached to his situation are such as must in a few years secure a very handsome competency.

He had under his command a principal agent who resided at the Island of Los Idolos; this officer has four hundred guineas per year, and a premium for every slave; all the other principal persons employed, receive also very good salaries, and possess a proportionate interest in the affairs of the society.

I have already observed, that the English factories had almost always at their disposal a great number of boats, and light vessels; that of Sierra Leona possessed, besides, a very fine vessel of eight hundred tons burden, which generally remained at anchor at the entrance of the creek; it carried twenty-four guns, and was on the whole armed as a ship of war.

The most valuable merchandizes, the principal effects, and the ammunition was placed on board this ship, where the chief of the factory slept every night; this vessel also served as an infirmary, because experience had proved that the coolness of the sea air was favourable to invalids.

The factory of the creek of Sierra Leona received every year at least ten vessels, sent from England with ample provisions...and they had constantly nearly two millions* of merchandize in their magazines.

* Of francs.

We found in the anchorage of the English creek of Sierra Leona five English vessels, and one three masted French ship, commanded by Captain Rousseau, dispatched for the execution of a treaty concluded in January 1785, between the Liverpool Society, and a Society of Havre, composed of Messrs Bachelor, Forbisson and Carmichel.

According to the conditions of this treaty, the English factory of the creek of Sierra Leona was to deliver to Captain Rousseau, in the course of a year, three thousand slaves, to be chosen by him of both sexes and all ages at the rate of six hundred franks per head. Half the price agreed on was to be paid on the day of delivery; the other half by bills of exchange at ten months.

Captain Rousseau arrived in this river the twenty fifth of September, 1785, and by the first of May, 1786, he had sent two thousand slaves to our sugar colonies....*

This treaty was inimical to the political principles of a great commercial state,† because it took out of the country a sum of money amounting to eighteen hundred thousand franks; besides this first disadvantage we had again, that of paying to the English at the rate of six hundred franks per head for slaves, which would cost us only three hundred franks per head, if we had traded for them ourselves....

Similar treaties were again concluded in 1787, and 1788, between the same society of Sierra Leona and the same houses of Nantz, but on the conditions of paying ready money, and at the rate of thirty guineas per head for slaves....

But our carelessness left all the commerce in the hands of the English, and the operations of their factory, in the creek of Sierra Leona, were increased during the year 1785 and the first five months of 1786 to a sum of more than eight millions. It will be seen that the affairs of the English society, established at the fort and isle of Bence, in the river of Mitombo, were nearly as advantageous.

The river Mitombo, which the Europeans voluntarily call the river Bence, from the name of the fort and isle of Bence, which is situated in it, and which contains a very fine English factory, arrives from a very distant Country of the interior of the continent....

...M. de Pontdevèze...rendered himself master of this island and fort in 1779.... There was not a single face, flank, or curtain of this fort, which had not been bombarded from top to bottom; and these damages were not repaired at the time when I visited them in 1786....

The largest vessels may anchor at the island of Bence.... In the month of May, 1786, I counted sixteen ships in this road, namely, three English vessels of six hundred tons burthen, five brigs, and six boats of

---

\* The French colonies.          † I.e. France.

the same nation, together with two Danish three masted ships of seven hundred tons burthen....

The factory of the island of Bence was totally distinct in point of interest from that of Sierra Leona; but they nevertheless mutually assisted and supported each other on every occasion.

...Although I was a Frenchman, and consequently the countryman of M. de Pontdevèze, who had done an irreparable injury to the English, it was impossible to meet with better treatment than I received from them at Bence, where I visited several times....*

The administration of this factory was established nearly upon the same principles and in the same manner as that of the factory of Sierra Leona....

The agents, merchants and clerks of the society of Bence, spread themselves over the upper countries along the course of the Mitombo, by which they procured nearly two thousand slaves per annum, as well as a quantity of ivory and other valuable articles.

By means of the light boats and vessels that composed their little but well organized maritime establishment, which were almost entirely manned by blacks, this factory kept up a very active trade on the coasts comprized between Cape Sierra Leona and Cape Palmas, from which they derive a considerable advantage. In 1785, and during the first five months of 1786, they delivered to the Danes more than three thousand blacks; besides which they had sent to the English colonies nearly five thousand. The general operations of this factory produced a much larger sum than the affairs of the creek of Sierra Leona....

SUMMARY TABLE

Of the produce of the commerce of the river of Sierra Leona and its dependencies during the year 1785 and the first months of 1786....

|  | Slaves | Value in franks |
|---|---|---|
| The English factory established in the creek of Sierra Leona, sent off slaves to the British colonies, to the number of - - | 3,200 |  |
| In conformity to the treaty made with a society of Havre, it delivered to the French Captain, Rousseau - - - - - | 3,000 |  |
| Total | 6,200 |  |

* In spite of its ruinous state, the factory must still have been in use.

|  | Slaves | Value in franks |
|---|---|---|
| Estimate of slaves sold to the colonies at the rate of twelve hundred franks per head |  | 7,440,000 |
| The said factory disposed of ivory, raw hides, wax, indigo, cotton, hard soap, rice, millet, tamarinds, aromatic seeds, chemical drugs, dyeing, colouring, and building wood, pieces of cotton cloths, mats, and other articles, including ambergrease and gold, to the amount of, according to the European value |  | 1,200,000 |
| The English factory of the island of Bence dispatched to the British colonies, and sold to the Danes, slaves, to the number of | 7,000 |  |
| Value of these slaves, at the rate of twelve hundred franks per head | | 8,400,000 |
| The said factory disposed of ivory, raw hides, wax, indigo, cotton, hard soap, rice, millet, tamarinds, lemon juice, pepper of different kinds, cassia in the cane, and other chemical drugs; tortoise shell, dyeing, building, and colouring wood; mats, pieces of cloth, spermacetti, ambergrease, and gold, for a sum, amounting, according to European value to | | 1,400,000 |
| Captain Basteresse* purchased three hundred slaves, and several other articles, which might amount in toto...in European colonies to | | 400,000 |
| M. Ancel...traded for 142 slaves, and other articles of commerce... | | 200,000 |
| Total estimate.... | | 19,040,000[151] |

In 1793, when the British settlement was already established on the peninsula, the French abandoned Gambia Island and in November 1802 a detachment of the Royal African Corps, some Nova Scotians and a few Maroons, were sent to occupy it.†

Meanwhile, events in England and America were to result in another settlement in the Sierra Leone river; this time it was for humane reasons. In England the Chief Justice's decision of June 1772 meant that any slave landing in England became auto-

* A merchant captain from Martinique.
† Bunce Island was abandoned by the owners in 1810; in 1812 it became a depot for the West India Regiment, part of which arrived in that year.

matically free. In America the end of the war with the colonists meant that many loyal Negroes had no longer any homes, so that some of them were brought to England in 1783. London, already full of freed slaves, was therefore presented with an additional number who did not like the climate and who were unable to find work, and compassionate men began to wonder what might be done for them. Doctor Henry Smeathman, in 1783, seems to have been the first to propose any specific plan for a colony in Africa, although he did not at that time suggest any definite place. He intended to finance the scheme from the profits which he expected to make from his experiments in improving air-balloons, forerunners of our modern aircraft which had caught his fancy when he studied them in Paris. In 1786 he published his 'Plan of a settlement to be made near Sierra Leona...under the direction of the committee for relieving the black poor, and under the protection of the British Government'. This envisaged a primarily agricultural settlement upon land purchased in Sierra Leone, although provision was made for hired labour and for setting up in trade. The colonists were to have a doctor experienced in tropical diseases—Smeathman, a schoolmaster, a schoolmistress and a clergyman. All were to be 'under the protection of the British Government' and disputes were to be settled amongst themselves 'according to the laws, by their own peers,* in a town meeting'.

Granville Sharp had been fighting for the same ends for many years, and when Smeathman returned to England after four years in Sierra Leone he found that the committee for relieving the Black Poor had been formed already. Accordingly, the first colonists arrived at Frenchman's Bay, or St George's Bay—the present Kru Bay—on 9 May 1787. On the 11th they saluted King Tom with thirteen guns before Captain Thompson went ashore to pay his respects. On the 14th payment was made to the king for land upon which the settlers should live. The next day everyone went ashore to cut a clearing through the bush to the present Fort Thornton, where they hoisted the Union Jack on the bare hillside. This settlement they called Granville Town, after their benefactor, but in 1789 their houses were attacked by the Temnes, probably egged on by the slavers in Whiteman's Bay, so that the settlement was moved from the shores of Kru Bay to Cline Bay—as it is now called. In 1792 Freetown was founded.

* I.e. their equals.[152]

CHAPTER IV

# THE KINGDOMS OF SIERRA LEONE

Except that the forest was thicker, the population smaller and big game such as bush-cow, elephant and hippopotamus much more numerous, we know very little about the history of Sierra Leone before the Portuguese arrived. The thickness of the forest which even seventeenth-century Europeans noticed particularly is, however, important because it limited the settlement of the country virtually to the rivers and estuaries. The Arabs, who for nearly one thousand years before the beginning of our period had travelled about the Sahara, feared to leave the open spaces to which they were accustomed and enter the dark forests. Islam and consequently Arabic writing came in strength to Sierra Leone only about 1750; the Vai script has an early nineteenth-century origin and the Mende script came some hundred years after that; there are no written records of this country before the Europeans came about 1460. Therefore our only sources for the early period are first the stone tools, carvings, metals and crude pottery used by former peoples and secondly tribal tradition and customs. The stone artifacts and pottery tell us that the early inhabitants believed in gods, cultivated simple farms where they grew millet, used leather for domestic purposes, wore beads for decoration and that some of them had migrated into Sierra Leone in a general south-westerly direction following the rivers. Since no expert study has yet been made of these the historian must rely primarily for early sources upon oral tradition.

The first Europeans voyaging down the west coast of Africa understood almost nothing of the hinterland; they had not come to settle, but to discover a route to the rich spice lands of the East. Even at the end of the eighteenth century, when the slave trade had begun to decline in Sierra Leone—where it had never been very extensive—foreigners still knew very little. There are four main reasons for this ignorance.

First, the Portuguese when they made their early maps were concerned only with providing sailing directions from one prominent landmark to another; any account of local customs, even of those people who lived along the coastline, was more in the nature of an entertaining digression than part of the real narrative. Secondly, to erect forts and trading stations was expensive; to maintain them was more so, not only from the purely financial point of view, but also because of the high rate of mortality amongst the European garrisons exposed to the dangers of fever and dysentery. Thirdly, as Mungo Park and others after him found, many kings looked to trade for a good part of their revenue; each caravan travelling to and from the coast was expected to pay a toll according to the value of its cargo as it crossed the frontiers of the various kingdoms. Consequently, European travellers into the interior were looked upon with disfavour as persons likely to break into a hitherto lucrative monopoly. Finally, tribal organisation along the west coast did not encourage large-scale European settlement. The sixteenth and seventeenth centuries were a period of great European activity and conquest in the Americas and the West Indies because in certain parts the climate was suitable for European settlement; elsewhere the rewards to be had from an empire whose ruler could be made subservient to the conqueror, as in Mexico rich in silver and gold, were worth the rigours of an unsuitable climate and the consequent loss of manpower. But there were no empires along the forest belt of the West African coast-line when the first Europeans arrived off Sierra Leone; neither was it possible to create one amongst the swamps and trees where each tribe and even individual villages moved at will according to the needs of immediate agricultural requirements and the pressures set up by succeeding waves of immigrants. Later, the financial interests of planters already engaged in the sugar trade upon vast plantations on the other side of the Atlantic were opposed to any similar system in Africa which might rob them of their considerable wealth and profits.

The age-old caravan routes across the Sahara, which ran from the shores of the Mediterranean to Kano and Timbuctoo, like the lines of communication across the sea, stopped short at the forest belt, some three or four hundred miles before they reached the coast. Indeed, whether one approached it from the west by sea, or from the north and east by caravan, this tropical forest offered a barrier seldom penetrated save by wandering Muslim traders and encompassing an area full of mystery and rumour.

Between 1510 and 1512 a Moor from the city of Fez in north-west Africa made two journeys into the south, one to Timbuctoo and the other to the Lake Chad area. Upon his return he wrote a *Description of Africa* which was so much in advance of any which had gone before, and indeed of some that were to come after, that he has become known to history not by his own name—El-Hasan ben Mohammed el-Wazzan ez-Zayyati—but by a nickname, Leo Africanus or Leo the African. In his *Description* he says that earlier writers knew almost nothing of this area, although religious wars had already begun to bring together the two separate civilisations, especially after A.D. 1038, when those who dwelt on the north side of the lower Senegal river were forcibly converted to Mohammedanism, thus founding the fighting Muslim sect known to history as the Almoravids who, in the course of their *Jehad* against their neighbours further south, in November 1087, lost their leader in battle. Yet, although Leo Africanus was a zealous and careful observer, his account nevertheless reveals an unconscious mixture of fact and fiction and he was able to write only about those whom he divided into fifteen kingdoms living on the eastern fringes of the forest, or upon its western coastline. To Leo and his contemporaries in North Africa, just as to travellers from Europe at this time, the forest remained a mystery. One fact is quite clear, however; Sierra Leone had never been the origin of any military expansion; on the contrary, it was a retreat for those who, uprooted elsewhere amidst the clash of imperial armies, sought sanctuary in a land where they hoped to settle in peace. Writing of this land Leo says:

They make war upon no-one, and none sets foot outside his own country. Some worship the sun...others fire...fifteen kingdoms known to us stretch along the two branches of the Niger and their tributaries. They lie between two vast deserts, one of which begins in Numidia and ends in these parts, the other, farther South, runs as far as the sea. They possess a great many religions for the most part unknown to us, as much because of the length and dangers of any journey made to their countries as because of the diversity of languages and beliefs to be found there....However, some intercourse is conducted with those who dwell along the sea coast.

...The Mali kingdom lies along a branch of the Niger for a distance of perhaps three hundred miles. It runs Northward until it meets the kingdom I have just mentioned [i.e. Jenne], in the South it ends in desert and arid mountains. Towards the West it is confined by natural forests which stretch as far as the Ocean....Formerly each of these kingdoms had its own sovereign. But nowadays they have submitted to three kings, the king of Timbuctoo,* who rules the largest part, the king of Burno,† who has the smallest, and the king of Gaoga.‡ . . . Many others in the south have boundaries which adjoin these territories.[1]

Consequently, although they were able to write at some length of North Africa by drawing upon Roman and Arab sources, the early Portuguese accounts such as those of Fernandes and Pereira mention very little about the nations of Sierra Leone and what they do have to say is confined mainly to those people who inhabited the tidal waters. The Bulloms, they said, occupied most of the country inland from the coast as far as one might paddle a canoe. The Temnes dwelt around Kasseh on the river Scarcies, and the Susus were to be found some twelve or fifteen leagues from the coast. In the north were what Fernandes called 'Çapeos',[2] whose principal virtue from his point of view was their enthusiastic consumption of grilled puppies, for each of which they were willing to pay the Portuguese six or seven pounds weight in gold.

Later writers, when referring to these people, have often omitted the cedilla, writing instead: *Capez* or even *Kapez*. This has led to a quite unnecessary, but almost irreparable confusion over the origins of this nation. In fact these Çapeos, Çapes or Sapis occupied in the sixteenth century a large kingdom stretching southwards along the coast from just beyond the north of modern Sierra Leone and comprising the Landuman, their cousins the Tyapi, who gave their name to the Sapi confederation, the Temnes, Bagas, Limbas, Yalunkas and Bulloms. Over all these the Sapi alliance exercised some kind of loose-knit suzerainty, but at no time was it in any way comparable to the well-disciplined empires of the western Sudan of the same date. Setting village against village, tribe against tribe, war stalked the coast in a perpetual game of hide-and-seek amongst the marshes and between the trees.

The people to be found today in Sierra Leone speak two basic languages, the Mande and the West Atlantic respectively. To the former belongs the speech of the Susu, Yalunka, Loko, Mende, Kono, Vai and Koranko; to the latter that of the Limba, Temne,

---

* I.e. Askia Mohammed.
† Bornu in northern Nigeria.
‡ A huge territory running from Lake Chad to Darfour.

Sherbro, Kissi and Krim. Since the Mande-speaking peoples spring from the Sudan it would seem at first sight that the original inhabitants must have been of the West Atlantic group, and that later they were invaded by the Mande-speaking nations; unfortunately the explanation is not so simple as that.

Many say that when their ancestors first came to Sierra Leone they met no one; but this is to speak in general terms; obviously a country so rich in game, fish and wild fruits must have entertained at least small parties of nomadic hunters from earliest times. What the tribal traditions mean is that the ancestors met no close-knit community such as those of the Sudan or Benin.

Probably the first people, as we know them today, to enter Sierra Leone were the Limbas, and in so doing they pushed the Gbande eastwards into what is now Liberia, where they still remain. A traditional account of their origins says that the first Limba man who came to Sierra Leone was called Mansonfundu, who led an invasion into country then occupied by the Gbande people and stretching as far west as the Wara-Wara chiefdoms of today.³ The Gbandes are related to the Lokos and also to the Mendes; a Gbande tradition says that their brothers left them at an early date to fight a war in the west.⁴ This must refer to the Lokos—whom today the Limbas call *Gbandiŋ*—some of whom were either cut off by the Limba invasion or shortly after staged a counter-attack. Consequently, as we shall see, the Lokos knew and traded with the Temnes at a much earlier date than the Mendes and thereby acquired in their speech a marked Temne influence which today distinguishes it from pure Mende.

All this, it seems, took place before A.D. 1400, because although there is no certain chronology in any oral tradition, the story of the arrival on the coast—at first on the banks of the Rio Pongo—of the Susus leads one to believe that the Limbas were already here when they came. The Susus migrated to the coast from the banks of the river Falama, a southern tributary of the Senegal, arriving in the Futa Jallon district about 1400. They had been part of the Soninke kingdom—itself part of Ghana—until in 1076 the Almoravids overran the Soninke capital.

In 1235 the *Sosso* kingdom, the Fulani-dominated successor to Ghana and now embracing the Susus, was defeated by Sundiata, a Mandingo ruler. He soon transformed his conquests into the kingdom of Mali, the richest in West Africa and in its heyday covering the western Sudan from the north-east border of Sierra Leone to the far side of Timbuctoo. Some Susu were incorporated into the Mali kingdom, but others fled to the Falama area. At this time the Mali king was styled *Mandimansa*, that is, king or *Mansa* of Mande country,[5] and Pereira tells us that in his day the Yalunkas—cousins of the Susus, the name being a geographical distinction—were a numerous people with a king called *Jaalomansa*; *Ja* is a title used today on the Senegal[6] and *Mansa* suggests that at one time they were under the influence of the Malis. In fact the Yalunkas soon took refuge in the south, driven out, so tradition says, by a pale-skinned people who wished to Islamise them. Mansa Musa, the famous king of Mali who ruled from 1307 to 1322, was renowned for his pale complexion, whilst the Songhai emperors who succeeded to most of the territory of the Mali had Berber ancestors.

The first Susus to arrive on the coast from Falama were a band some two hundred strong led by King Kanfori Domin Konteh; they were composed of five families, all cousins of Konteh, called Bankole Kamara, Manga Koudjie, Baggan, Loumbe and Manga Laba. Later they were joined by others who followed different routes. Their traditions, like those of many other tribes, say that they followed the elephant herds, hunting them towards the setting sun; when they reached the sea, finding the country un-inhabited, they settled down. There they were gradually sur-rounded by the Bagas, close relations of the Temnes, who came from the east and north-east and later, when Konteh was a very old man, by the Yalunkas, who are of the same stock as the Susus, having today similar idioms, religions, customs and fetishes. Because Susu tradition does not mention the arrival of the Limbas in the north of Sierra Leone, who, by 1450, must have been surrounded on the one side by the Susus and on the other by the Yalunkas, one must presume that the Limbas were already in Sierra Leone before the Susus came. Similarly their southern neighbours the Bulloms are not mentioned in this respect; they too were here before the Susu. When King Konteh died he was succeeded by his son Manga Kombeh Balla, in whose reign arrived on the coast the first Portuguese. The traditional Susu story which follows, there-fore, gives us the approximate dates of the Susu, Yalunka, Baga and Temne migrations and also, by inference, of the Limba and

Loko movements. All these people entered the Sierra Leone area before the Europeans came:

The Susus were nomads and hunters. They went towards the West with their women and children moving slowly but never stopping, like ants. They stayed a month, a year, two years in a place and then set out again. They lived by hunting and by gathering corn, roots and wild berries. They were armed with arrows and accompanied by many dogs as fierce as leopards. When they halted they built shelters in the forest near running water and hunted until there was no more game; then they set out once more with their young men and the dogs in front. They also fished in the rivers, drying the fish and eating it on the spot.

When they rested the *Kanfori* set up his family round him in huts and nearby the other heads of families grouped themselves in the same way. These huts...were made of wood and fibre....The men hunted and fished; the women cooked, gathered wild fruits, prepared skins of wild animals for clothing and protection, made mats and water pots and fetched wood and water.

...They wished to expand towards the East but the Bankole branch of the family was turned back by another war-like people.

And so Domin Konteh lived at Domin-ya* which became the first capital. At length this town was abandoned and replaced by Thié when the Americans, Portuguese and English began to trade in slaves.†

One day...there was trouble in the North West. The Susus there met certain black strangers from the North who...were entirely naked, being tall and strong with teeth filed into a point; their women had shaven heads.... They lived especially by fishing in the sea of which they had no fear. These people were the Bagas.... After a period of fighting boundaries were settled between them by treaty and there was peace. The Bagas formed four small nations round the large one of the Susus.

Domin Konteh...was very old when there arrived from the Futa Jallon district people whom the Peuls called Yalunkas....They told them that the yellow Peuls of Futa Jallon had made war on them and that they had wanted to convert them to their fetish called Allah....

When Domin Konteh died his son Manga Kombeh Balla succeeded him....The first Portuguese traders arrived; to begin with they did not live in Susu country but on board their ships where they traded and then left....Manga Kombeh Balla persuaded the Portuguese to settle in the country...the first Portuguese who settled was Sittel Fernando who lived at Bramaya.[7]

* *Ya* is Mande Susu for 'a place'.
† Possibly a confusion has arisen between the slave-traders and their market.

Usually the rise and fall of empires in the western Sudan had little immediate effect upon the people of Sierra Leone although the backwash of a falling dynasty, like that of the Susu, would often lap about the tribal frontiers to throw up the half-spent ripples of some tribal migration. The Susus fled from the Malis, and so probably did the Bagas, Temnes and Sapi, but the Yalunkas, because they arrived later, had most likely migrated to avoid the conquests of Sonni Ali (1464–92) who began the expansion of the Songhai empire. By 1550 the Sapi alliance stretched some two hundred miles along the coast, temporarily swallowing the Susus, but, although the collective name of this confederation derives from the Tyapi, the dominant element seems to have been the Temne nation. *Tyapi* (singular), *Sapi* (plural) are Fulani words used today for the Landuma people. Portuguese descriptions of their communities and societies show that officials had titles closely resembling modern Temne; thus about 1500 their king who lived near the river Scarcies was called *Obe Vrig*—*Obe* is the equivalent of the modern Temne *Bai*—whilst the elders amongst the Sapi were called *Solategi*—perhaps the modern *Santigi*. The Bundu girls when the bush was 'pulled' gave public dances accompanied by a drum called then as now a *ta-m̄abɔrɔ*.* Although only the Susus in this confederacy were of Mande origin we are told that the Mandingo pattern of dress was universal; this need not confuse us because even today the Temnes weave little cloth whilst we are particularly informed that the Susus only imported cloth which they obtained from the Fulahs in the north; this of course was the coat and breeches of Mandingo pattern.†

In the south and west of Sierra Leone there dwelt the Sherbros or Bulloms, who speak a language descended like that of the Temnes from the West Atlantic group; further south lay the Kono kingdom which stretched inland from Cape Mount in a north-easterly direction. Portuguese travellers in the early 1500's knew of a large and well-established town called Krim Mano, in the Sherbro district, and also of a tribe which they called *Cobales*—possibly the Golas—and so it is likely that the Krims and the Golas have lived for a very long time in small numbers amongst the creeks which intersect the thick forest of the south.

Therefore, when the Europeans came, Sierra Leone was inhabited by the Bagas, Temnes, Susus, Yalunkas, Lokos, Limbas,

---

* See ch. I, p. 10 above.       † See ch. IV, p. 164 below.

Bulloms, Krims and Konos; because the Temnes and Bulloms lived along the shore, it was their languages which the Portuguese learnt and recorded for the purposes of trade. D'Almada in 1594 said that all nations under Sapi rule understood one another's speech; in those days the Bulloms lived along the coast as far north as the island of Bulama, which represented the approximate northern limit of this confederation, and it was, therefore, Sherbro which was spoken as the lingua franca.

The first account of the river of Sierra Leone and the inhabitants to the south which gives us any significant details is an unidentified English one written about 1568. In those days the two arms of the river were called Mitombo and Tagrin, and the English had called in at the latter to refill their water casks. They arrived in time to watch the struggles of a confederation of Sierra Leone chiefs to stave off the advance wave of an invasion by a people calling themselves Manis, but known to the Temnes as *Sumbas* or those who cause trouble. This movement had begun some hundred years earlier when the Temnes, originally part of the same migration, first pushed across the eastern frontiers of Sierra Leone. It seems that the Manis or Sumbas came originally from the Futa Toro district, because d'Almada was told that the supreme leader of the original Mani forces had been a woman. Presumably, like the Temnes, they had fled from the terrible wrath of an emperor motivated in part by Islam and determined to overrun his pagan neighbours. We know that the district south-west of Kano in Nigeria was invaded in the first half of the fifteenth century by armies from Futa Toro, led by a woman called Bakao-Tourounkou, and that a new capital city, whose ruins may be seen still to the south of Zaria, was named after her. Presumably some of these refugees from Mali and Songhai turned off towards the coast before the main body reached Nigeria and, forming an aristocratic nucleus of warrior chiefs, led those whom they encountered in the forest into Sierra Leone where they settled. D'Almada was told that the Bulloms were also a relic of an invasion previous to that of the Manis, the country having been overrun about a century before, and that the latter when they came met a people with customs similar to their own; these were probably the Temnes or the Lokos. The Bulloms have been here so long that they have no tradition of immigration. Significantly D'Almada adds that the Mani paid a tax called *Maref* to an overlord who dwelt 'far behind';

*Maref* is a Malinke word and points, therefore, to a Mande origin
of the warrior chiefs. At the end of the fifteenth century, the Kano
district being invaded by Askia Mohammed, emperor of Songhai,
whose kingdom when he died stretched from the middle Niger to
Tekrur, the Manis fled once more and this brought them to Sierra
Leone by way of modern Liberia.[8]

About 1567 the main body of the Manis had not arrived in
this country although it was stationed close behind in the river
Sestos area, from which groups were sent forward to spy out the
country and to harass the enemy when opportunity occurred. In
December one of these parties led by two kings, Sasina and Seterama, were cut off and besieged in the town of Bonga, lying on the
south side of the river just below Tasso Island; the English sailors
arrived in time to play a small part in the ensuing skirmish and to
help Seri, the king of Sierra Leone. The name Seri is an alternative
for the clan name Kamara, traditionally the earliest Mande clan in
the western Sudan. Mande influence was, therefore, already strong
in Sierra Leone.

Our generall...sent into the river of Magrabomba* which is the
sowthwarde of Tagarrine...to see what good might be done...came ii
embassadors with our messangers one of them from Sheri the kinge of
Serra Lione...the other from Thoma kinge of the [?Casseti]†...
against Sasina‡ and Seterama...these ii kinges that desired our
[general's friendship] had besieged the others in a town called Bonga on
the river of Tagarrine where we ridde [at anchor]...this towne was
walled [with] mighty trees...[and] in it soldiers that had come thither
150 leagues...abowte the 27 of January our generall sent up a small
shippe with certaine pinaces and in them 90 menne...to the ayde of
the ii kinges...there was for the espace of ii dayes divers skirmyshes
where there were above 20 of our menne hurte besides divers negros
our frendes...the kings Sasina and Seterama escaped...there was
slaine of the negros...our frendes Sheri Bangi the sonne of king Sheri
in the assault...the negro kinges sente him [i.e. the English general]
worde that...they departed but nevertheless our generall showlde sende
to the Castros and there they wold make readye negros for him....[9]

In 1609 Balthasar Barreira, a Jesuit missionary, speaking of this
invasion said: 'More than seventy years ago, a certain barbarian
nation, for want of land, set forth to look for more. These people

* Magrabomba was the name of the river Sherbro at this time, but travellers
often confused the names of places in the early days.
† Probably those living in Kasseh.     ‡ Also mentioned by d'Almada.

are called Jacas in the Congo, in Angola Grindas...and here they call them Çumbas, a nickname for Manes.' In the Congo the governors of Angola had used the Jacas as soldiers, but since they were cannibals this was unpopular. Barreira adds that they destroyed the Congo when it was ruled by King Bernardo and when Queen Catherine was Regent of Portugal; in the middle of the seventeenth century Coelho was told that after they had attacked Elmina the invaders took another ten years to reach Sierra Leone. Catherine was Regent from 1557 to 1568, so that it is to Bernardo I (1561–5) that Barreira refers.* D'Almada says that the Manis arrived in Sierra Leone some forty years before his visit in 1594, but all these dates are only approximate. It was, in fact, about 1564 that the Mani invasion of Sierra Leone began in earnest when, formed like a belt round the country, they stormed the southern frontiers and, attacking the Bulloms, soon encountered the Temnes in strength. The Temnes, it seems, had earlier made themselves masters of part of Sierra Leone, setting themselves up as an independent nation and neglecting to pay homage to their Mani overlords, some of whom had remained close by whilst others ravaged the coast further south. The Temne kings of Sierra Leone, looking for allies, found them amongst the Bulloms and Limbas whilst the Manis, meeting their former vassals, came upon them and their new Bullom allies in a mood of bitter revenge.

The invaders at once made a two-pronged attack, one force moving inland whilst the other, led by Chief Masariko,† advanced along the coast. The latter fell into an ambush prepared by Bamfora the Bullom king and here he was killed. The right wing, however, eventually settled down somewhat inland, intermarrying with the local population to become what we know now as the Kissis. A study of languages has shown that the class system of nouns amongst the Kissis and Sherbros is closely related and it is likely that it was only at this time that the two peoples separated. Place-names suggest that all Kono country, much of Mendeland and part of Vai territory as we know them today were occupied at one time by the Kissis,‡ who soon after their arrival in the

---

* In 1556 William Towerson had noticed that—like the Manis—the inhabitants of the town near Elmina Castle had short bows; d'Almada noticed that the invaders had short ones whilst the defenders' were long.[10]

† Cf. the modern Mende *Maha*: chief.

‡ E.g. *Langrama* and *Peje* in Mende country suggest the Kissi *Laŋ*: mountain; *pey*: river.

sixteenth century separated the Konos and the Vais, once a powerful confederacy.

About 1568 reinforcements sent up from the south caused the Bulloms to retire and many took refuge upon Portuguese ships and so became slaves involuntarily. The kings Sasina and Seterama before they sailed away to the south had sent word to the English that they had slaves for sale and now, as the Manis advanced, this traffic became greater:

Of those who fled before the enemy many were forced to take refuge on board Portuguese ships; small boats like birds of prey hovering over the burning bush went in search of fugitives who were in despair and brought them to the larger vessels. The Mani themselves sometimes brought prisoners alongside our ships, and offered them in exchange for as little as a belt, a red cap, or a piece of cloth worth seven pence in the Cape Verde Islands.... On one occasion, some Mani who had reached a Portuguese ship at nightfall heard the music of a flute played with great skill. They enquired whence came such sweet sounds and said that they must surely have a celestial origin. When they learnt that the music came from one of the crew, they wished to know if his masters were ready to part with him and at what price.[11]

Advancing further, but avoiding the Limba and Yalunka who, they had learnt, were practically invincible since they lived in fortified caves in time of war, the Mani came upon the Susus. These had made an alliance with some Fulani and now they decided to stand firm. By this time the Mani had been joined by two Portuguese and a half-caste named respectively Francisco Vaz, Salvador da Costa and Paulo Palha. Da Costa brought with him three muskets. The Susus were drawn up with seven Fulah horsemen in the van, whilst the main body of archers was protected to their front by a company of spearmen whose job it was to guard the flank. At the first charge the Mani barricades, which they had thrown up on the far side of the river running between the two armies, gave way, and after a brief fight, when da Costa did not have enough time to reload, the Susus and their allies were left victorious upon the field. The main body of the Manis sought refuge at sea.

We are told that as the Manis advanced they impressed for military service the young men of every nation which they over-ran. By now they had subjugated the Temnes because foremost among the rout at this time ran the Bulloms and Temnes. The

Bulloms, lying further south and so among the first to receive the Manis, capitulated early, although in 1582 Bamfora was still fighting Sasina and his ally Sherabola whilst Farima, the Mani king of the Lokos, was at war with the Limbas.[12] Coelho, a Portuguese amber merchant, looking back on the conquest after one hundred years, wrote:

They say the subjugation of the Temnes by the Manis took three years. At the end of which, tired of war, and seeing their numbers diminished, they decided to settle...encouraged by the fertility of the country.... The Manis who settled in Sierra Leone, for the sake of security and peace intermarried with the original inhabitants (but there is still a difference in language). They divided the country into two groups: the Manis and the Bulloms.[13]

By 1600 the Temnes and Bulloms had merged with the Manis, and the country was divided roughly at the Sierra Leone river—Loko, Susu, Yalunka and Limba against Temne, Bullom and Mani. The low-lying shore on the north side of the river is known today as the Bullom shore and when Coelho said that the country was divided Mani against Bullom he meant those living on the north side of the river against those on the south; besides, a few Bullom lived, as they do now, along the northern coast as far north as the Iles de Los where Coelho met them, but he had never visited the southern territories.

Some of the original Mani leaders were still alive at the beginning of the seventeenth century and one of the most famous was Tura* or Don Pedro—king of the Manis as he was still called—who ruled over the Temnes. He married into the ruling houses of King Fatima of Bullom and of Don Felipe, king of Sierra Leone and son of Farima, the first Mani king of the Lokos; an English visitor in 1607 said Felipe was called Borea by his own people. Pedro and Felipe are Portuguese names and these two kings had been baptised by Barreira the Jesuit missionary. They are the first Christian kings of Sierra Leone. Felipe's sister, one of Pedro's wives, was also baptised when it was thought she was on her deathbed, but she recovered. In spite of his dynastic alliances Don Pedro, being invited to certain funeral celebrations, remained apart with his

* There is today a clan-name amongst the Temnes called *Turé*; this is widespread also in the east of Sierra Leone. *Tura* is Mande for 'a bull' and has been borrowed by the Temnes as *-thura*.[14]

The Manis, showing relationships between the rulers of the Lokos, Bulloms and Temnes

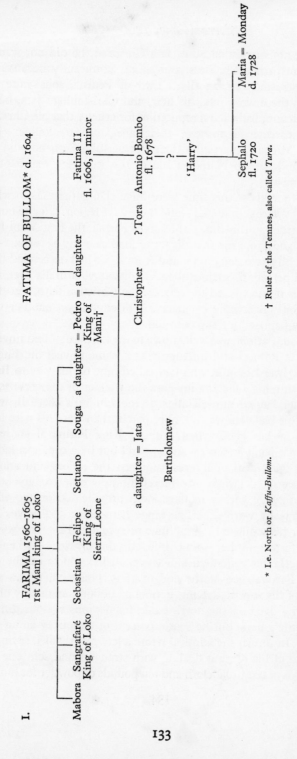

I.

FATIMA OF BULLOM* d. 1604

FARIMA 1560–1605
1st Mani king of Loko

Mabora | Sangrafaré King of Loko | Sebastian | Felipe King of Sierra Leone | Setuano | Souga | a daughter = Pedro King of Mani†

Fatima II fl. 1606, a minor

a daughter = Jata

Christopher | ?Tora

Antonio Bombo fl. 1678

Bartholomew

?

'Harry'

Sephalo fl. 1720

Maria = Monday d. 1728

* I.e. North or Kaffu-Bullom.

† Ruler of the Temnes, also called Tura.

II. SASINA fl. 1560–1582
SETERAMA fl. 1560 } in Sherbro.
SHERABOLA fl. 1582

133

warriors, not merely because, as a Christian, he did not want to participate in heathen rites, but more significantly because the kings distrusted one another. Two of Pedro's sons were also baptised; these were Jata, his heir, and Christopher: Jata, before his conversion, had such a reputation for cruelty that his Christian subjects threatened to give their allegiance to Felipe. Jata, baptised Michael, married a daughter of John Setuano who was brother and heir to Felipe; a son of this marriage was baptised Bartholomew.

Royal funerals at this time were huge clan gatherings to which all relatives were summoned—and these were legion. 'For instance', wrote Barreira at this time, 'the son of Farma, the first Mani King of the Loguos, told me that his father had as many as seventy-two sons and fifty-two daughters, and from these had descended three thousand persons'. Such exuberant polygamy naturally presented difficulties if one wished to embrace the Christian faith, but these were adroitly overcome by marrying in church yet another wife, especially baptised for the occasion.

Farma, or Farima, was well known to the Portuguese and English; he lived at Robaga and in August 1582 came to visit the English admiral Edward Fenton who had called here on his way to Brazil in order to refit. One can imagine the wonder of the crew as the old warrior hauled himself aboard; the admiral's chaplain wrote of him: 'his bad cote was no more patcht than were his bare leggs splotted, he has goodly lips...under King Farma al go naked nether is ye King knoen by any apparel but by a cap.' In fact he caused a great deal of interest amongst the sailors and another account says: '...when any merchant desyrethe to buy bonde slaves the kynge within 10 dayes wyll provide 300 or 400 which they wynne by warres....The kinge hathe 2 or 300 wyves who worke for his wealthe in gatheringe of ryce etc. The fyrst wyfe is the cheyfeste and her sonne inioyeth the crowne...when the kynge dyethe his concubynes or wyves shalbe sent to deathe with hym.'[15] Farima died at the end of 1605, poisoned, it was said, because of his severity. King Fatima of Bullom, an enemy of the Manis who lived on the north bank, for obvious reasons did not visit Fenton's fleet, but he sent a present of a monkey and a tusk of ivory. In return the admiral wrote a letter of thanks, saying he had heard of his upright dealing with strangers and sent one and a half yards of red broadcloth and ten pounds of powder for himself

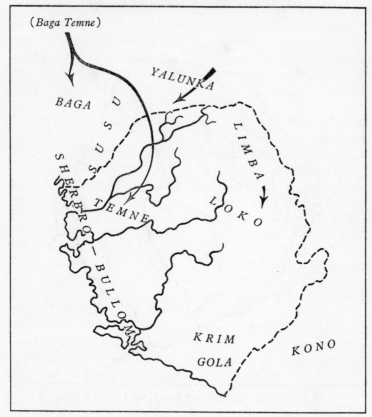

Routes of the main invasions into Sierra Leone: *c.* 1400

and a smock 'of Russia worke' and a 'tuppeny looking-glass' for his Queen.[16]

One of Farima's sons was called Sangrafaré; after his father's death he went into exile at the court of Don Pedro, king of the Manis. Pedro may have been contemplating some military alliance at this time in order to renew the war, because Sangrafaré was not the only important visitor to be received:

The third who visited Don Pedro was Sangrafaré, pretender to the kingdom of the Loguos, which belonged to his father, the great Farma. His people gave him the cap,* that is possession of the kingdom, but

* Nowadays a new Temne chief is presented by the Alpha with a white turban in a calabash; this is the crown.[17]

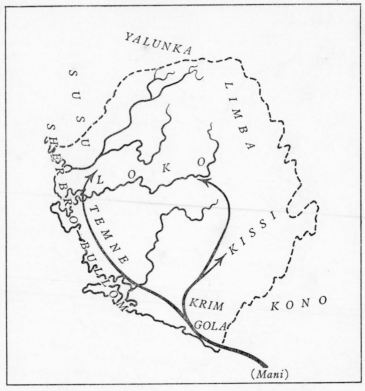

Routes of the main invasions into Sierra Leone: *c.* 1600

he was driven out by his brother who now reigns and against whom he is now gathering a following in preparation for war; because, although he had been named to succeed his father, he had been unable to do so because of his elder brother. The latter is not wanted by his people because he is cruel and has killed some of his own brothers in order to reign more securely.[18]

After a few months' fighting, Sangrafaré obtained his inheritance at the end of 1606. Pedro's other two visitors were Filau, who owed allegiance to King Fatima II of Bullom, and King Fatima himself who lived somewhere up the river Sierra Leone, on an island then called *Caracore*,* two days' journey from his capital town. His father had died in 1604 and, anxious it seems to make

* *Caracore* is possibly the modern Ma-Kurubulai, on the Port Loko Creek.

136

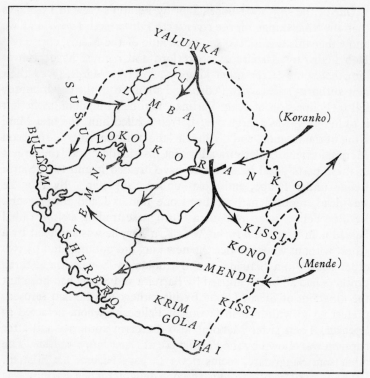

Routes of the main invasions into Sierra Leone: *c.* 1800

peace with the Manis, Fatima II brought with him a sister whom
he gave in marriage to Don Pedro. Since this was a ceremonial
visit, it is very likely that he had also in his entourage a German
trumpeter, originally captured by pirates off the Iles de Los and
sold into slavery. Barreira had met him previously in the Mellacourie district further north and had offered to intercede with
Fatima for his release, but this the German had begged him not to
do because, he said, he was content to stay where he was and to
continue his school for young trumpet players. Fatima himself
may well have attended his music classes because he was still a
youth when he visited Don Pedro and his uncle Besse was ruling
as Regent. Like Sangrafaré he too may have been seeking sanctuary, for we are told that at this time he went in constant fear of
poison.[19]

One of the ship's log-books kept by Fenton's crew in 1582 says that the chief kings on the river were *Farma* and *Torria* and we know that this was indeed so. Tura, king of the Manis, christened Don Pedro by Barreira, was overlord and it must have been to him that some of the other kings, themselves Manis, owed their new authority. But when Pedro died about 1610, the paramountcy fell to Felipe, son of King Farima. Farima's kingdom, as he left it to his sons, was a large one; Barreira called him 'the first Mani King of the Loguos' and d'Almada 'the principal ruler of the Lion Mountain range'. Barreira adds that his kingdom was 'the largest in these parts', and he seems to have divided it into two: Sierra Leone under Felipe, and Loko under Sangrafaré. By 1605 he was dead, reputed to have lived one hundred and thirty years. Besides Felipe, who lived in a Portuguese trading station called Salvador in what we now know as Kru Bay, he was survived by a sister, without whose advice the new king did nothing, and by two other sons, John Setuano and Bartholomew Souga; these three brothers had all been baptised by Barreira and Souga had been left the kingdom of Sierra Leone by his father; this he had refused, preferring to withdraw in favour of Felipe, to whom he acted as Speaker. Their sister Mabora* also exercised authority and after baptism was known by the Portuguese as *Dona Filipa de Leão*. The other son, Sangrafaré, seems never to have become a Christian. Felipe himself had three sons and one daughter when Barreira was here and he lived on the south side of the river. In February 1606 he wrote to the king of Spain granting permission for the building of a fort on part of his land near the mouth of the river; this was intended to give protection to the Portuguese traders against pirates who infested that bank of the estuary, compelling smaller boats requiring less depth of water to hug the mudbanks on the northern shore in order to avoid their deeper-draughted enemies.[20]

It is evident that a considerable *entente* had sprung up amongst the former members of the Sapi confederation now allied to the new Mani overlords and isolating the Limbas and Susus; Pedro had married into the Bullom and Loko ruling houses so that, at one time or another, the Loko King Felipe was both suzerain and brother-in-law to the ruler of the Temnes. Moreover, when Fatima of Bullom came to visit King Pedro he had already been preceded by his vassal Filau, another member of the confedera-

---

* Mabora's duties may have been ritual ones like the modern *Bom Poro*.[21]

tion. By his encouragement of the exiled Sangrafaré, Pedro seems to have been in doubt as to the permanency of the Loko alliance and in this he was probably right. Seventy years later, in 1678, a European observed that the Sierra Leone river separated the two hostile camps and the Lokos had ceased to pay any allegiance to the Bulloms, most of whom had been driven into the south-east corner of the country by the Temne advance into the peninsular area.[22]

It is not easy, at this distance, to discover what new habits and customs the Manis brought into Sierra Leone. D'Almada, writing only thirty years after the invasion, said that he was unable to distinguish between the invader and the vanquished; unfortunately he does not mention what distinctions the inhabitants themselves made, though obviously there were several. A contemporary English account, written when John Hawkins on his second voyage visited Sherbro* early in December 1564, is more explicit. It tells us that the 'Samboses'—Sumbas—had been living there for three years, that they had enslaved the Sapis and made them tend millet, rice, roots, pumpkins, chickens, goats, palm-trees, gather wild fruits and prepare dried fish—none of which they understood themselves[23]—and that they did not file their teeth nor scarify their bodies and limbs like the Sapis who lived farther north.† Nowadays rice is seldom empoldered by the Bulloms, but a British ship's captain in 1794 saw crops being grown in this manner by the Temnes in the north of Sierra Leone. What Hawkins saw was almost certainly hill rice. D'Almada also noticed that the Sapi, a Temne-dominated confederation, filed their teeth whilst the Manis did not; according to Susu tradition this custom was introduced into the north by the Bagas about 1400.

From all accounts the Manis were polygamous—not always giving succession to the eldest son—pagan and cannibalistic; they encouraged cannibalism amongst their slaves. These were most likely captured originally round Zaria and other parts of the western Sudan from cannibal tribes known to the Arabs as *Dem Dem* or *Nyam Nyam*. This was where the ancient State of Ghana obtained its slaves; and the Fulani emirs of Kano and Zaria used them as

---

* Sambula Island in the text.

† In 1582 Madox drew the tattoo marks of a woman on the river Sierra Leone; the linear and keloid patterns have been equated with those of Portuguese Guinea. On the other hand, a conventionalised scorpion resembles the art of Nigeria—Benue valley.[24] The large pattern round the hips leads one to suppose she was a Limba.

executioners; one was still a member of the emir of Kano's house-hold as late as 1925.[25] The Sapis, Hawkins noticed, were not cannibals, but lived mainly on fruit and cattle.

The bow and arrow which the invaders used were of a different pattern from those of the defenders, being smaller; otherwise their weapons were similar. The boats still used in the south-east by the Bulloms are generally unlike those elsewhere—unless under Bullom influence—and it may be supposed that these too were introduced by the Manis. The Bullom canoe, called *sala*, is narrower than the so-called Bullom boat of today, although it is similar in design. Hawkins, in Sherbro, saw boats some 24 feet long, carved and painted red and blue; in calm water they could carry sixty people, elsewhere twenty or thirty, and they were rowed from a standing position. In the Sierra Leone river Fenton, however, saw canoes like 'a lyte swynes trou' (a pig trough); they were used by the three Portuguese who had come to make a formal call—surely if they had had a bigger canoe they would have used it.

One would not expect the Manis, who used canoes extensively, to have any cavalry, but the Susus living on the borders of the desert borrowed seven Fulah horsemen from their neighbours. These seem to have demoralised the invaders and probably contributed largely to their defeat on the river Scarcies. These horses alarmed the Temnes just as much as the Manis; horses were not common here until 1800.

At the death of a Mani king sacrifices were made as part of the funeral celebrations, as they were in more recent times upon the death of the Ashantiheni. This was not so amongst the Sapis: 'This people bury their dead within their houses, and they bury them with such gold ornaments as they are wont to carry....Rulers are buried along the footpath outside the village, and the reason given for this is that having administered justice they should be buried where all can see them. A hut is later erected over the grave.'[26]

The Limba and Yalunka have always remained apart from the rest of the peoples in Sierra Leone, and d'Almada treats them as such in his description: 'The Limba and the Yalunka are astounding for their warlike qualities.... They have underground shelters in which they take refuge after having set fire to their villages. When the bewildered enemy retreat, they sally forth and attack them.'

Of the invading Manis we are told:

The invaders call themselves Manis...they represent but the van of an enormous army whose rear halted when they were warned that their comrades had decided to settle down in a most fertile country which they had subdued.... The invaders surpassed themselves in destructiveness and ferocity. They had actually trained some of their followers, not themselves Mani, to devour human flesh...and used them to a great extent to strike terror into the hearts of their enemies. As to what the Sapi have to say about their country having been overrun before, I am inclined to see a confirmation of this in the fact that when the Mani arrived they came across a local group with the unusual customs just mentioned. To this day the Mani continue to pay allegiance, in the form of a tax they call *maref*, to some overlord far behind.... They say the supreme leader of their original forces was a woman; but I have not been able to verify this.[27]

*Maref*, a Malinke word which leads one to suppose that the warrior chiefs who led this invasion were of Mande origin, means 'something kept in a store'.

A comparison of certain stone carvings, often of steatite, or soap-stone, called *nomoli*,* found almost exclusively amongst the Temne, Mende and Kissi peoples shows very definite affinities with the wooden figures made today by the Bagas in Guinea. Especially similar is the treatment of the head, where the natural space between the ears and the nostrils is greatly exaggerated, terminating in a large hawk-like nose. This feature occurs also in certain carvings found in Nigeria. In the absence of further evidence it seems reasonable to suppose that this art-form came in by the same route as did the warrior kings who led the Temnes and Manis to victory in Sierra Leone in the fifteenth and sixteenth centuries; that is, by way of Futa Toro or Nigeria and from thence to this country.

Sierra Leone tradition says that *funde*, or Hungry rice,† came into this country: 'at the time of the civil wars. The Temnes and Lokkos who waged war with the Susus and Fullahs, were the first to discover its cultivation in those countries.... The Susus and Fullahs say in their turn, that it came into their countries from the North.'[28] This grain was cultivated in the Sudan in the fourteenth century, and by 1582 it was being grown in Sierra Leone.[29] The Lokos, as we have seen, were conquered by the Manis and drawn

---

* *Nomoli* is a Mende word; in Kissi: *pɔmdo*.
† *Digitaria exilis.*

into their confederation which included the Temnes, although they soon rebelled and rejoined the Susus, with whom they have linguistic affinities. Tradition says that some time after the Limba had occupied Gbande country a war arose in that district between the Lokos, who were the aggressors, and the Limbas and Susus; it lasted three years until: 'Sare [a Limba warrior] appealed to Momodu Musa and Musa Tagira, recent immigrants from Susu Tamiso, to help him against the Lokos. They agreed and together they drove out the Lokos.'[30] This episode sounds like another version of the Mani subjugation of the Temnes which we are told also took three years. If this is so, the Lokos lived at that time further north than they do now.

When the Susus defeated the Manis near the Scarcies soon after 1570 they seem to have occupied Port Loko, because another tradition says that the Lokos were driven from the Port Loko area by a Susu warrior called Brimah Konkorie. After a while Pa Kargbo, a Temne, sent a message to Moriba Bangura Nes, a hunter who lived nearby, asking for help in driving out the Susus. He consented, and on his arrival at Port Loko sent to Megbele, a town on the other side of the Rokel river, to seek additional help from Brima Fatima, who had been born in Port Loko. Assisted financially by Pa Mela Bangura, otherwise known as Ansumana Mela, a brother of Moriba Bangura Nes and a wealthy trader, they routed the Susus. Moriba Bangura was crowned king of Port Loko and Brima Fatima returned to Megbele. We are then given a list of twelve kings which represents a span of some three hundred years, so that it was about 1600 that the Susus surrendered Port Loko to the Temnes, who named the place *Petifu* or New Town.[31] Shortly after the death of Bai Farima, first Mani king of the Lokos, his people, now allied to the Susus, recaptured the town, and the Temnes, therefore, changed its name to Baké Loko, or Wharf of the Lokos. This Susu drive to the south ended by separating the Bagas from the Temnes, so that, whilst the Temnes have become a Sierra Leone people, the Bagas are part of Guinea. Sangrafaré's Loko kingdom probably included most of what we know today as Loko territory, as well as the original land in the north near the modern Wara-Wara chiefdoms. The Manis, it seems, in their march westwards had enlarged the Loko kingdom, setting up Farima as king of a huge territory which he divided at his death amongst his sons.

Indeed Port Loko has had a very chequered history, difficult to describe exactly, because it lay on the border between the two hostile confederations which grew up after the Mani invasion. Sometimes it fell to one side and sometimes to the other. The story is further complicated because of the prolonged rivalry between the European traders who came to the Sierra Leone river and who, for their own advantage, set one people against another. Soon the various nations which strove so constantly for power along the waterways of Sierra Leone found that they could play off one European power against another and in no time everyone was engaged in a titanic game of beggar-my-neighbour.* There was, for instance, a Portuguese settlement at Port Loko; this the settlers guarded closely, allowing no other European traders to do business there. The other Europeans, therefore, were forced to operate at the river mouth where it was noticed that those on the north shore preferred to trade with the English, whilst the south favoured the French. The English had a factory on the river about 1663, but they were obliged to move it three times as a result of attacks from both European and African rivals before they settled finally upon Bunce Island about the year 1672. Even there they suffered constant interruption and, within sixty years, the Royal African Company virtually abandoned it. Inter-European rivalry was, of course, just as traditional as that of the African, but it was further inflamed by continental European wars. For example, on New Year's Eve 1666, Abraham, the English factor for that company known as the Royal Adventurers into Africa, fell a victim to exactly this kind of complication. On 12 September 1664 a Dutch fleet had arrived in the river and de Ruyter, the admiral, landed at King Jimmy, where he caused his name to be carved on a large rock, before sailing upstream to Tasso Island to sack the English fort there. By 1665 the

---

* This is not to say that, when the time came, those who dwelt further inland did not do the same; but, until the late nineteenth century, the European powers did not become involved to any extent in the hinterland. When Franco–British rivalry occurred about the frontier in the north-east, in 1893 Kouroua Ouara, a Kono chief, set one against the other for his own advantage. Thus, of the affair at Waiima in that year, a French report says: 'I endeavoured to secure Kouroua Oura, who was the sole cause of the incident, and who, well knowing that the English were occupying Waiima, arranged to set one force upon the other and to join himself with the victor. It was a favourite method of his and had served him well hitherto. Thus he had used Porequere's Sofas against the Mende, Lieutenant Maritz against the Sofas, and the British against the French.'[32]

war begun out here by de Ruyter's hostile acts along the coast had spread to Europe, so that feeling between traders of the two nations who encountered one another in the river, although they were merely private merchants—often trading without their country's permission—ran high. Abraham, who seems to have been curiously unsuspicious of his country's enemies, was invited to dinner aboard a Dutch ship then lying in the river and promptly kidnapped. Luckily for him, he had struck up a friendship with Antonio Bombo,* son of the then king of Bullom, who ransomed him for nine hundredweight of ivory.[33]

By this time it was more than one hundred years since Bai Farima had installed himself as king of the Logos and there had grown up a generation to whom the great Mani invasion was but a legend. Moreover, such was the impact of their attack that it is generally difficult to uncover traditional accounts of the various nations which precede it.

About 1600 the alliances and dispositions of the peoples in the south-east of Sierra Leone which had grown up after the Mani invasion were disturbed by a further wave of immigrants, which, divided into three separate movements, descended on Sierra Leone between 1600 and 1725. First the Konos and Vais, already a nation in decline, were attacked by Flonikerri, a Kru king recently subjugated by the Deforo, or Folgias as they were called by Europeans at that time.[34] These were part of the Songhai empire of Gao, attacked in 1591 by Judar, commander under the Sultan of Morocco, who led 4000 men across the desert from Marrakech. Meanwhile, Manimassah, brother of Mendino, king of Manow, driven into exile, had set out westward and with the aid of Flansire, king of the Folgia, made himself master of Flonikerri's people; together they all attacked the Golas and, as a reward of success, Flonikerri was permitted to overrun the Cape Mount area. As a result the Vais were separated from the Konos who remained behind, though driven somewhat to the westward into Sierra Leone, whilst their comrades were pushed towards the coast led, so tradition says, by two brothers Fabule and Kiatamba. Today certain Mendes call the Vais *Karos*, the very word used by Barbot, and it is possible that this 'Kru' invasion represented the advance of another branch of the Vais.[35]

---

* Antonio was said to be about 40 years old at the time. In 1678, seven tusks of ivory, weighing 112 lb., were paid for a hogshead of claret.[36]

Kissi tradition says also that, coming from the upper Niger before 1600, when they drove the Limba westward, after 1600 they were attacked by the Korankos who, once driven north of the Niger, now crossed over again in strength and attacked the Kissis. Presently, the whole of the east was in turmoil, and the *Mendes*, representing the second of the three invasions begun between 1600 and 1725, followed upon the Krus. Today those whom we call collectively the Kru people are in fact a mixture of Krus and those who have been assimilated, so that the entire group has become a somewhat miscellaneous designation rather arbitrarily constructed by scholars to hold a number of races which do not seem to fit elsewhere. These include the Queah, Quoja or Givi,* a people of Mande origin; *Koi* is Mande for a chief.

The Frenchman, Jean Barbot, who wrote in about 1680 of his voyages on the coast of Guinea, spoke of the first and second parts of this movement, which by that time had been completed. He says that the Bulloms paid homage to the Quojas at Cape Mount who in turn were subject to the Folgias; these acknowledged the suzerainty of the emperor of *Manow*. This empire represented the rearguard of the Manis settled somewhere to the north of modern Liberia and the name exists still as that of a small Mande group of people.

The Country inland from...Cape Monte is called Quoja. It is inhabited by the Vey-Berkoma,† and Quoja-Berkoma, who were both subdued by the Karows. The Vey-Berkoma are the Remains of the ancient Inhabitants of...Cape Monte; once a populous and warlike Nation, extending as far as the Country of Manow, but at present reduced to a Handful of Men...Quoja-Berkoma, that is the Land of Quoja, [borders] on the North and North East with the Galas, Vey-Galas, Hondos,‡ Konde-Quojas, that is High Quojas...and have a Language different from that of the Quojas.[37]

In fact, what had happened between 1600 and 1680 was that the Quojas, who had subdued the Bulloms, Krims and Temnes, appointing in those countries viceroys or *Dondaghs*, were subsequently overrun by Flonikerri's brother and successor, Zilly-mango—who also conquered the *Quilliga* (i.e. Gallinas) area, the

---

* D'Anville's map of 1749 marks the country: 'Folgia d'ou sont sortis les Carous' and 'Royaume de Qoja ou des Carous'.[38]

† Barbot says Vi or Vey signifies half a nation and Berkoma means land.[39]

‡ A people living to the north.

Bulloms and the Krims—and lost their hold upon the south and east of Sierra Leone. Zillymango's son, Flansire, completed the rout by subduing all the coast westwards to the river of Sierra Leone and appointing in his new territories viceroys,\* including one Kandaqualle in Sierra Leone and, further south, one Selbore from whom, says Dapper, Sherbro took its name.[40] This may well be so; as far as Europeans were concerned Sherbro and its derivatives are names which do not appear in maps before the seventeenth century.† But nearly a hundred years earlier Bamfora, king of the Bulloms, had defended the south against a hostile warrior chief, whom Edward Fenton called Sherabola, allied to the Mani leader Sasina. If Sherabola was also a Mani, which is probable, and if Dapper is right when he says that the second invasion from the south had imposed a viceroy called Selbore upon Sierra Leone, then it is possible to link Flonikerri's expansion northwards with that of the Manis and to consider the second invasion merely as an extension of the first in 1564. The third attack from the south by the *Mendes* had certainly a direct connection with the second and one is tempted to believe that both the Mani and 'Kru' invasions represent a preliminary occupation of this country by those whom we know today as Mendes. Certainly the appointment of military viceroys is more typical of Mende organisation than that of any other nation then predominant in Sierra Leone. Traditionally, the role of a Mende chief seems to have been that of a military leader—like the Mani's—with absolute powers in secular matters although some of this authority was delegated to lieutenants in other parts of the chiefdom. On the other hand, for example, the semi-sacred nature of a Temne chief's office restricts his authority and divides his functions amongst a large number of officials.‡

It was said of this *Kru* invasion:

As soon as they arrived at Cape Monte, on the south-Side about the Town of Tombi, they invaded the Vey-Monow, (or People of Vey-Berkoma) who being numerous and fierce, were not easily mastered: But their Weapons being only Darts and Assagayes, or Lances, they

---

\* The Gallinas area was placed under a viceroy called Sytre. *Karo*, Gallinas and Vai are today synonymous.

† D'Anville's maps of 1749 and 1775 mark what today is Sherbro Island as *Farulho* or *Massacoy*; *Serbora* also appears marking the west end of Turner's Peninsula.

‡ Moreover, these viceroys were soon deposed—see below—and whilst the deposition of a Temne chief is rare, it is not infrequent in Mende country today.

were so gauled at length by the continual Onsets and poisoned Arrows of the Karows, that, repairing with their Hoods on their Heads to Quolm, a Fort of the Karows, a little Eastward of Tombi, they sued for favour. This Flonikerri granting they lay down on their faces, according to Custom...and he trod on them with his Feet. After this, he made an Agreement with them, the Conquered swallowing a little of the Blood of Hens killed in Preference of them all, in token of the same. Then the Hens were boiled, and the Flesh eaten among them: Only the Legs were reserved, as a Memorial, to be shewn to any who should violate the Compact....

But scarce were the Minds of the Veys and Karows united, before Miminiko, son of Manimassah, forgetting his former Obligations to Flonikerri, came with an army of Galas and others to attack the allied Nations.... The Galas at first by their Numbers, having put the Karows to a disorderly Retreat, Flonikerri...rallied and renewed the Charge with such Fury, that they soon became Masters of the Field...Zilli-manko, being chosen to succeed his Brother, pursued the Victory and... advancing to Quoja Monow...the Inhabitants submitted without Opposition.[41]

At the height of their power the Quojas, led originally from the north by one known in tradition as Luseni, had also appointed viceroys or *Dondaghs*, amongst the Bulloms—such as the *Dondagh* of Sherbro known as *Massaquoja*, or Massaquoiah—and these *Dondaghs*, no longer supported by stern authority, now lost all control; consequently, about 1650 the *Dondagh* of the Sierra Leone Bulloms who was appointed by the overlord in Cape Mount was overthrown and fled to the Banana Islands.

At the same time the provincial governors appointed by Flansire in the Gallinhas area betrayed him by a conspiracy, and after much fighting they divided his territory between them and, at the same time, threw off the foreign yoke. Flansire's eldest son, Flamburre, before he succeeded his father, helped him to restore order temporarily. By 1670, christened Philip by the Portuguese missionaries, he had settled his four brothers as rulers along the river Sierra Leone; the eldest lived five miles beyond Baga, the second, Don Andreas, at the second watering-place from the river mouth, the third, Don Jeronimo, at the third point on the south bank, and Don Thomas at Tumba. However, they rebelled also, fighting mainly amongst themselves; thus fell the only State in Sierra Leone modelled, like many in the Sudan, along semi-feudal lines with some kind of sovran power vested in the emperors of

Manow and delegated by them to their principal vassals the Folgias, who in turn had subjugated the Quoiahs, themselves overlords of the Bulloms, Krims and Temnes. Other rulers lived up and down the rivers and creeks of Sierra Leone, but little has come down to us except their names.

The Bulloms, having freed themselves from the viceroy, continued to quarrel amongst themselves; even in their heyday it is not likely that the viceroys exercised any strong control over such a large area, covered as it was with forests and swamps which made communication difficult. 'Each of these petty kings', wrote Barbot, 'has an absolute authority in his own districts, and can make war or peace, without consent or approbation of this, or of any of whom they hold.'[42] Many kings, virtually independent even before the rebellion, now appear to have sought the paramountcy for themselves, and cryptic entries in the Royal African Company's journals give us occasional glimpses into these intrigues: '4th April 1728. Some time this Week Old Py* returned empty from the Yongree Bolloms, there is a Difference between them and the Bollomms of Sangraferry's Province and a Warr like to ensue, Occasioned by the Palaver between me and them, upon which the King sent Old Py home....'[43] The palaver between the Bulloms and Walter Charles, factor at Bunce and writer of the extract above, was centred in Sherbro and it is possible that Sangrafaré also came from that district; another entry in Charles's journal mentions 'the lower Boloms, whose King, Lewis, was poison'd in drinking fetich Water, by Sangraferry's means'.[44]

At this period the Royal African Company's agent on York Island was Thomas Corker, who had come down from their factory in the Gambia in 1698. Even then he was no stranger to that part of the country because in 1695 he had founded a factory on the river Boom; in 1688, presumably as a junior officer, a memorandum was made that he was 'to be encouraged by advance of sallary'. He was still in Sierra Leone in 1713.[45] Two other names, both equally well known in the history of that area, also occur in these records; they are Rogers and Tucker.

In February 1681 an inventory was made of the effects of Zachary Rogers, recently deceased agent at Sherbro. He left at least one son, also named Zachary, who later fell out with the company with whom he had previously worked, joining the inter-

* 'Old Py' must have been a company's servant.

lopers at Sherbro and forming an alliance with the pirates on the Banana Islands.[46]

In November 1699 Peter Tucker was the company's agent in Sherbro and in March 1716 we hear of one hundred bars, being two years' salary, paid to John Tucker senior. He was illiterate and could only make a mark upon his receipt.[47] It is the descendants of these three who, tradition says, came together from Europe into the Sherbro area about the year 1740. One, Cleveland Caulker, stopped at Shenge, another, Abraham Tucker, at Bar Hall, and the third, Charles Rogers, settled in Meena Town on the Kife river.[48] In fact, as we know, these three were not strangers but probably the first generation born in Sierra Leone. Confusion has arisen because some at least went to Europe for education and travel before returning home to set up as traders. For example, we are told of one of the Tuckers in 1757:

...who has aquired a great fortune by his skill and some other abillites in the way of trade. He commonly goes by the name of Henry Tucker and lives upon the same shoar as we do [i.e. south of York Island] about a mile distant. He has been in England, Spain and Portugall and is master of the English tongue; he has 6 or 7 wives and a numerous of-spring of suns and daughters; his strength consists of his own slaves and their children, who has built a town about him and serves as his gre-metos upon all occassions. This man bears the charectar of a fair trader among the Europeans, but the contrary among the Blacks. His riches sets him above the Kings and his numerous people above being surprized by war; almost all the Blacks ows him money, which brings a dread of being stopt upon that acount, so that he is esteemed and feared by all who has the misfortune to be in his power. He is a fat man and fair spoken, and lives after the manner of the English, haveing his house well furnished with English goods and his table tolarably well furnished with the country produce. He dresses gayley and commonly makes use of silver at his table, haveing a good side board of plate.[49]

Henry's eldest brother, Peter Tucker, was not so fortunate at this time and often received financial help from him; this made Peter jealous. About 1754 he plotted, unsuccessfully as it happened, to kill him and in 1758 he persuaded some of the kings to refuse to trade with any of Henry's boats and 'to take goods out by force under colour of duty, to make his innocent brother as poor as himself'[50]—that is to say to seize some of Henry's merchandise on the excuse that he owed the kings customs duty, as we should call it today. At this time we are told that both brothers had been in Sierra Leone about forty years and that Peter had several children all of whom at one time or another had been clothed by Henry.

Another descendant of a former Royal African Company servant was Zachary Cumberbuss, chief of Jamaica Town in 1726. He and the company fell out with the king of Sherbro, whose name is unknown, with the result that the king of Sherbro was deposed in favour of his 'senior captain', called Maximo, because his people feared to lose the company's favourable trading posts which brought them so many toll duties.[51]

On the north side of the Sierra Leone river, not far from the place now occupied by the town of Kumrubai, lived Bai Samma whom Barbot in 1678 called the principal king of the country and to whom he said other rulers paid homage. A mile east of Robaga on the south bank lived King Semaura, whom a contemporary described as an ill-natured man always quarrelling with his neighbour, the king who lived in Serboracasa, a town on the southern tip of the river mouth. Further up on the same bank lived John Thomas; he was strategically placed for collecting the tolls which it was usual to levy upon visiting ships trading up the river and these he levied in Bai Samma's name. An entry in the account-book kept in the factory at Bunce reads: 'Charges to Brandy, given John Thomas and sent the King by Samma att severall times 4 gallons.'[52] One of King Philip's brothers told a French merchant in 1668 that John Thomas was a 'mutineer and a rebel' and Thomas's alliance with Bai Samma was probably the cause of this remark. Possibly he became the leader of the rebels who freed themselves from the jurisdiction of the emperor of Manow. Because the river divided the two main political groups in Sierra Leone at this time, Thomas's business with the north shore must in any case have appeared sinister.[53]

Not all who worked on Bunce Island were slaves, and amongst the freemen employed by the Royal African Company at this time was a young man called Sephalo who, when King Harry his father died, succeeded him in a Bullom chieftaincy somewhere on the Bullom shore. His sister Maria, some of whose relatives were living in Sherbro in 1728, married another servant of the company called Monday who, planning to seize the factory in 1728, was caught before his scheme was ripe; he was hanged by the company as a traitor, from a tree at high-water mark upon the back of the island. Maria remained faithful to the company, helping in many ways as an interpreter and peacemaker. By 1729 she had founded a town at the north end of Lumley Beach:

...at 6 past noon we are close in shore with the Sandy bay without Cape Sierra Leone, the Cape then bearing North about 3 Miles. We have the Vistos of Cape and Cockle Bays both open and can see thro' the trees on both them necks of Land, into Sierra Leone River, about this time we see a great fire on shore, upon which I conclude it to be Seniora Maria's, whose town is on the Neck Land at the bottom of Cockle Bay....[54]

Thus wrote Charles in his journal as he returned by ship from the Banana Islands.

By the time that Seniora Maria had settled near the modern Aberdeen the Bullom confederacy, still fighting for the paramountcy, ran from the south-east of Sierra Leone to the Sierra Leone river, terminating in the vassal kingdom of Burré, and separating the Lokos from the Susus who still dwelt along the northern coastline. The Loko kingdom stretched inland until one came to the country of the Limbas; beyond that again lay the Concho in the north.[55] This confederacy, of course, included the Temnes, overrun nearly two hundred years before. To the north-east lay the Yalunka, and to their east the Korankos. The kings of Sierra Leone at this time were: King Betura, who flourished between the years 1698 and 1721 and King Bernard, who was dead by October 1723.[56]*

A few years later there ruled three kings in Sherbro and under them a number of section chiefs. Over all ruled Suri, king of Sherbro, with King Sheffra and King Sumana as his vassals. In the middle of the eighteenth century this kingdom stretched from the peninsula of Sierra Leone to Shebar Strait, south of Sherbro Island. Nicholas Owen, an Irishman who traded for ten years in this area, wrote towards the end of his time there:

...as for the inland parts I have not yet learn'd, only as to thier respective nations which stands thus by thier own account. To the eastward of the Bulums lies the nation of the Timnes or Timines, which

---

* Other kings and headmen at this time include: King 'Matchivella'[57] and King 'Byballa',[58] both reigning in 1684–5; Bayaka, King of Kiddam, and the kings of 'Sangra', 'Shee', 'Nunquebah', 'Yong' and 'Cockbilly', all in the Sherbro area.[59] Cockbilly is probably Kagboro (Shenge). In 1886 Lawson, Government Interpreter, referred to the 'Sheys or Sherbros'.

seems by thier quantity of slaves to be a peopleous nation; this nation speakes a langauge of thier own far diffr't from the Bulums, but I am not able to give any acount, as they lie so far inland and we have no tradeing among them. Next to these inland is the Banta, next the Cono, and the Tene,* all these lies eastward of the Kingdom of Sherbro....[60]

In 1785 Lieutenant Matthews, R.N., who made a trip into Sherbro to mediate between two kings whose quarrel had involved all that country, drew a map of Sierra Leone in which he put the Temnes to the east of Port Loko creek; eastward of the Rokel river lie first the Bulloms and then the Sherbros. To the north of the Rokel along the coast are the Susu and inland the 'Mandingo'.[61] It will be noticed that neither of these two writers yet mentions the Mendes and that the dispositions of the other peoples in Sierra Leone have changed little since 1600, except that the Temnes have been pushed westward across the Rokel river by those beginning to crowd behind; in their advance they have driven the Lokos northwards. Also the Bulloms are now confined to the south-west of the country, having lost whatever control they had had over the Loko and Temne chiefdoms in the days of the *Dondagh* viceroys.

But the flourishing trade at Sherbro, Bonthe and Cape Mount had soon attracted the attention of the emperor of Manow, who was jealous of those who paid him what can only by now have been a nominal homage. John Ogilby, writing in 1670 and drawing largely upon the accounts of the Dutchman Dapper, tells us that the inhabitants of Quoja country acted as middlemen between the inland nations and those on the coast, exacting tolls upon everything sent to, or brought up from the seaports. Consequently, the emperor now summoned his war boys who pushed the Krus eastward and the Sherbros towards the west so as to prepare a path for more direct trade with European ships. The subjects of this emperor were called Mende, says Ogilby; he is the first English author to mention the name and Barbot, who copied him—but fortunately not *verbatim* because there are obvious slips†—wrote: 'The Folgias depend on the Emperor of Manow....The Folgias as well as the Bulom and Silm [Bullom and Krim] call the subjects of this emperor Mendi, that is, Lords.' Furthermore, Ogilby wrote a long description of Society customs, drawn mainly from Dapper's information in the Sherbro area. Thus he uses the

* The Tene are a Liberian tribe today.
† Especially a confusion between Folgias and the Quoias in this passage.

Sherbro word *Soggono*, modern *Sokonc*, for the leader in Poro or Bundu, but he also uses the words *Sovah*, *Pilly*, *Billy* and *Sande*.[62] These are terms employed by the Mendes today.* Ogilby gives us, therefore, our first Mende–English vocabulary. The Vais and Mendes have very close affinities—most Vais today understand the Mende language—and it is evident that during the *Karo* or Vai invasion of the mid-seventeenth century, a branch, now known as Mendes, entered Sierra Leone for the first time in large numbers. This thrust, which represents the second act in the realignment of the east begun by the Krus shortly after 1600, was part of the final collapse of law and order in the Songhai empire, begun by the invasion of El Mansur, the Moroccan emperor; today the Sherbros still call a great man *Songé*. This emperor's troops, led by Judar Pasha, a Spaniard, and largely composed of European slaves, had soon discovered that the wealth of Songhai was founded not on the possession of gold-mines as they had believed, but upon extensive trade protected by the efficient armies of the Askia emperors. These armies had now vanished before the Moroccan onslaught and on all sides the invaders, wasting away from tropical diseases and weary from the long march across the desert, saw the vassals of the former Songhai empire rising in revolt. Their own army was too small to re-establish order throughout this vast domain; they were content to hold in fee only the three major centres of Gao, Timbuctoo and Jenne which lay along the northern elbow of the river Niger. Elsewhere Fulani and Malinke warriors plundered at will.

Askia Mohammed of Songhai, upon his return from Mecca in 1497, had attacked and forcibly converted to Islam his pagan neighbours, including the Mandingo, Fulani and Koranko. His successors, when they were not fighting among themselves, continued this crusade and before 1590 they had already begun to drive the Korankos back across the Niger towards Sierra Leone where they soon occupied the eastern provinces of Limba country. Now the Fulani and Mandingo descended upon the country; this in turn set the other nations fighting amongst themselves. The Mendes did not penetrate deeply into Sierra Leone until late in

* *Sowah* is used in the Sande and Bundu societies for the head official and also in Poro during the initiation of young men. *Sande* is a society amongst the Golas, Konos, Vais and Mendes. Barbot says the Golas introduced it. Bundu is a similar society amongst the Sherbro and Temne. *Bili* is the Mende circumcision, *Pili* means one who throws a charm.

the eighteenth century. Nicholas Owen, who traded forty miles up the river Jong, never heard of them, but after his death in 1758 they attacked the Sherbros and presently the war drums beat outside the very gates of the new colony in Freetown.

This last act in the movement begun just after 1600 was started by the Muslims of Futa who drove the remnants of the emperor of Manow's subjects, the Mendes, across the frontier into Sierra Leone. About 1725 Alpha Ba of Koranko, styling himself *Alimami* instead of taking the usual title of military leaders who were known as *Siratiks*,[63] declared a *Jehad* against the animist pagans of Futa, mainly Susu and Yalunka. Upon his death the war continued under a theologian and soldier, the former Alpha Ibrahima of Timbo, usually known as Karamoko Alpha. The traditional story of this *Jehad* says:

The Gehad, or Holy War, began at Talangsan: the people who started it were twenty-two; some of these were Arabs, who afterwards formed the Foulah tribe. Ten of them were Mandingo or blackmen....

The Foulahs...came from Fars and sprang from the Arab race. Two principal men called Sayidi and Sayree left Fars on a tour to a country called Jakaba, where they came in contact with a leading Mandingo priest named Alhaj Salieu Swarray....After having obtained blessings from the Alhaj, he told them to go and reside in a country called 'Futa Jallo'....The descendants of Sayidi and Sayree convened a meeting at the eldest son's house (Alimami Sorie) for the purpose of waging war throughout Futa. In the meeting it was agreed that they should make a start. Alimami Sorie went to a town called Wosogoromah, where he met the heathens celebrating a great feast: he took out his knife and burst the drum of the Jalloonkahs (as the inhabitants were called). These people got enraged and pursued the offender, who crossed over to Timbo where his elder brother, Karamoko Alfa, then lived....A message was there and then sent to Fugoonba, where the large family resided, informing them of Alimami Sorie's action: they sent back another message that they should rally together and march against these heathens: they met at Talaasa, where the first battle took place. During a long and hard fight, the Foulahs won the victory....The eldest of the party suggested that Karamoko Alfa be installed as their chief and it was unanimously agreed upon....He reigned for eighteen years; during his reign, he waged war against the neighbouring heathen tribes, whom he conquered, and the whole country was converted to a Muslim country. After his death the crown was given to Alimamy Sorie, his younger brother. This chief was a famous warrior...first he set out against the Sankarah people, Kuronko, Kissie, Warsolonie, and on to the Red

Water,\* also Joema and Moria countries and Bambugu and Barjar, and
conquered these countries....He was succeeded by Alfa Salieu....He
was succeeded by Alimamy Bardambah....He fought a fierce battle
against the Jallonkas and was victorious...he fought with the Susus and
Limbahs, the Sulima and Falaba countries...and right on to Bundu and
Bambarra countries....After having conquered all these countries he
crossed over to the Niger country and then returned to the Gambia
River....[64]

The Muslims had fought from Futa Jallon to the headwaters of
the river Moa in the south-east yet they met no Mende people.
However, the fighting in the Niger district must have driven the
Mendes south because Owen, trading up the river Jong, knew of a
King *Musolum*, a Mandingo who in March 1758 had 'come down
from the inland kingdoms' and 'made 2 or 3 pety kingdoms subject
to him'; also his observations upon the quantities of slaves supplied by the Temnes suggests that they must have been at war for
some years with a people in the north and east.[65] About the year
1786, so we are told:

..A Foulah Mohomedan, from the Futah country, journeyed into the
Mendi country, and, residing there, in time became wealthy and renowned for the efficacy of his charms, which were reputed to have more
power than any other medicine man in that part of the country in which
he resided. For this reason they styled him Foulah Mansa, or the Foulah
King, and, marrying many wives, he soon became allied to most of the
principal Chiefs of the country, and the owner of many slaves. At his
death his eldest son, adopting his name, took to war as his occupation,
and in time became a great warrior, and conquered a vast extent of
country now known as the Yonnie district, and bounded on the east by
various Timanee districts, on the south by the Mendi and Bompeh
Sherbro countries, and north and west by the Quiah and Masimerah
districts.[66]

Two years later the Mendes attacked the Temne country in the
Rokel district:

About the year 1788, one of the slaves named Combo Smart, a Lokkoh
man, belonging to the slave dealers at Bance Island, was stationed at this
place [i.e. Rokon], and the Timanees, observing his conduct with dis-
satisfaction, took measures to drive him out of the country, and put him
to death. They united in this under the leadership of Alikarlie Fatmah

---

\* The 'Red Water' is north of modern Sierra Leone; Falaba and Sulima are
in the extreme north of this country.

Brimah, of Port Lokkoh, and made war against him for several days,
when, finding that he could no longer stand against them, he endeavoured
to escape to the Kossoh country; his sisters and brothers making their
escape to Sierra Leone and Bullom.... They took him unawares...and
cut his throat.

His eldest sister, Yenken* Magbachee,...went to the Yama country,
and got the Kossohs to overrun the Timanee country....[67]

*Kosso* is a Temne word for a Mende person, not now used because
it has developed an impolite meaning although it occurs in mid-
nineteenth century treaties signed by the Mende leaders themselves
apparently without objection. The word has nothing to do with the
*Concho* of d'Almada, Barreira or Cuelho; the *Concho*, or Mori-man,
lived north of the Limbas in a land containing much gold which
Sierra Leone has never yielded in any quantities, whereas the mines
of Futa Jallon were already extensive in the eighteenth century.[68]

In 1803 Thomas Winterbottom said that the Temnes occupied
the river territories from Freetown to Port Loko and Rokel,
running inland for a considerable distance where they subdivided
into Temnes, Lokos and Korankos. Major Laing, later murdered
in Timbuctoo, in his map of 1824 clearly marks the area at present
occupied by the northern Mendes as being part of Koranko
country, so that the latter nation must have preceded the Mendes
as settlers in Sierra Leone, sweeping quickly down as far as Port
Loko from the north-east.[69] He says:

The extent of the Timanee country, from east to west, may be computed
at ninety miles. It is bounded on the east by Kooranko, on the west by
the colony of Sierra Leone, part of Bullom and the ocean, on the north
by the Mandingo and Limba countries, and on the south by Bullom
and Kooranko.... The Kooranko country...covers a large extent of
ground, but is not powerful in consequence of its numerous divisions
into small and separate states; it is bounded on the W. by the Bullom,
Limba, and Timanee countries; on the N. by Limba, Tamisso and
Soolima; on the E. by Kissi, the river Niger, and by countries yet
unknown.

Very soon the new invaders were engaged in warfare against the
Limbas, the Temnes (especially when the Mendes, Konos and
Korankos were in alliance under a supposed natural son of the
first Combo Smart who had adopted the same name) and the
Sherbros.[70]

* *Yenken* is now a Temne and Sherbro society name for a dancer.

By 1825 Sir Charles Turner, governor of Sierra Leone, the struggle having reached the frontiers of the colony, was expressing apprehension for the safety of the settlers amidst a 'cruel and destructive war', as a treaty with Banka, king of Sherbro describes it, which had 'for several years raged between certain tribes of the Kusso nation and the inhabitants of the country bordering on the Sherbro Bulloms'.[71] Obviously such a bitter state of affairs made any permanent settlement by the new invaders quite impossible along their main battle-front, and one is not surprised to learn that, wherever their warriors might be, true Mende country lay divided almost equally across the Sierra Leone–Liberia frontier of modern times. In 1843 Doctor Robert Clarke, assistant surgeon to the colony, gave the exact limitations of the Mendes as described by a friend with some twenty years experience of Sierra Leone: 'The Kussoh country appears to lie between the parallels of 7° and 8° 15′ north latitude and in a south east direction, between the degrees of 10° 30′ and 12° west longitude.' That is to say, east of the river Jong and south of Mongeri. Giving further particulars of Mende land, Clarke says:

This country is said to be divided...into several principalities or states, or head towns; it is bounded on the north by the Timnehs, on the east and south by tribes of which I have not yet got any account, except that one on the east is said to be the Konah nation; on the west by the Sherbro, Krim, or Kittum, and the Fye or Vye nations.

...The Sherbro country, commencing at the Ribbie...river on the north, and ending at the sea bar on the south, runs east to the Kussohs.

The.Orim or.Kittam, is a small tribe between the Fye and Sherbro, on the banks of the Boom and Kittam rivers.

The...Vye country, commences at Gallinas, and extends to the south east, to about Cape Mount.[72]

Meanwhile the Temnes, under pressure from the east, drove the Lokos northward where, driven further west by the invading Korankos, they met head-on the Limba, also seeking fresh ground. In this vast reshuffle of territory many old alliances were broken and many old enmities forgiven. By 1800 new ideas and new blood had been injected into this country from both the east and the west; the new Christian settlement in Freetown had its Mohammedan counterpart elsewhere.

# CHAPTER V

# CLOTHING AND WARFARE

Quite soon every civilisation produces three kinds of dress. There are clothes for everyday wear, those for war and those for ceremonial purposes. In a warm climate, of course, one tries to combine modesty with the greatest comfort; the exception to this is the dress of ceremony which is often hot and heavy.

A description written about 1507 by Valentim Fernandes, a German author working on information gathered by Portuguese travellers, speaking of the mouth of the Sierra Leone river, says that the inhabitants of the surrounding country were Temnes. He describes their dress as well as their houses:

The houses of the poor are made of stakes stuck into the ground, plastered with mud and covered with straw and rushes.

The houses of the rich are built of mud and brick; inside they are well white-washed; the outside is of chalk or white clay. Outside they are well made, being the best houses in all *Guynee*. Some are filled with rich matting; on these mats, of which they are just as proud as we ourselves are of carpets, the Africans place as seats three legged stools, very well made and covered with ox-skin.

Their furniture consists of bowls, pots and earthenware pans.

Their bed is a mat near which they keep up a fire all night.

The clothes of the important men are cotton shirts and breeches.

The poor have a cloth made of wood-fibre with which they cover their loins.

The women have a cloth around their loins....[1]

In 1594 d'Almada, writing of the Sapi, whom the Mani invaders had found scattered along the coast from the Rio Nunez to Cape Mount some fifty years earlier, says:

The Sapi possess an attire of their own made of cotton in the form of a loose gown and breeches for the men. The women have their distinctive dress also. Their weapons are spears, swords and arrows. The articles that our traders barter among them include cotton cloths, black cloth from India, hangings from Arras, red caps, black hooded cloaks for the leading men, hats, dyes, bloodstones, beads from India, curtains, trumpets, brass basins and salt.

...This people bury their dead within their houses and they bury them with such gold ornaments as they usually wore when alive in their ears, round their arms, and through their nose. Their ear-rings or *ma-suko* weigh up to thirty crusados [i.e. about 3½ grammes; a Portuguese coin so called because marked with a cross].²

This striped loose gown which d'Almada saw was universally popular. William Finch, an English merchant who came to Sierra Leone in 1607, said of the people he met:

The King keepeth his residence in the bottome of the Bay [i.e. modern Kru Bay], and is called by the Moores [i.e. Africans] Borea....Hee hath other pettie Kings under him...Boreas Dominions stretch fortie leagues into the land; he hath tribute of Cotton-cloath, Elephants teeth and gold; he hath power to sell his people for slaves...and some of them are by Portugall Priests and Jesuits made Christians, and have a Chappell....The King, with some about him, are decently cloathed in Jackets and Breeches, and some with hats, but the common sort go naked, save that with a Cotton girdle about their waste they cover their privities; the women cover theirs with a Cotton-cloath, tucked about their middles and hanging to the knees, wrapped round about them; the children goe starke naked. They are all, both men and women, raced and pinked on all parts of their bodies very curiously, having their teeth also filed betwixt, and made very sharpe...the haire of their heads they cut into allyes and crosse patches; others weare it jagged in tufts, others in other foolish formes; but the women shave all close to the flesh.

Their Townes consist of thirtie or fortie houses, all clustered together...covered with reed and enclosed with mud-walls,...having at the entrance a matte in stead of a doore...not fearing robbery....In stead of a carved bedsted, they have billets of wood laid overthwart, upon which, in stead of a fether-bed, they spread a matte or two. Some are so proud, that they have their (Arras) hangings also of mattes about the walles, yet most about their beds betwixt them and the wall. Their other furniture, is two or three pots of earth to keepe water in, and to boyle such meate as they can get, a gourd or two to fetch Palme-wine, and a halfe gourd for his quaffing cup, earthen dishes for their loblolly,* a basket or two by the walles for his Maria [i.e. wife] to gather cockles, with a snap-sacke for himselfe made of rindes of trees to carry his provant,† with his Tobacco and Pipe, and thus is their house furnished. When they goe abroad each weareth one of those snap-sackes on his shoulder, wherein he carrieth his provision and Tobacco (which in no

* I.e. stews and other cooked dishes.
† I.e. provender or food.

wise must be long from his mouth) with his do-little sword by his side, made by themselves of such iron as is brought them; having also his bow and quiver full of poysoned arrowes, pointed with iron in forme of Snakes-sting, or else a case of Javelins or Darts, pointed with iron of a good breadth and sharpe; and sometime with both.... When any dieth, a little thatched shed is set over his funerall hearse, under which in earthen pots they continually keepe fresh water, and in earthen platters set divers meates, sticking about them some three or foure bones. To the South of the Bay, some fortie or fiftie leagus distant within the Countrey inhabiteth a very fierce people which are man-eaters, which sometime infest them...tobacco is planted about every man's house, which seemeth halfe their food; the boll of their Tobacco-pipe is very large, and stands right upward, made of clay well burnt in the fire. In the lower end thereof they thrust in a small hollow cane, a foot and a halfe long, thorow which they sucke it, both men and women...each man carrying in his snap-sack a small purse (called Tuffio) full of Tobacco and his Pipe. The women do the like in their wrappers, carrying the Pipe in their hands.... They have a fruit called Gola...this fruit they set much by, chewing it with the rinde of a certaine Tree...to which they attribute great vertue for the teeth and gummes*....[3]

The patterns of these 'shirts' and 'wrappers' have scarcely changed since 1500. In 1698 the Royal African Company traded especially in the blue and white striped cloth called Cape Mount shirts. In 1726 the king of Sherbro was wearing 'his Cape *Mount* Surplice, which is a sort of Garment made and worn by the natives of Cape *Mount*, being of Cotton, striped with Blue and White; the Shape is justly describ'd by the name'.[4]

The usual dyes, then as now, were yellow, blue, red and black. Yellow, so the Swedish botanist Afzelius said on his visit to the colony in 1794, was made from the Butter fruit tree;† today the Konos use a plant which they call *gbasi*.‡ Blue is made from the indigo plant, red from camwood and sasswood.§ A description of Ndawa, a warrior chief in 1880, says 'His dress was of cotton dyed in reddish brown with sasswood, and he wore a black cap with strong war-charms in ram's horns about him. His sword rested in a bark scabbard well-rubbed with beeswax.'[5] The black

---

* Today, for the teeth, many sticks are used, including lime and guava.

† *Pentadesma butyracea.*

‡ *Terminalia ivorensis.* The Mende use what they call nyεlε—*Craterispermum laurimum.*

§ Camwood is *Baphia nitida*; sasswood, or red water tree, is *Erythrophleum guineense.*

dye for cloth is made from the boiled seeds of the Christmas Bush★ mixed with the oil of boiled and crushed oil-palm kernels. Another kind is made from the crushed leaves of what the Mendes call *Dɔwɔ*.†

From contemporary accounts it is noticeable that weaving and dyeing was practised in the north-east and south of Sierra Leone rather than in the centre. Cloth was also imported from the north by the Susus and d'Almada noticed that this nation exchanged dyes, cotton cloth and ready-made clothes for salt. In 1821 Major Laing noticed the same trend whilst travelling through Temne country:

I could percieve no traces of a characteristic costume amongst those resident in their own country; every individual, according to his fancy or ability, clothes himself after the fashion of other tribes. Most of the head-men were habited in the Mandingo shirt and trowsers, with a cap of red or blue cloth; others wore the shirt, with a pair of trowsers of satin stripe, reaching as far down as the ancle, and nearly as tight as pantaloons; some the shirt only; but...few possessing more than a small square piece of coarse cloth, or woven bark attached to a string, and tied round the middle. This tegument, scanty as it may be, was, I apprehended, the only covering used by the whole of the Timannees previous to their acquaintance with Europeans, as the manufacture of country cloth among them is very limited, being even now only known to a few individuals, who possessing more energy than their neighbours, have ventured to the country of Kooranko, where they have learned the art of weaving....Kooranko is the first country to the eastward of Sierra Leone, where the manufacture of cloth is common, but it is in general of a coarse quality. As the traveller advances eastward, he finds the natives improve both in the texture of the cloth and size of the loom. In the country of Sangara [i.e. beyond the modern north-east frontier of Sierra Leone], very handsome and large cloths are manufactured... and form an important article of trade among the interior nations. I have seen cloths similar to those of Sangara on the Ivory and Gold Coast....I should presume the art of weaving has been introduced from the eastward....[6]

In that same year Catherine Hutton, who fused the accounts of Golberry and Winterbottom to form a pretended visit of herself to Africa, wrote:

The dress of the Timmanees, who inhabit the south and the Bulloms who inhabit the north side of the river Sierra Leone is such as has been

★ *Alchornea cordifolia.*          † *Pseudospondias microcarpa.*

often described, the wide cotton shirt for the men, and the cotton cloth, forming a petticoat, for the women, with a second cloth thrown occasionally over the shoulders. The ornaments are beads, coral, gold, and silver, in the ears, and round the neck, large silver rings upon the arms, and small bells at the ancles. The dress of the men is not complete unless it be laden with gree-grees [i.e. charms]. Children go entirely naked...but their hair is neatly plaited, and a string of beads, coral, or a piece of European silver coin is hung round... the neck, ancles, or wrists. From this time till they are married, the girls wear a narrow piece of cloth, the ends of which hang down behind and before, nearly to the feet; the dress of the boys is the same, except that the ends do not hang loose.... The women ornament their foreheads with squares, triangles, and other figures of blue, red, or white paint.[7]

This disinclination of the Temnes for weaving is true, generally speaking, today. The smaller Mende loom, which is portable, is used now by the Mende, Sherbro, Vais, Krim and Kono people. The heavier, more permanent, Mandingo loom from the north is favoured by the Limbas, Korankos, Upper Kissis and Upper Konos. Sherbro mats called *bicas* were well known to the early Portuguese, and they were in great demand in seventeenth-century England; Laing may well be right when he says that weaving was introduced into Sierra Leone from an easterly direction. At any rate that was the general route of later migrations in our period. Such trades as weaving and basket-making—besides the tests of endurance and a certain knowledge of toxicology—are taught during the initiation of the young men into their Society law and customs, and this westward drift of cultures still continues; for instance, it was only about 1950 that the Snake Society—so called because of its members' serpentine dances—was introduced into Kono country from Liberia.[8] A late eighteenth-century description of Sherbro Society dancers says: 'On their heads they wear a monstrous fabric of bamboo, adorned with feathers; on their legs a number of iron rings that jingle as the wearer moves; the rest of their clothing is a petticoat of grass. When one of these men comes into the town, the young women form a ring around him; while he throws himself into a variety of the most fatiguing attitudes....'

Usually, it is the more formal occasions which have been recorded by visiting Europeans, and our best description of the dress of a

Temne king is one of 1784, when Forbana* came to Gambia Island
to sign a treaty with the French ceding part of his territory:

A cap of blue cotton covered his head, and two pieces of the same colour
formed his dress; the one hung over his shoulders, and the upper part
of his body; while the other covered his loins, and fell down behind, like
a woman's petticoat, as low as his heels; beneath this he was naked, and
he had in addition only a narrow belt of blue cotton, which was fastened
round his hips and the upper part of his thighs.[9]

Forbana had arrived on the island at ten o'clock in the morning,
accompanied by his wife, in a canoe some fourteen feet long
manned by twelve rowers; as soon as he arrived he received a three-
gun salute from the French, who, after entertaining him to a meal,
presented him with European clothing:

The first suit consisted of a scarlet dress, richly embroidered with gold,
four inches broad; a poppy coloured silk waistcoat...red breeches,
embellished with golden knee bands; crimson stockings, shoes with red
heels, large silver buckles, a shirt with long laced ruffles, a neckcloth of
the same, and an enormous cocked hat, ornamented with a red feather,
about three fingers in breadth.... To this first suit...there also belonged
a very large sword, with a richly worked handle, and a belt of crimson
velvet, embroidered with gold; and a bamboo cane, four and a half feet
long, ornamented with a silver head...as large as that of a drum-
major's; and lastly a silver chain, which served as a string to the walking
stick.

It is interesting to hear of this forerunner of today's Paramount
Chief's staff. The other suits were green laced with gold and 'clear
blue, embroidered with silver'. Possibly this last one changed hands
either by purchase or in return for some benefit; at any rate it
sounds very like what King Jimmy wore some twelve months later
when he met Lieutenant John Matthews on the shores of Kru Bay.
Matthews had come to obtain permission to build stores and workmen's houses for his company, and he said afterwards of his
meeting: 'Image to yourself the shore of a little sandy bay covered
with black men, women, and children. Under the shade of a tree

---

* Forbana was king of the islands in the river, including Bunce and Gambia
Islands; he succeeded in 1775. *Gbana* in Temne means 'big'; it is a name given
to the senior Poro candidate at any initiation ceremony; cf. King Niambana
whom the settlers of 1787 parleyed with. But *forbana* is a word used by the
Mendes for a type of flowing (blue) cloth or gown which has come from far off.
However, possibly Panaboure (above, p. 48) = Gbana Burré, i.e. King of Burré.

sat the king in an arm-chair, dressed in a suit of blue silk, trimmed with silver lace, with a laced hat and ruffled shirt, and shoes and stockings. On each side sat his principal people, and behind him two or three of his wives.'[10] By this time, of course, the Fulahs were firmly established in Sierra Leone, mainly as traders, and the early colonists must have seen many of them:

The dress of the Foolahs and Mohamedans in general, is a wide shirt resembling a surplice, of white, or sometimes blue cotton; very wide drawers, reaching a little below the knee; sandals; and a red or blue woollen cap. If a man have two patches of red set upon the drawers behind, in the bend of the knees, and a cotton cloth rolled round the bottom of the cap, he assumes an air of conscious superiority. The silver ornaments worn by some of the chief women were said to be of twenty pounds value.[11]

Laing, who was a better observer than our previous informant, said:

The costume of the Mandingoes is extremely plain, simple, neat and becoming; consisting of a cap, shirt, trowsers, and sandals. The cap is composed of blue or red cloth, is conical in shape, and neatly worked with different coloured threads; the shirt, which hangs loosely over the trowsers, is truly simple in its construction, being formed of about a fathom or more of blue or white baft [i.e. 6 feet or more of coarse cloth] doubled, with a small hole cut in the top to admit the head; the sides are sewed up about half-way, leaving sufficient room for the play of the arms; trowsers of the same materials reach merely to the knee; they are made very wide, and gathered round the loins with a strong piece of tape. The width of the trowsers is a great mark of distinction among the Mandingoes; hence the common expression among them, Koorte Abooniato, 'large trowsers', which is synonymous with 'great man'. To such an extent do they carry this fashion, that I have known a head-man with a whole piece of baft, being about twenty yards, made into one pair. The females wear a pang cloth of baft about a yard in width around the waist, impending as far as the calf of the leg; and a shawl or some fancy cloth suspended from the head, and covering the neck and shoulders, if they are not at work....[12]

Obviously everyday dress varied very little amongst the inhabitants as a whole, if only because it was so scanty. Contemporary observers of the Mani invasion did not make any distinction between the clothing of either side because they seem to have seen only the war dress:

Al the Samboses [i.e. Sumbas] have white teeth as wee have, far unlike
to the Sapies, which doe inhabite about Rio grande, for their teeth are
filed...and [they] doe iagge their flesh, both legges, armes and bodies,
as workmanlike as a Jerkinmaker with us pinketh a ierken....The
Sapies and Samboses also, use in their wars bowes and arrowes made of
reedes, with heads of yron poisoned with the iuse of a Cucumber....In
their battles they have target men, with broade wicker targets, and
[darts] with heades at both endes, of yron, the one in forme of a two
edged sworde, a foot and a halfe long, and at the other ende, the yron
long of the same length,...to counterpease it, that in casting, it might
flee level....And when they espie the enemie, the Captaine...crieth
*Hungry*, and they answer *Heygre*, and with that every man placeth
himselfe in order, for about every target man three bowemen will
cover themselves.[13]

The Mani tactics, however, differed somewhat from those of the
Sapis because whenever they halted they built barricades of stakes
for their protection. An English expedition, bound for the New
World* about 1567, arrived in the mouth of the Sierra Leone river
to find an advance party of Mani warriors besieged in their
fortified town by those whom they had invaded:

Our generall...sent into the river of Magrabomba which is sowthwarde of Tagarine...to see what good might be done...ii kinges that
desired our [generall's] friendship had beseiged the others in a town
called Bonga...this towne was...very warlik and was walled [with]
mighty trees bownd together with great wythes; in it soldiers that had
come thither 150 leagues...it had in it of principall soldiers negros
6000....Abowte the 27 of January our generall sent up a small shippe
with certaine pinaces and in them 90 menne...to the ayde of the
ii kinges...there was for the espace of ii dayes divers skirmyshes where
there were above 20 of our menne hurte besides divers negros our
frendes for the negros of the towne issued out divers tymes and shewed
them selves verrye valorous....Our generall...gave assaulte by that
parte of the towne which adjoyned to the river; the negros had made
many engines as false diches covered with lighte stickes, leaves and suche
trumpery to overthrowe our menne in and with their invenimede
arrows and dartes so defended themselves, having made loopes in every
place to shote owte at for their savetye. Our generall was everye where
incoraginge his menne whoe were so overmatched that allmost all [were]
wounded and some...having 7 or 8 woundes together...abowte this

---

* This is probably from another version of Hawkins's third voyage, but it
cannot be identified for certain. The MS. has been damaged by fire. The siege
took place on the banks of the river Sierra Leone.

tyme our generall...seying that the breache was made comaunded to lyghte fire pykes...and fyre workes and shotte them into the howses... and so the kinges our frendes brook doune the walles and entred with their hole campe fynding no resistence....[14]

Thirty years later d'Almada wrote further of their skill in war:

It is clear that the Mani come from a nation that lies like a belt around the others. I would say that they bear some relation to *Mandimansa* for whom all the other nations of Guinea shew such fear that when the name is spoken they take off their hats. For one thing, they seem to speak the same language; also they use exactly the same clothes and arms, the latter easily distinguished from those of other people by their smaller size so that their enemies cannot use their short arrows on their own long bows whilst they, on the other hand, can profitably use their enemies' arrows. They use shields made from cane and rushes, large enough to cover a man standing up. Their other weapons are short swords, daggers, one hanging by their side and one strapped to the left arm, and iron spears pointed at both ends. In war-time they carry two quivers. They poison their arrows with the sap of just one plant, unlike other people who make up their poison from several plants. Their dress consists of a loose gown open at the neck, with the sleeves reaching to the elbows, breeches wide at the top but narrow below the knees, and to finish caps decorated with feathers which also adorn their shirts.[15]

Like the English before him, d'Almada noticed that the Mani never halted without digging entrenchments and putting up fortifications called *atabanka*.* This, it seems, was never done by any warriors in Sierra Leone before the Mani came. In the great fight near the river Scarcies, when the Susu and a few Fulah horsemen routed for the first time the invaders, the Susu leader addressed his warriors beforehand telling them that their cause was just and victory certain.

This said, he ordered a group of musicians to begin their war-march, and the army set out to meet the Mani, every man determined to fight to a finish. The Mani, as if in doubt about their next move, had stayed within their fortifications; only a few isolated groups attempted to molest the Susu flanks. But these remained in tight formation: the spearmen in front and guarding the flanks, the bowmen in the centre. Ahead of all rode seven Fulo horsemen, mounted on small horses with saddles and bridles and draped with cloaks whilst large bells hung from their necks.

* Possibly a Temne word. Cf. *Atobankere*: a Temne custom connected with rice growing.[16]

At the first charge, in which the horsemen played a notable part, th barricades, or *atabanka*, gave way. But the Mani stood their ground, for they had the advantage of numbers; yet not for long.... When the Mani saw that the day was lost, like the excellent seamen they were—having sailed all the way along the Coast of Malagueta so as to reach Sierra Leone—they took to the water, the Bulom and Temne at their head.

Although the *atabanka* had failed the Mani in their last fight, other nations must have been impressed with the idea; of the people in the north-west of Sierra Leone d'Almada said: 'once weak and faint-hearted, by contact with the Mani they have developed into good soldiers.... They have developed the habit of enclosing their villages with palisades; some have acquired artillery and hand-guns.'

Once this form of defence had become widespread it was neces-sary, just as it is today in modern warfare, to develop measures which would render it ineffective. Hitherto battles seem to have been fought in daylight—no one could manage a horse at night in such thick uncertain country—but now it was found more satis-factory to have specially selected warriors advance under cover of night and attack at dawn. Thomas Winterbottom, surgeon to the colony of Sierra Leone, describes how a number of Mandingo slaves were besieged in 1795 in a town called Yangheeakurree in Susu country; on this occasion the barricades were used not only for defence, but also as part of the attack:

During the two first months of the siege of Yangheeakurree the allies were very active, and made several attempts to force the wall, but were repelled with so much loss, that their chiefs resolved to change the siege into a blockade. For that purpose a strong palisade, about ten feet high, was carried round the town, about twenty yards distant from the walls. Before this was done, the slaves had the side of the town next the mountains quite open, and could go out to hunt and procure provisions and vegetables; but when I visited it in March 1796, it had been com-pletely invested near two months. In order to annoy the besieged, stages about twenty feet high were erected behind the palisades.... These stages formed only two sides of a square, and were composed of four strong spars fixed in the ground, the intermediate spaces being filled up with small stakes secured by withes. They were prevented from falling forwards by the long shoots of the mangrove tree, which were fixed to the upper part of the stage on the inside, and fastened to strong stakes driven into the ground. Before the erection of these stages the inhabitants had used to pass a great part of the moonlight nights in dancing and making merry in the open air, but afterwards they did not dare to move out, except during the gloom of night, for fear of being shot at. From one of these stages I had a complete view of the inside of the town. The thatch of the houses nearest the walls had been set on fire by the besiegers, by firing from their muskets pieces of iron made red hot in a smith's forge; and, to prevent the others sharing the same fate, the inhabitants had pulled off the thatch.

...About a fortnight before I reached the camp the Soosoos had cut down a large pullom tree, which grew just within the line of their intrenchment, and causing it to fall towards the town, it broke down about twenty or thirty feet of the wall. During the confusion which succeeded, two of the besiegers entered the town by the tree, which served them for a bridge, and brought away the war drum as a trophy. No further attempts were made to penetrate by this breach, nor did the besieged endeavour to rebuild it. The approach of the rainy season rendered it at length necessary for the besiegers to take more active measures, and with infinite labour they brought, from a distance of twenty miles, two or three pieces of old rusty cannon, carrying one and two pound balls, slung by means of poles upon men's shoulders. Pieces of iron bars, about six inches long, were fired from these guns, and, after having beat down a great portion of the walls, they rushed in, and, as I was afterwards informed, cut the throats of the wretched inhabitants who survived.[17]

Such tactics as these, introduced by the invading Manis from the south-east, have been used in Sierra Leone within living memory. A modern writer has recorded the gist of conversations held in the 1930's with three old warriors from the Kailahun district as they remembered the wars of their youth:

In the days of which we speak there were no Paramount Chiefs as we know them to-day and there were certainly not so many towns, and even they were few and far between. A town of about 150 houses would be the largest, and probably the majority of 'chief' towns would be under the 100. Each town would have its own chief who would, perhaps, rule over a few outlying villages, his position depending upon his prowess in war or the prowess of his warriors. Farming was the chief occupation with Hunting and Fishing, and the spasmodic gathering of palm kernels. War served as a kind of interlude, waged either by an angry chief or one who was anxious to increase his prestige. Raids would be paid upon neighbouring tribes who, in their turn, would raid for themselves. Thus in Luawa there would be raids on the Kissis, Balus, Gbandis, Kɔnɔs; and they in turn would raid Luawa.

# Clothing and Warfare

On the whole there does not seem to have been much fighting between the Luawa chiefs themselves, although one or two instances are on record. It was rather perhaps that they united against a common enemy, or perhaps a threatened chief would appeal for help, such help being willingly given on the payment beforehand of six country cloths and one gown. In such wars the spoils were not inconsiderable and an enterprising chief could quickly become rich and his prestige amongst the chiefs increased. Slaves, women, cattle were the common spoils of war in those days and would be shared according to bravery in the first place and position in the second. In this connection it is interesting to note that if a chief desired to call a truce, he would send as his ambassador a woman of light-coloured skin (*nyaha gowole*) with a white country cloth, a gun, and salt to intercede on his behalf. She would probably be his daughter, or at any rate one of his most valued women, for she automatically became the wife of the conqueror.

For the most part these wars would be waged during the darkness. Guns were freely used, but as they took a long time to reload they were not much used after the first volley. Swords and spears were the main equipment, also a sort of shield called 'Kafa-lowoi' or fork of a Kafa tree which was very hard. Strips of iron were fastened across the fork and the whole shield was used to ward off blows of a sword or the flight of a spear. Apart from these necessary weapons, there were the numerous charms hung over every part of the body. Charms chiefly procured from the Muhammadans to guard the life of the wearer, for it was believed that even a shot from a gun was made harmless by them.

There does not seem to have been much actual training for warfare, as the methods then adopted guarded against, to a great extent, the novice entering the firing line. To elucidate this it will be necessary to explain the methods of warfare adopted when a town was attacked. The attacking forces were composed of the following:

1. The Miji (Needle) or Jumper-down (Hitɛmɔ)
2. The Fande (thread)
3. The Kanyɛi (wax)
4. Hakahoumɔ (holder of the ladder)
5. Four Kokoyagbɛbla (drivers from the fence)
6. Kɔgugbanga (warriors)
7. Ngɔmbuhubla (men in midst of battle)
8. Gbamai (ordinary men—sort of reserve)
9. Kɔjokoliisia (war sparrows; young recruits who were carriers and might be called upon to fight)

The order of attack was arranged as follows: before the fight the Kɔgugbanga were called upon to range themselves among the Miji, Fandei, Kande, or Kokoyagbɛbla. There does not seem to have been any definite number for each leader, but perhaps the average would be about twenty, depending of course, on the size of the force. If the Miji thought that not enough men had chosen to follow him. he might choose from those left. As the fighting generally happened in the dark, two watchwords were given, say, two names such as 'Vandi' and 'Buakai'; thus if two men met and one said 'Vandi', the answer was 'Buakai'; if no answer was forthcoming then he knew it was an enemy. The town was approached as silently as possible and if there were two or three stockades to get over (as was generally the case) the Miji led with the others following close behind. As they approached the last stockade, the Hakahoumɔ would rush forward with the ladder which he would hold firmly for the others to ascend. The Miji was the first to ascend and then on his own, had to jump down calling out at the top of his voice his name; he would quickly be followed by the others—the Kokoyagbɛbla splitting into twos and going around the inside of the stockade to prevent anyone from escaping. Until the warriors heard the Miji cry out 'A wa-o' (all come), which was the sign of victory, no one was allowed to partake of any looting. It was of course impracticable for all warriors to ascend by means of the ladder, but once the leaders were over, the rest followed as best they could. All this would take place very quickly, and the Gbamai and Kɔjokoliisia were allowed to do what they liked and follow when and how they could. The Chief—known as the 'Kɔmahɛi' (war chief)—did not take any part in the actual fighting, unless things were going wrong.[18]

In this account one can see many of the old-established Mani war tactics. Guns had been used in the battle at the Scarcies, but then too there had been no time to reload. Moreover, they were always inaccurate—Frederick the Great of Prussia, who studied such matters with the greatest care, about 1750 ordered his troops to aim ten paces in front of the enemy because he reckoned that the heavy kick of the explosion would automatically raise the muzzle to the right elevation. Also, against a strong stockade the light bullets then used would have little effect whilst in the half-light of dawn they would have been a danger to friend and foe alike. For the same reasons the bow and arrow would have been very uncertain weapons, though in skilled hands they were probably more accurate.

D'Almada particularly mentions the small size of the Mani bow and this too was adopted by those whom they had conquered. About one hundred years after, Barbot, a French company agent, remarked that the people he saw along the banks of the river carried small bows and arrows.[19] Poisoned arrows have a very ancient origin; in 1585 one of Thomas Cavendish's men was killed in this way whilst attacking a town on the south bank of the Sierra Leone river. At the end of our period a Fulah bow was described as: 'made of bamboo...very elastic and strong....The cord is composed of a thin piece of bamboo split lengthwise.'[20] The arrows, tipped with iron, unlike those found further down the coast, were not feathered.

One of Barbot's drawings shows two men carrying spears about eight feet long and fish-spears some four feet long, barbed like an arrow. Fernandes, writing about 1506, speaks of 'huge canoes carrying 120 warriors, with their spears, shields, arrows and provisions'.[21] Another Portuguese at this time said that these large canoes were made only by the Bulloms, who carved them from a single tree trunk. Such boats are still used in Sierra Leone today, together with the small indigenous ones which have been used in the north of this country for more than five hundred years.

Like the nineteenth-century chiefs, when a truce was called after the first Mani conquest defeated rulers hastened to offer their daughters in marriage to their conquerors.*

By the eighteenth century, probably under European influence, a particularly vicious kind of cudgel had been invented. In 1728 when Walter Charles, chief agent at Bunce Island, was driven out by a surprise attack at night he received a crushing blow from one of these which he afterwards described as 'one of their man-dukes (large sticks made of heavy Iron Wood and tapering towards the end; 2 inches in thickness more than at the part they hold in their hands)'.[22] By this time, of course, heavy guns had been imported into Sierra Leone for more than two hundred years and their use was well understood; Charles's enemies, once they had captured the fort, turned the cannon on the company's servants as they fled. Later, the more powerful kings made a point of keeping one or two cannon, but they must have been an awkward load on a bush-path whilst corrosion soon made them dangerously weak in the barrel; Major Laing, early in the nineteenth century, visited Rokon where the headman Pa Kombo—or Kombo Smart—who was out of town when he arrived, asked him to fire a salute from

---

* In West Africa defeated tribes have always tended to occupy their usual habitat and to become tributary to their conquerors; in East Africa the defeated tended to move out of their district altogether.[23]

the four guns which lay about the compound so as to mark his entry. Laing says: 'The salute was accordingly fired; but he was by no means satisfied with the reports, as I had not put in much powder, under the supposition, that from their exposed situation, they might have been honeycombed.'[24] Nonetheless, soon after the end of our period the old methods of fighting from stockades had to be adapted to the needs of the modern firearm. A French account of an attack upon Tecuyema, a town near Waiima in the north-east of Sierra Leone, in 1893, shows how this had been done. Lieutenant E. Maritz, in charge of the French troops, described the town as it had been fortified by Porequere the Sofa leader in Sierra Leone who received his orders from Alimamy Samory—or Samodu:

Porequere's base is composed of a central *diarsa* [i.e. a fence; *diarsa* is a Malinke word], which he uses as his private enclosure; a second encircling the first encloses the houses of the Sofas and their wives. A third encloses women captured in the country and guarded by a body of Sofas. Porequere has eight horses and each morning he summons his Sofas and organises small revictualling expeditions. The rest of his troops stay under arms prepared for any attack from local warriors.

...Arriving at dawn before Porequere's *diarsa*, I endeavoured to muster the hordes...behind us. I had only succeeded in drawing up some 50 warriors when a Sofa, coming out of the *diarsa*, raised the alarm. Forced to hasten the attack, I sent my detachments towards the gateway, but it was very strong and to scale the *diarsa*, which was at least 18 feet high, was unthinkable. The Sofas had begun to put up a heavy fire.... I then fell upon another gateway, which we carried.... The second and third *diarsas* were forced and fighting was carried into the village.... The village is very large, composed of big mud houses joined together by lines of stockades.... The village was fortified in this way:

A first wall, very solid and unscalable, with a sentry walk; a second wall with sentry emplacements every 24 or 30 feet with, near each of these emplacements, revetments for riflemen, made of stone or of large blocks of wood, leaning against the stockade with a platform above for a second line of riflemen. Finally a third wall, 1200 feet in circumference, encloses the village where the houses are joined together in groups either by the walls or by the stockades.[25]

# CHAPTER VI

# FOOD

'It seems to mee', wrote Nicholas Owen at Sherbro in 1757, 'that the blacks on this coast retains their ancient custums without alteration in any thing, except thier cloathing, which alters a good dail by the help of Europain cloath[;] swords and household furneture, likewise has made some adition to thier granduer with our goods in general.'[1]

But Owen and his contemporaries knew only the fringes of Africa; they had heard little of Arabic influences or of the migrations such as that which had brought *funde* into Sierra Leone. Unaware of these they were, of course, not able to judge properly the exact effect of three hundred years of European trade upon the west coast; much of what Owen called 'ancient custum' had in fact a modern origin. This was especially true of edible fruits and herbs.

Although a botanical collection had been made at Cape Coast Castle in 1697 by the Reverend John Smythe whilst working for the Royal African Company, it was not until July 1725 that Doctor James Houston, Chief Surgeon at Cape Coast Castle, visited Sierra Leone and made a note of certain medicinal plants used for poultices and disorders of the stomach. However, as he admitted himself, he was no botanist: 'Had I been a Windle-straw-man, I might have made a Collection of different Plants here...; but as my Genius never led me to the Study of Specu-lative Botany...I freely own, my Knowledge in the Vegetable, Animal and Mineral kingdoms extends no farther than what's comprehended under the *Materia Medica*.'[2]

In 1771 H. Smeathman began a study of plants in Sierra Leone, but of those on the Banana Islands only; Lieutenant J. Matthews, R.N., made a small collection of some mainland plants, but the first scientific undertaking here was that of the Swedish professor Adam Afzelius, in 1792. Inevitably there were many plants which he was unable to identify, and not all of these were indigenous.*

* In 1791 three planters and several overseers with experience of tropical agriculture were sent out to Freetown at the company's expense. Three estab-lishments were formed; the first was a cotton plantation at Thompson's Bay

A recent survey of five hundred of the flora of the Belgian Congo proved that 377 of these had an Asiatic and 107 an American origin. Moreover, one hundred of them are used today as staple foods.[3] In fact, like any other peoples, West Africans had been experimenting with foreign dishes long before Owen came to Sherbro. More than a thousand years ago Arab influences had brought in such plants as the sugar cane, Asiatic rice, onions, the Creole *Crane Crane* and *Greens*, benny seed—now used for frying—and certain kinds of wheat. Other species, such as the banana and coco-yam, seem to have spread westwards naturally from the African shores of the Indian Ocean. It is likely that bananas have been known in Sherbro for over four hundred years; the word used for a banana in Sherbro is *bana*. The bananas of Africa, mostly of the related genus *Ensete*, are hybrids of the wild forms *Musa acuminata* and *Musa balbisiana* of India and Malaya. Although modern bananas are seedless, this is due to selective breeding; at one time they must have been propagated by seed and there is therefore very good reason to believe that the banana in Africa is an importation. There are wild yams in Africa, but these are only different sub-species of the Malayan *Dioscorea alata*, *Dioscorea bulbifera* and *Dioscorea esculenta*. Similarly, the coco-yam, *Colocasia esculentum*, is not found in Africa in a wild form. All are importations,[4] but it is practically impossible to assign to them a date. An Indonesian migration to Madagascar occurred probably some three hundred years before the beginning of our period—at least by then the east coast was substantially settled—and although their imports are seldom found further inland than the west of modern Kenya traders may well have brought their fruits across the continent at a very early date.

Few plants cultivated by the American Indians were known to Asia, Africa or Europe before the New World was discovered at

which by 1794 had failed because the planter returned to England. Another planter died and the third, James Watt, began the Clarkson Plantation on the Bullom shore, planted with sugar cane, cotton, rice and vegetables. In 1795 Graham, a sailor now in charge of this plantation because no one else was available, was sent to St Thomas and Princes Island for new seeds and plants. He returned in November with coffee, cinnamon, Brazil tobacco, Guinea grass and other things. The coffee plants went to Clarkson Plantation except for a few reserved for the Garden of Experiment, established by Afzelius near Freetown in April 1794 but given up in December 1795 for financial reasons, and some which were presented to Bunce Island and the head men of factories and a few local towns.[5]

the end of the fifteenth century.[6] The introduction of these new species more than doubled the food supply of the other continents.*

Food is acquired in four main ways: by gathering fruits and vegetables, by fishing and hunting, and by cultivation.

From accounts of visiting sailors it is obvious that there was never any lack of fish along this coast; at Bunce Island the Royal African Company even considered producing isinglass, which is obtained from the air-bladders of certain fish. The earliest methods of fishing here were by hook and line, by using a variety of baskets and traps made from local fibre, by spearing, by building walled tidal enclosures and by poisoning. The first hooks were made, as they are still, from the bones of certain fish; these are sharpened at one end but they are not, of course, barbed. All hooks, whether of bone or metal, are called by the Mendes *ndoli*; metal hooks, now sometimes made locally, were imported originally from Europe. The short traps, made from palm fibre and placed under the bank with the mouth facing downstream, are called *mbumbui* in Mende and in Temne *katunk*. There is also a longer one, similar in build, which the Mendes call *vaimɛi*. Most inland fishing is done by women, but a trap made to close up at the mouth when a fish enters, used only by men, is called by the Mendes *ndosi*. The hour-glass shaped creel carried by women to hold their catch as it is taken up is called in Mende *piyɛi* and in Temne *ralɔma*. Except at sea, fishing is usually a woman's task and perhaps the oldest kind of tackle is the women's net called *Tumo* in Sherbro and *mbembe* in Mende and Temne. It is a cord scoop-net about eleven feet long having no handle and it is used in shallow creeks and rivers, often by two women at once, one on either side of the wide mouth.[7] In certain places it is forbidden by the fishing society called *Tuntun*.† Other fish-traps and baskets are made of fibre in many shapes and sizes, but there do not seem to be any plunge baskets in Sierra Leone, although they are known in the Gambia, amongst the Kissis of Guinea, and in Ghana. These baskets are made to be plunged quickly by hand over a fish in shallow water and they have a small opening at the top to allow the fisherman to put in his hand and catch his prey. How-

* In North America alone some 400 species were used.
† A ban or taboo is often placed by the Poro Society upon certain pools; this is called by the Temnes *waŋka* and by the Mendes *hale*. This taboo, which is a powerful one, is used also on other occasions; there are others still with different names. In general the *Tuntun* dislike all nets, especially the seine net.

ever, ordinary baskets are sometimes used in this way, but the fish must be seized by inserting the hand at the bottom of the basket as it rests on the river-bed.

The tidal enclosures, often called *minnow wells*, are made of loosely piled laterite boulders set just below high-water mark; when the tide ebbs the water drains away through the holes in the walls leaving the fish struggling in shallow water.

A variety of poisons is used on the coast*—altogether some fifty have been identified—and many of them have a tannin base which affects the fishes' breathing. Just after the end of our period Lieutenant Clarke, assistant surgeon to the colony, described a Susu method:

> The following mode of fishing is practised amongst the Soosoos. They collect a quantity of the leaves of several narcotic plants, called by them 'Makey Jeakey, Jur' etcetera,† and pound them, when they proceed to the banks of the river, and spread the mass over the rocks and stakes by the water edge. As the tide rises on the mass, the water becomes saturated with the narcotic principle of these plants, and in about half an hour the effects are perceptible. If successful, the women and children, who alone follow this occupation, raise a general shout.[8]

When the bow and arrow was used regularly in Sierra Leone no doubt fish were shot either from the bank or from a canoe. A spear with a permanently fixed one-barbed head, used also on land against deer, is still employed as a harpoon in Sherbro. Just below the head, which is bound to a shaft some nine feet long, is a strong cord to the other end of which is fastened a wooden float. It is used from a canoe with one man in the stern paddling and another standing in the bows with the harpoon raised for the strike. Often very large fish are caught in this way.‡ This method is sometimes varied by taking a cutlass to slash at fish in shallow water—often the blunt side of the blade is used as the striking edge but even so great care is needed to see that the water does not deflect the blade on to the user's legs.

All these ways of fishing probably preceded the discovery of net-making on this coast. For instance, the cast-net was intro-

---

* The general names for fish poisons—e.g. *Adenia lobata, Tephrosia vogelii*—are *tawi* (Mende), *katɔl* (Temne). They are seldom used in Sherbro but, for large fish, the Kissis poison their arrows with sasswood.[9]

† Possibly *Adenia lobata*; the Mendes call it *jumuke, maŋɔnyi*.

‡ Barbot shows the same type of spear in one of his drawings.

duced first by the Portuguese although each European nation brought its own variety of fishing tackle as part of an expedition's normal equipment. As a result European twine must have been known on the coast for five hundred years, but it is unlikely that it was bought generally by local fishermen much before the end of the nineteenth century.[10]

With the discovery of netting came first the draw-net (called *pel bono* in Sherbro) and then, developed from it, the Bullom set-net, called by the Creoles *Pin-chain-net* because of the stakes which stick up from it above water. The draw-net is a small wall net, used by two men, only in shallow water, who drag it ashore by two strong poles fastened at each end. The net is kept upright by vertical sticks some four feet long. The set-net is much bigger and is used from canoes working in pairs—sometimes called chain boats—when a shoal of fish has been sighted. The vertical stakes, longer than those of the draw-net and projecting from each side of the net, are driven into the sea-bed so as to surround the shoal and cut off its retreat in a creek or bay. The Bulloms call these nets *pel banka*, *pel baha* or *pel bobo*, according to the size of the mesh.*

Drift-nets, called *pel kuku* in Sherbro and shot from a drifting canoe, are used mainly at night when torches are carried to attract the fish; they are made usually of palm-fibre and are supported in the water by cork-like floats.†

Lines of stakes are set up in the rainy season. At the end of the line, which runs out at right angles from the coast, is set a net to trap any fish trying to pass up- or downstream and, finding its way blocked, nosing its way along the stakes. Deep-sea fishing, which means being at sea for two or three days on end, is said to have been introduced by the Nova Scotians. The seine net is first mentioned by Lieutenant Clarkson in 1792 and it is another European importation.‡

Although Englishmen in the 1560's saw fish being dried in the Sherbro district, there is no reason to believe that fish-curing in early times was ever as extensive as it is today, especially because there were no roads, so that distribution must have been more difficult. Now,

* *Pel bobo* has a mesh of 1¾ inches and is used to catch *bobo* fish—the Creole *adarei*—see J. Hornell.[11]

† Probably *Musanga cecropicides*—the Umbrella Tree, called by the Mende *ngofui*. The Breadfruit Tree—*Artocarpus communis*, Mende *befui*—is also used for floats.

‡ This net reached Ghana only about 1907.[12]

for example, a pall of smoke may be seen drifting a mile or so down-wind from the curing sheds on the Plantain Islands. Here the *bonga* is dried and partially cooked—it is placed very close above the flames—for some thirty-six hours over a smoky fire of mangrove wood. One of Barbot's drawings of 1678 shows a fish suspended from a convenient sloping dead branch above a wood fire.[13]

Indigenous wild fruits and vegetables are hardly within the historian's range and it is, perhaps, enough to say that certain dishes still used—such as the Creole *bologie* and *Crane Crane*—were known to the first inhabitants of this country because they grew wild and that Barbot lists about two dozen trees used for making canoes, cloth, dyes, fuel, magic, medicine, mortars, poisons and soap.[14] *Crane Crane*, of the Jute family, is Asiatic in origin and was probably acquired at a very early date from the Arab and other traders. Seven hundred years after the Arabs came the Portuguese; new roots and seeds, lying in the holds of their ships, began to cross the oceans from India to America and Africa, and from America to this coast. A fifteenth-century sailing ship was small, and the uncharted open seas a constant menace. Supplies of water soon ran dry—especially if there were horses on board—and captains preferred to sail as far as possible in sight of land. Consequently, whether they were bound for China or Peru, a crew's first experience of foreign parts beyond Europe was always the West African coast. Gazing for days at the lifeless cliffs which drop down from the Sahara desert, sailors were glad to come again to vegetation and a safe anchorage. Thus in 1506 a ship came to Portudal, south of where Dakar stands today and at that time graced by a large wood of tall green trees: 'Opposite this wood there is anchorage for a small ship...with a good bottom of gravel and coarse sand, lying about half a league from the shore....Formerly a good trade in slaves was carried on here, when one could obtain ten as the price of a horse, but now, due to mismanagement, they will not pay six. One may buy plenty of meat, "milho",* "feyxões"†, water and wood....'[15] Further south the tropical rain forests offered a diet different from that of the arid north; more or less where Bissau stands today the early Portuguese found a people with 'great quantities of rice, "milho", yams, hens, cows and goats'.[16] Here too, by the beginning of the sixteenth century, were limes and lemons, which had found their way across Africa and

* See below.     † I.e. groundnuts.

which the Portuguese lost no time in carrying further down the
coast. They planted some limes at King Tom, where they were
flourishing in 1582; at the end of the eighteenth century this
orchard was still visited by sailors. By 1700 the private traders
living there were planting orchards in their gardens. Doctor
Houston wrote: '...down where the River opens into the Sea,
where the Ships lie in Harbour, there are high Lands inhabited by
several Englishmen, separate Traders from the Company; where
I have seen Citron Trees in their Gardens, bearing Fruit to
Perfection without any Cultivation, only the Seed put in the
Ground....'[17] Afzelius unaccountably mistook these for a
plantation of lemons, remarking that the fruit had 'degenerated so
much as almost to resemble Limes'. He may have been misled by
the English sailors who referred to both these fruits as lemons.
The Creole 'lemon', of course, is a tangerine. At the end of the
sixteenth century d'Almada said that oranges were plentiful in
Sherbro, but until after 1700 oranges, either sweet or sour, were
uncommon in the Sierra Leone river estuary.[18]

About 1510 a Portuguese said that the people of Sierra Leone
ate rice, 'milho', yams, 'macarras',* haricots, fish and shellfish
both boiled and roasted.[19] The exact translation of 'milho' is often
difficult because great confusion existed in the minds of early
European travellers regarding maize (Indian Corn—*Zea mays*) and
the two main species of millet—Small Millet (*Pennisetum*) and
Large Millet (*Sorghum*). Maize came originally from America
and was introduced into San Thomé by the Portuguese some
time in the sixteenth century. The Small Millet was first grown
in the Sahara region; Large Millet was known to the Arabs,
who had grown it for centuries before the Europeans came to
Africa. Today the word *milho* in Portuguese may mean either maize
or Large Millet, but *miglio zaburro* seems always to have meant
Large Millet. It would seem that neither species of Millet was
known in the forest belt of West Africa until the Portuguese took
it there.[20] Significantly Cadamosto saw both kinds growing in the
Gambia in 1455. A hundred years later it was the staple diet in
that country: 'To grow varieties of millet—which we call "zaburro" the general food of these peoples—they clear the silt left
by the floods, then scatter the seeds without further tillage, and
cover them with a thin layer of sand.'[21] At this date one begins to

* I.e. groundnut—*Voandzeia subterranea*, Bambara groundnut.

hear of these seeds spreading all along the coast and it is possible that the following, taken from an account of an anonymous Portuguese pilot written about 1540, is an early reference to maize: ' At the beginning of August they begin to sow grain, which they call "zaburro", or, in the West Indies "mehiz". It is like chick pea, and grows all over these islands and all along the African coast, and is the chief food of the people. It is harvested in 40 days.'[22] In fact maize was being spread at this time by the Portuguese ships trading down the coast. Those bound for San Thomé and the Gulf of Guinea in search of slaves were permitted by royal ordinance to put in at the ports in North Africa in order to take on maize with which to feed their slaves on the next leg of their voyage. But this and other grains could be used also for trade:

I send you sixty head of slaves...I send them at this time out of necessity, since there are so many slaves, because besides those which are thus sent I still have here in the factory one hundred and thirty head of slaves. Therefore, I have to inform you that you must at once send me one hundred 'moios' of corn, because little remains available for use here...for they take it each day, and they need it both for trade and to eat.[23]

At the end of the seventeenth century, maize seems still to have been scarce and trade in millet as a food for slaves continued:

...first of the corn called *Milhio*.
The large 'Milhio'...when grown up...is one and a half or twice a Man's Height....*
The second sort of *Milhio*, called by the Portuguese Maiz†... grows in the same manner as the great *Milhio*, only the Stalk is not so thick, nor the Ears covered with Leaves as the other is....
I have seen it bought, and have also bought myself, one thousand Stems or Stalks for six, seven, eight and nine *Takoes*, each *Takoe* amounting to about Four Pence Farthing *English* Money....This Corn, in Time of Peace, is the cheapest of all Provisions; but in War-Time, it sometimes rises to an incredible Price.
...To which the Laziness of the *Negroes*...contributes very much, as also the great Number of *English* Slave-Ships which yearly come to this Coast; for these not being so well victualled as we [i.e. the Dutch], they are obliged to buy *Milhio*, which yearly carries off many Thousand Sacks.

* I.e. maize.                    † I.e. millet.

...It is told me as Truth, that before the *Portuguese* came to this Coast, the *Negroes* subsisted themselves with...two Fruits [i.e. yam and potatoes], and a few Roots of Trees; they being then utterly ignorant of *Milhio*, which was brought thither by that Nation.[24]

It is probable that maize, by about 1550, was being grown sporadically on the coast between the Gambia and Ghana. One cannot be certain since no specific reference to an Indian Maize has been found before 1600 when the Dutch trader Peter de Marees saw it for sale in the Gold Coast together with 'oranges, limons, bannanas, backovens,* potatoes, indianias [i.e. pineapples], millia [i.e. *milhio*], rice, manigette [i.e. Guinea pepper], hens, eggs, bread and such like necessaries'.[25]

Further confusion has arisen because some writers mistook certain cereal crops which they saw on the coast for wheat. For instance, in 1554 John Lok, the English explorer, wrote:

They have very faire wheate, the eare whereof is two handfuls in length and as bigge as a great bulrush, and almost foure inches about where it is biggest. The stemme, or straw, seemeth to be almost as bigge as the litle finger of a man's hand, or litle lesse. The graines of this wheate are as big as our peason, round also, and very white, and somewhat shining, like pearles that have lost their colour....I told in one eare two hundred and three-score graines. The eare is inclosed in three blades, longer then itselfe, and of two inches broad apiece.[26]

This, however, cannot be wheat because wheat does not have such large bracts, or blades, enclosing the ear as those which Lok describes; it is probably maize.

The Mende names for maize—*nyɔi*—and pennisetum—*pele nyɔi*—suggest that maize was known to them before pennisetum; that is, having already a name (*nyɔi*) for maize, when they discovered a corn which resembled it, they gave the new crop a name (*pele nyɔi*) derived from the older one.

Although corn, yams and sweet potatoes have been grown for many centuries in this country the Sierra Leonean has never been so fond of them as he is of rice. The Nigerian student at The University College of Sierra Leone sometimes complains of the lack of yams in his diet, and indeed the best yams have always been found further south; an anonymous Portuguese pilot wrote:

The roots, which the Spanish Indians call *batata*, are called *igname*, by the negroes of San Thomé, who cultivate them as their principal food....

* Backoven: banana: plantain.

There are various kinds of these roots, yams *cicorero*, a large quantity of which is taken by the ships which come to San Thomé to obtain sugar. This kind remains fresh for many months, and will not spoil, if kept a whole year. There are three other kinds of yams, one from Benim, another from Manicongo, and a third yellow variety; but these do not keep so long. That from Benim is more delicate in flavour.[27]

In 1786 Lieutenant Matthews, writing from Sierra Leone to a friend in England, said 'Indian corn and millet both thrive extremely well, but are little cultivated'. A few months later he wrote again: 'The customary food of the natives is rice, which they always boil quite dry, and either eat it with palm-oil poured over it, or a strong gravy made of fish, flesh, or fowl, and vegetables boiled together, highly seasoned with pepper and spices, and palm oil. They use very little animal food, and in general prefer it smoke dried rather than fresh. . . .'[28]

Bitter cassava was introduced into the Congo basin from South America about one hundred and fifty years after the discovery of the New World. Here it remained for over two hundred years before spreading along the coast in any quantity, but from then on its distribution was very rapid. The reason for the original delay is because, to extract the prussic acid which is contained in bitter cassava, it is necessary to press or pound the roots. The South American Indian had invented a fibre tube which, when filled with cassava and then stretched, acted as a press; no such machine was known on the West African coast. In this part of the world people, as we have seen, were accustomed to boil most of their food and if someone merely boiled this cassava without pressing it they must have made themselves very ill.

Sweet cassava has a longer history on this coast although this is not easy to unravel because early travellers sometimes confused it with yams and sweet potatoes. It is cultivated extensively in the northern part of West Africa and in Lower Guinea and after it has been peeled it may be eaten raw or merely boiled. It does not make such good *fufu* as the bitter variety. It was being grown in the Sierra Leone river in 1725; Doctor Houston, caught in the rain on Tasso Island, took shelter in the hut of an old woman who was a Royal African Company slave. He says: 'The poor old Creature was sitting over a Fire, baking Bread; the Meal was made of the Roots of a Tree pounded, which she called *Jamming*, in her Dialect, between two Stones. I tasted of the Bread when baked,

which she called Manioco; it had much of the taste of a roasted
Potatoe.... This poor Creature had nothing but this Bread, or a
roasted Plantane to live on, and was vigorous and strong considering her Age.'[29]  In 1786 the bitter variety was still unknown
in the colony area:

To save labour, which the natives studiously avoid as much as possible,
they plant their cassada, or manioc, amongst the rice after they have
weeded it; it remains about four months in the ground, and is then fit for
use. The young roots are very good eating either roasted or boiled, and
are next to yams as a substitute for potatoes. The Abbé Raynal, in his
history of the European settlements in the West Indies, says the manioc
is twenty months in the ground before it attains perfection, and that it
is a strong poison before it has undergone the preparation necessary to
make it into bread; but this is by no means the case with the African
manioc, and it is eaten raw with as much safety as roasted or boiled.
Indeed the children are very fond of it raw, as it is very sweet when
young.[30]

It is evident from this account that the author did not know that
there was already more than one kind of cassava in West Africa,
because the Abbé was quite right; sweet cassava matures in some
three months, but the bitter variety takes four times as long.  In
1751 Nicholas Owen and his brother were marooned accidentally
for a night upon a sandbank off Cape St Anne near Shenge 'without
any other comfort then a sword and some cassada root to keep us
from starving' and this too, since they had no mortar, must have
been the sweet kind of cassava.  On the other hand it is said in
Shenge that bitter cassava has always been known there and that
the sweet kind was introduced only some forty years ago. There is
nothing unlikely in this account since Shenge, and of course
Jamaica Town, have been trading directly with the New World for
some four hundred years.  It has been said that it was from this
district that the Portuguese, about 1500, took bananas to San
Thomé; they may well have introduced bitter cassava at the same
time. The opening up of the Shenge hinterland with the construction of roads began some forty years ago and this may have brought
in for the first time sweet cassava from Guinea whilst permitting
the Sherbros to export the bitter variety.  Significantly there is a
species of bitter cassava grown in the Northern Province today
which is called *Shenge*.

The settlers who first came into the colony would of course have learnt how to treat bitter cassava in the New World and, finding that none grew in their new home, they must have soon taken steps to acquire some; this they may have done by importing it directly from the West Indies, but it is just as likely that they got it from Sherbro. Certainly in modern Sierra Leone there is more demand for the bitter varieties near the coast and along the railway line—where one might expect the influence of Sherbro and colony customs to be strongest—than there is in the interior.

The coconut was another late-comer to the Sierra Leone peninsula, and it too was probably brought up from Sherbro. It was taken to Cape Verde by the Portuguese about 1540; the *Account of the Colony of Sierra Leone*, published in 1795, says laconically: 'Cocoa trees grow in Sherbro where they have been planted.' Barbot's account of the Sherbro area in 1678 carries a picture called *Bridge in the Quoja's Country* and this shows clearly four coconut trees.[31] John Atkins, who visited Sierra Leone in 1721, also mentions them, but he does not say specifically that they grew in the peninsula area: 'The Shores hereabouts, like those of *Sweden*, are rocky, and without any Cover of Earth almost, yet produce large Trees, the Roots spreading on the Surface. The chief of them are the Palm, the Coco, and the Cotton-Trees.'[32] It is noticeable that these trees are not often shown in eighteenth-century pictures of the colony area; Smith's *Prospect of Bense Island* (1721) depicts what is certainly an oil-palm in the centre of the island.[33] On the other hand, Lieutenant Matthews's *View of the entrance into Sierra Leone River* (1788)[34] contains what is obviously a plantation of full-grown coconuts.*

The Europeans on the coast naturally tried to grow the vegetables which they were used to at home, but these efforts ended usually in failure. Often the seeds sent out from home were spoilt before they arrived; usually the soil and temperature of the tropics were unfavourable and the hours of daylight insufficient to allow plants to grow which were used to longer hours of sunshine in the northern summers. For example, about 1455 a visitor wrote:

No corn, rye, barley, spelt,† or vines grow in this Kingdom of Senega, nor from thence onwards, in any regions of the land of the Blacks. . . . Although they have attempted to sow these grains (which they have

---

* It is very likely that coconuts found their way to Sherbro in the same way and about the same time as did bananas.

† Spelt: a species of wheat.

obtained from us Christians) they will not grow because of the great heat....It appears that they grow various kinds of millet, small and large, beans, and kidney beans, which are the largest and finest in the world. The kidney beans are as big as the long hazel nuts familiar to us, all spotted with different colours, as though painted, and very beautiful to the eye. The beans are broad, thin, and of a bright red colour, though there are others white in colour, very beautiful.* They are sown in the month of July, and harvested in September....They drink water, milk or palm wine.[35]

About 1506 Fernandes, writing of San Thomé, said: 'The corn sown in this island grows as high as sugar cane. It produces neither seed nor cob, the leaves are like that of the cane. Green shoots sprout from the roots all the year round, just as from the cane in this area.'[36] In the middle of the sixteenth century an anonymous Portuguese pilot wrote: 'During their working days, they sow millet zaburro...and yam roots, and many household herbs, lettuce, cabbage, radishes and bran seeds. When these are sown, they grow abundantly in a few days, but the seeds the plants produce cannot be sown again.'[37]

There were, of course, the usual wild animals on the coast, but they were much more numerous than they are now. In the sixteenth century Sierra Leone was already famous for its herds of elephants as well as for its high standard of ivory carving: 'In *Serra Lyoa*, the men are very skilful and ingenious;† their ivory work is truly marvellous, compared with any other thing which one may ask them to make....In this country there are a great number of elephants and it is from their innumerable tusks that they produce their fine handiwork. The elephants are not trained to work as in India; they kill and eat them.'[38]

In May 1728 the factor at Bunce noted in his Journal: 'A Drove of Elephants Six or Seven in Number swim'd over from Tasso to the Bago Shore this Day, seen by all the People.'[39] This observation that they were seen by all the people gives perhaps an indication of the elephant population at this time. One imagines each man on the island calling his friend from work to see what he considered a rare

* The beans are probably *Phaseolus lunatus*, which are said to have a South American origin, but it is not impossible that they should have been carried there by the Portuguese from Africa.
† 'très habiles et très ingénieux'; cf. W. Fagg, *Afro Portuguese Ivories*, Kegan Paul 1959, *passim*; these are all pictures of salt-cellars, dagger handles or spoons, the very objects mentioned by Fernandes.[40]

sight, so that presently all were exclaiming in wonder at something unusual. However, elephant were still to be found in the colony area in the mid-nineteenth century when a few visited False Cape.

In 1721, according to Atkins, hippopotamus ivory was still common in Sierra Leone.[41] In the mid-sixteenth century, hippopotamus were caught along the river banks here by felling trees across the game paths and in Sherbro their flesh was reserved for kings. The hippopotamus, with his short forelegs, cannot jump more than a few feet, so that finding an obstacle, as one account of 1568 says, 'unto the which when they come and cannot passe over they stande still where eyther the negros kill them or they dye themselves being lett [i.e. cut off] from the river without the which they cannot live'.[42]

In August 1582 a party from the English Admiral Edward Fenton's fleet of four ships made a small excursion into the hills of the peninsula. Here they found three 'turkey cocks' and two beasts 'of a brown color with short tayles and round flat hornes as byg as 3 yer old bullocks very grosse and fat'. Later, they came upon elephant droppings near Aberdeen point, and they expressed surprise upon seeing 'hens just as owrs'.[43]

The horned bullocks were probably bush-cow, or what Matthews, in 1786, called buffalo: '. . . in the interior parts, and in some places near the sea, there are very extensive Savannahs, where the grass, known in the West Indies by the name of Guinea Grass, grows to an amazing height; and feeds and conceals vast numbers of deer, buffaloes, and elephants.'[44]

Except for elephant, most animals could be snared, trapped or caught in nets. Deer feed in the early morning and by following their tracks a crowd of hunters can discover where they are lying up during the heat of the day and surround them with long nets, four or five feet high, hung on trees. The beasts are then driven into the nets. Small animals can also be driven into nets placed along specially built hedges set usually in a zigzag with holes at various places covered with a net.

Leopards are often caught in box-like traps made of stout branches and creepers, sometimes baited with a goat; when the trap is entered a support is released and a heavy door falls down behind the quarry.* Animals may also be caught in a hole in the

---

* A similar device is used with a semi-circular trap having its arc along the shore for catching fish.

ground, camouflaged with sticks and grass and sometimes having
sharp stakes placed upright in the bottom. Snares with a noose are
placed on the ground and also, for monkeys, in the trees. Those
on the ground are often attached to sticks bent over and held down
until the animal enters the noose, whereupon the stick is released,
springing back into an upright position and so tightening the
noose. The monkey-trap is built so as to prevent the monkey from
following his usual tree-top road and to force him to walk into the
noose, which is usually tightened by a weight.

There are, of course, many variations in the size and design of
these traps and snares, according to the size of the game they are
intended for, but all are very old and were in use long before the
gun or rifle came to West Africa.

The bush-cow, a very uncertain animal and cunning like the
true buffalo, must have been a problem before firearms were
generally known in Sierra Leone. Possibly he was dealt with in
the same way as the elephant; a hunter would lie in the fork of a
tree above a known elephant path and as the beast passed by would
spear him with a heavy-shafted spear, the tip of which had been
dipped in poison. The animal was then followed until it dropped.*
In the sixteenth century the favourite morsels were the toes, the
trunk and the penis.[45]

It was, of course, the settlers at the end of the eighteenth
century, brushing larger areas of farm-land than ever before, who
drove the last of the bigger indigenous animals further into the
interior. In 1816 rice, cassava, plantains, coco-yams, coffee, maize,
bananas, oranges, limes, pineapples, groundnuts, guavas, paw-
paws, horses, cows, bullocks, sheep, goats, pigs, ducks† and fowls
were for sale daily in the market in Freetown. In that year 8352
bushels of cassava were sold to the colony Government—mainly
for the support of the 525 children and infirm persons receiving
relief—for £522. An average of 660 bushels were sold weekly for
1s. 3d. a bushel, those on relief using it as a substitute for rice.
A clergyman, Mr Johnson, has left us a picture of the colony as it
was in that year:

On the banks is a meadow for the cattle belonging to our people which is
always green. Our House, the Church, and the School-Houses for the

* In Ghana sasswood is used to poison pools where game are known to drink.[46]
† Muscovy duck, although Dr Houston saw some in Sierra Leone in 1722,
were still rare at the end of that century.[47]

Boys and Girls, stand together, in a large enclosure on one hill. The remainder of the hill contains about twelve acres, and has been brought, with the help of the Children, into a state of cultivation. I think we shall have nearly enough provision from this Farm, next year, to supply the Schools. We have now planted it full with cocos, cassadas, plantains, banana and coffee. In front of our House, on another hill, is a part of the Town, which extends on our right and left. Behind us, on a higher hill than ours, the Governor has erected a Cottage. From every part of my House I can see the whole Town. Around the Town are the people's Farms.[48]

Although some of the plants grown by these settlers were indigenous, or at least naturalised, several dishes nowadays old favourites in Creole households were introduced in the first place by the settlers or by slaves taken from the slave ships after the trade was made illegal in 1807. *Crane Crane* and *Greens* both have an Asiatic origin and may be considered as being well established by the beginning of our period. *Beni* seed is a Mandingo word for the botanist's *Sesamum indicum* and this too must have reached Sierra Leone at an early date. Ruftin Plum (*Parinari excelsa*) is indigenous and may be found from the west coast to Uganda and East Africa.

The Freetown Registers of Liberated Africans—which contain the names of all those rescued from slave ships after 1808 by the British navy—show that a large number of these were Yoruba in origin; many chose to settle in the new colony where they soon introduced their own tribal customs. The dishes known as *bologie*, *egusie* and *awusa**[*] all have a Yoruba name, although the plants to which these are now given were sometimes already known in Sierra Leone.

Naturally some Creole dishes were derived from the West Indies, such as *sweet sop* and *mammy supporter*. Both were brought in by the early settlers at the end of the eighteenth century.[†]

Briefly, the more common foods available in our period were as shown in the diagram opposite.

* *Bologie*: *Crassocephalum biafrae*—some indigenous; *egusie*: there is an indigenous *Cucumeropsis edulis*, but it is rarely seen now and *egusie* is now used for the water-melon—*Colocynthis citrullus*; *awusa*: *Tetracarpidium conophorum*—a Nigerian plant.

† *Sweet sop*: *Annona squamosa*; *Mammy supporter*: a corruption of *mammea sapota* with which the Sierra Leonean *mammea americana* has been confused.

# Food

| | Sixteenth century | Seventeenth century | Eighteenth century |
|---|---|---|---|
| Avocado pear | | | — |
| Banana | — | — | — |
| Beans | — | — | — |
| Breadfruit | | | — |
| Cassava sweet | | — | — |
| Cassava bitter | ··· | ··· | — |
| Coconut | ··· | ··· | — |
| Cola | — | — | — |
| Cashew | | — | — |
| Coco-yam | — | — | — |
| *Funde* | — | — | — |
| Groundnut | — | — | — |
| Guava | — | — | — |
| Lemon, lime | — | — | — |
| Maize | — | — | — |
| Mammy apple | | | ··· |
| Mango | | | — |
| Millet | — | — | — |
| Oil-palm | — | — | — |
| Okra | ··· | ··· | — |
| Orange | | — | — |
| Paw-paw | — | — | — |
| Pepper | — | — | — |
| Pineapple | — | — | — |
| Plantain | — | — | — |
| Plum (country) | — | — | — |
| Pumpkin, melon | — | — | — |
| Rice | — | — | — |
| Soursop | — | — | — |
| Sweetsop | | | — |
| Sugar cane | — | — | — |
| Tumbler | — | — | — |
| Yam | — | — | — |

The dotted line stands for the probable, but uncertain, existence of foods in Sierra Leone at any given date.

# CHAPTER VII

# CONCLUSION

The period before 1787 was one of change and experiment; tribal invasions had altered the political map of Sierra Leone; Portuguese influence had given way to French, Dutch and English; a succession of chartered companies had failed; Christianity and Islam had begun their first crusades; fashions in clothing and food and methods of warfare were continually changing. It could hardly be expected that this pattern would be altered overnight by the establishment of yet another settlement on the peninsula. Indeed, for a few years it did not seem likely that the settlement would last as long as had many others.

It is true that all the peoples of modern Sierra Leone—except the later settlers—were dwelling already within its future frontiers and that there were to be no more devastating invasions. Moreover, whereas the early economy had been primitive because the population was small, travellers in the 1790's saw rice-empoldering on a scale which could have been produced only by a complex social organisation; those interested in peaceful trade saw infinite possibilities in this.

But the prolonged warfare begun in the seventeenth century by the Mende immigration and spread in the eighteenth by an Islamic *Jehad* continued with increasing ferocity throughout the nineteenth. Also the French fleet, following custom long established on the coast, attacked the rival European settlement in 1794. Subsequently the Sierra Leone Company built considerable defensive bastions; although these were never used again against an enemy at sea they show how the heritage of international rivalry along the coast haunted the new enterprise.

In fact, during its early days, the settlement at Granville Town—the apotheosis of the anti-slavery movement in England—struggled in poverty whilst the private slave-traders and timber merchants on Bunce Island, who had succeeded the Royal African Company there in 1752, flourished. Small factories had been built by three London merchants—Alexander Grant, John Sargent and Richard Oswald—on the neighbouring islands. In 1758 treaties were made with Bai Samma, of North Bullom; in 1766 with King Sumana. In 1785 these merchants leased Bunce to Captain Bowie, agent of the notoriously cruel slaver Ormond.* It was not easy to get rid of the bad type of European resident who, ever since the days of the Portuguese renegades, had battened all too often upon this coast. In August 1808† Governor Perronet Thompson wrote in despair to his future wife:

I have been all last night and to-day making out my report for England. There is much that is very doleful and some that is good. The state of European manners is bad beyond description. The black subjects are infinitely more orderly and decent. So much for this religious colony. And while the white inhabitants are roaring with strong drink at one end the Nova Scotians are roaring out hymns at the other.‡ But there is worse than this; you have heard me speak of Macaulay's apprentice-ships; and it is as I suspected, that these apprenticeships have after sixteen years successful struggle at last introduced actual slavery into the colony. In March last, two slave ships were taken on the coast and brought in here; the slaves were landed and the men and children... apprenticed to the inhabitants and twenty dollars§ were received for each; the women were given away. A number of the men were reserved for the service of government and worked...for nothing but their provisions. Some of the neighbouring natives soon began to say to them 'Where you are, is plenty work and no money; come to us and we pay you for your work'....[1]

At this stage the prime need was not so much trade as agriculture to support those who were to become the future merchants of the country. Thompson wrote: 'We are all tradesmen and the consequence is that we have nothing to trade in and very little to eat. We are masons, and there is nothing to build; or carpenters and there is nothing to frame; but very few of us cultivate the ground as we ought to do, because we have been apprenticed to easier callings.'[2] If long-term plans were to be made it was also necessary

---

* Ormond came first to Sierra Leone as a cabin boy in 1759 and was then hired as an assistant in the slave factory at Bunce. In 1792 the grandson of the first Cleveland—from the west of England—had a big slave factory on the Banana Islands from which he traded up the Sherbro river. He had sublet part of the island to another trader called Bolland 'who has factories all over the Coast, and is supposed to have made a great deal of money'.[3]

† Thompson had been only three days in Sierra Leone when he wrote this.

‡ Thompson was a Methodist; he married Nancy Barker in 1811.

§ £4. 10s.

to have a less impermanent administration than that so far pro-vided by a series of indigent chartered companies. About this time Samuel Swan, an American importer, wrote home: 'The Governors of Sierra Leone have generally been elected by the prevailing party at home concerned in the African Trade. This in a great measure accounts for their invariably undoing what each predecessor has done.'[4]

However, this was the darkest hour; in 1809 Thompson wrote again:

If anyone asks what we have done with all our money, we have built three batteries, and finished two which were begun, we have made roads in the streets of the town*...we have improved the watering place—bought a civil store and filled it with goods;† cut a large road into the country—cleared a new settlement‡—clothed the militia and furnished them with arms§ and cleared some hundred acres for the health and safety of the town which we mean to plant this year with rice and cotton....All these expenses I hope are incurred once for all, and will not come over again like the wooden houses and batteries of the Sierra Leone Company.[5]

The settlement had been saved from oblivion; it was no longer an appanage of yet another chartered company, but for a year now had been a crown colony. The way was open for greater commercial expansion dependent no longer upon one company alone; treaties of peace and trade were made between the English crown and the local kings within an ever-widening horizon.

Henceforth, if Sierra Leone was to become anything more than a coaling station for foreign ships she had to show by her own prosperity that foreign investment could earn a satisfactory dividend. In 1885 Sir Samuel Lewis, an eminent Sierra Leonean, said:

The Settlement has reached a crisis which enlightened statesmanship in even the earliest period of its history had discerned as an ultimate and not very remote fate of its contracted area, and of its capacity to main-tain its population by its own natural resources. If this colony which

* Thompson gave them names instead of numbers.
† The cost of living had soared because there had been too many middlemen; the new store reduced the cost of rice from 8s. to 4s. a bushel.
‡ Notably Leicester village.
§ Thompson formed a brigade and devised for it a 5s. uniform.

has a magnificent position for centralizing the resources of the vast interior of West Africa...has failed in answering these expectations, it must not be supposed that the necessary knowledge is wanting in those in authority here, to suggest for correcting the cause of failure, effectual methods in regard to which however, for now nearly sixty years there has been a conflict of opinion,...between the Imperial Government and the local administration of this Settlement.

It is impossible to shut our eyes to the fact that whatever the future possibilities of Sierra Leone...the main source of livelihood at present...is trading....

Let us frankly admit the unpleasant fact that after nearly a century of contact with this Settlement, the aboriginal inhabitants bordering on this coast are unable to forget the lesson of rapine and bloodshed, taught or fostered in them under the now obsolete European slave-trade system....As Sierra Leone is not a producing centre, but must carry on its trade with the industrial populations of the interior...our trade is entirely at the mercy of this intermediate obstacle to steady progress....

All travellers concur in the assertion that in the interior of the continent, you find the moral as well as the mental character of the people undebased by the effects of Western civilization....Rapacious even as the Mendis are held to be when they come near the coast, they are in the very heart of their country represented as fair specimens of orderly, industrious, and peaceful interior Negroes....To have an effective jurisdiction reaching as near as possible such interior industrious tribes would be a boon to the British trade.[6]

Like Owen and other eighteenth-century traders, Lewis blamed the warlike state of the immediate hinterland for the failure in trade; he pressed impassionedly for 'annexation by means of purchase' of this territory. There was, of course, friction between settler and tribesman, trader and farmer, Christian and Muslim but Lewis's vehemence had led him—probably purposely—to exaggerate these differences. To another eminent African, looking back on these early years, there was infinite hope of a happy and prosperous partnership. In 1888 E. W. Blyden wrote:

The settlers gradually died out, and there being no further accession from America, the recaptives and their descendants naturally and properly came to the front, until now they own most of the valuable property in the colony....But this element, which has superseded the Nova Scotians and Maroons is not exactly indigenous. As the negroes from across the sea gave place to them, so they, receiving no accessions, will give place to the indigenous tribes. But this fading away will be less marked if, by judicious intermarriages, the Creoles blend with the surrounding tribes. And I am glad to learn that this process is gradually going on, especially in the villages.* Timnehs, Susus, and Mendes are now uniting in marriage with Eboes, Akus,† and Congoes, so that in the course of time the tribal peculiarities, which have often been a source of misunderstanding and disunion, will be happily effaced.[7]

* I.e. in the Colony.   † I.e. Yorubas.

# REFERENCES

CHAPTER I, pp. 1–27

1 Alvares d'Almada, *Tratado breve dos Rios de Guiné* (1594), ed. L. Silveira, Lisbon, 1946, author's translation.
2 Hakluyt Society, 2nd ser., vol. LXXX, p. 78.
3 Fernandes, *Description de la Côte Occidentale d'Afrique*, ed. Th. Monod, A. Teixera da Mota and R. Mauny (Bissau, 1951), p. 81.
4 Purchas, *His Pilgrimes* (Glasgow, 1905), vol. IV, p. 2.
5 Pereira, *Esmeraldo de Situ Orbis*, ed. R. Mauny (Bissau, 1956), p. 85.
6 Sierra Leone Archives, Minutes of Governor's Council, fos. 123 and 172; also for 1838, 7 December, fo. 125. I am indebted to Dr N. A. Cox-George, Fourah Bay College, for this reference.
7 Fernandes, *Côte Occidentale d'Afrique, passim*; Pereira, *Esmeraldo de Situ Orbis, passim*.
8 G. R. Nylander, *Grammar and Dictionary of the Bullom Language* (London, 1814).
9 B.M. Add. MS. 33976 B, fo. 3v.
10 *The New English Dictionary* (Oxford, 1919).
11 C. F. Schlenker, *An English-Temne Dictionary*, London, 1880.
12 *Tratado Breve dos Rios de Guiné* (Lisbon, 1946), chs. XIV and XV.
13 P.R.O. MS. T 70/10, fo. 27r.
14 Hakluyt Society, 2nd ser., vol. LXXXVI, p. 29.
15 B.M. Cotton MS., Otho E viii, fo. 26r.
16 *Tratado Breve dos Rios de Guiné*, ch. XIX.
17 Quoted in Purchas, *His Pilgrimes*, vol. IX, p. 262.
18 F. de Coelho, *Duas Descricões seiscentistas da Guiné*, ed. D. Peres (Lisbon, 1953), p. 228.
19 Purchas, *His Pilgrimes*, vol. VI, p. 248.
20 Hakluyt Society, 2nd ser., vol. CXIII; *Fenton's Journal*, ed. E. G. R. Taylor (1957).
21 Purchas, *His Pilgrimes*, vol. IV, p. 7.
22 B.M. Cotton MS. App. xlvii, fo. 43.
23 *Ibid.* fo. 142r.
24 *Ibid.* fo. 28r.
25 F. Guerreiro, *Relação Annual das Coisas...os...Padres de Companhia de Jesus*, 3 vols., ed. A. Viegas (Lisbon, 1942), vol. II, ch. IX.
26 *Ibid.* Author's translation.
27 J. Barbot, *A Description of the Coasts of North and South Guinea* (London, 1746), p. 94.
28 *Ibid.* p. 106.
29 *Africa* (London, 1670), p. 373.
30 *A New and Accurate Description of the Coast of Guinea* (London, 1721), pp. 444f.

CHAPTER II, pp. 28–61

1 B.M. Cotton MS. Nero B i, fo. 242.
2 Jobson, *The Golden Trade*, reprint (Teignmouth, 1904), p. 112.
3 K. G. Davies, *The Royal African Company* (London, 1957), p. 43, and B.M. 8223 e/12, p. 3—report of 1706—and P.R.O. MS. T 70/10, fo. 4r.
4 B.M. Add. MS. 34329, fos. 24r, 26r, 27r.
5 B.M. Cotton MS. Nero B i, fo. 149r.
6 *Ibid.* fo. 89v.
7 Cotton MS. Galba C iv, fo. 22r, June 1570.
8 Quoted from W. R. Scott, *The Constitution and Finance of English, Scottish and Irish Joint-Stock Companies to 1720* (New York, 1951), vol. II, p. 4, from Hakluyt's *Principal Navigations*, vol. VI, p. 141.
9 W. R. Scott, *Constitution and Finance*, vol. I, p. 298.

10 Greenwich Library MS. 550/73.
11 Hakluyt Society I, vol. LXX, p. 15
12 P.R.O. MS. T 70/1, fo. 19v, Zachary Rogers to Directors, Royal African Company.
13 B.M. Cotton MS. App. xlvii, fo. 32r.
14 *The New Cambridge Modern History*, vol. VII, chs. XXII and XXIV *passim*.
15 Astley, *Voyages* (London, 1745), vol. II, p. 379; F. de Coelho, *Duas Descricões*, p. 234.
16 P.R.O. MS. T 70/1465, 29 Feb. 1728/9.
17 P.R.O. MS. T 70/10, fo. 3v, 25 June 1678.
18 J. Newton, *Forty-One Letters* (Aberdeen, 1822), p. xliv.
19 P.R.O. MS. T 70/1, fo. 37r.
20 P.R.O. MS. T 70/11, 24 March 1686/7.
21 *Ibid.* 19 Oct. 1688.
22 P.R.O. MS. T 70/60, 9 July 1724.
23 P.R.O. MS. T 70/590, fos. 133 and 139.
24 J. Barbot, *North and South Guinea*, p. 429.
25 P.R.O. MS. T 70/362, 1 Jan. 1720/1.
26 P.R.O. MS. T 70/11, 24 Jan. and 9 Feb. 1691/2.
27 P.R.O. MS. T 70/18, July 1711.
28 *Ibid.* March 1712.
29 P.R.O. MS. T 70/3, p. 90, Jan. 1714/15, Richard Smith to Directors.
30 P.R.O. MS. T 70/11, 1 and 6 March 1683/4, 9 April 1684.
31 Astley, *Voyages*, vol. II, p. 517.
32 Quoted from *A History of the Colony of Sierra Leone*, J. J. Crook (London, 1903), p. 11.
33 P.R.O. MS. T 70/52, p. 77, Directors to Freeman at Sherbro.
34 P.R.O. MS. T 70/51, p. 152.
35 P.R.O. MS. T 70/53, p. 130.
36 Astley, *Voyages*, vol. II, pp. 317 and 464.
37 *Sierra Leone Studies*, O.S. vol. XI (1928), p. 16.
38 S. M. Golberry, *Travels in Africa*, trans. W. Mudford (London, 1803), vol. II, p. 177.
39 J. Newton, *Forty-One Letters*, p. xlii.
40 *The Journal of a Slave Trader*, p. 72.
41 *Ibid.* p. 75.
42 *A Voyage to Guinea, Brasil and the West Indies*, J. Atkins (London, 1735), p. 36.
43 N. Owen, *Journal*, p. 80.
44 Quoted from Davies, *Royal African Company*, p. 220.
45 Owen, *Journal*, p. 104.
46 Davies, *Royal African Company*, p. 221.
47 P.R.O. MS. T 70/1465, 8 August 1728.
48 B.M. Add. MS. 12131, *Mr J. Strands Journal of Occurences*.
49 National Maritime Museum, Greenwich, MS. 53/035.
50 E. A. Robertson, *The Spanish Town Papers* (London, 1959), p. 129.

CHAPTER III, pp. 62–119

1 Hakluyt Society, 2nd. ser. vol. LXXXVI, p. 78, ed. J.W. Blake (1942).
2 B.M. Add. MS. 33976 B, fo. 3v.
3 Harris, *Voyages* (London, 1764), vol. I, p. 719.
4 *Sierra Leone Studies*, N.S. vol. XI, p. 174.
5 B.M. Cotton MS. Nero B i, fo. 88v.
6 B.M. Cotton MS. App. xlvii, fo. 37, *Madox' Journal*; Otho E viii, fo. 208r, *Walker's Journal*.
7 F. Guerreiro, *Relação Annual das Coisas*, vol. II, p. 208.
8 *Ibid.*
9 Coelho, *Duas Descricões*, p. 232, author's translation.
10 *Cal. S.P. America and West Indies, 1574–1660*, 9 April 1651.
11 Hakluyt Society, 2nd ser. vol. CXIII, p. 105, ed. E. G. R. Taylor (1957).
12 Coelho, *Duas Descricões*, p. 234.
13 P.R.O. MS. T 70/10, fo. 59v.
14 R. F. Burton, *Wanderings in W. Africa* (London, 1863), vol. I, p. 249.

15 Guerreiro, *Relação Annual das Coisas, passim*; Coelho, *Duas Descrições*, pp. 76 f.

16 John Atkins, *A Voyage to Guinea, Brazil and the W. Indies* (London, 1735), pp. 51, 256; Astley, *Voyages*, vol. II, p. 509.

17 *Duas Descrições*, p. 235.

18 P.R.O. MS. T 70/1, fo. 20v.

19 Astley, *Voyages*, vol. II, p. 375.

20 P.R.O. MS. T 70/18, Nov. 1690.

21 P.R.O. MS. T 70/61, 21 Jan. 1689/90.

22 P.R.O. MS. T 70/50, fo. 108r.

23 Astley, *Voyages*, vol. II, p. 312.

24 B.M. 816m/11 (43).

25 P.R.O. MS. T 70/1, fo. 19v.

26 P.R.O. MS. T 70/902, 14 Aug. 1688.

27 *Ibid.* 4 Feb. 1696.

28 P.R.O. MS. T 70/591, loose folio at Aug. 1713.

29 P.R.O. MS. T 70/902, 16 April 1691.

30 P.R.O. MS. T 70/18, 8 December 1708.

31 Astley, *Voyages*, vol. II, p. 317.

32 Barbot, *Description of the Coasts*, pp. 118, 277.

33 *Some New and Accurate Observations on the Coast of Guinea* (1725), p. 53; B.M. 1045, f. 6 (2).

34 *Ibid.* p. 5.

35 P.R.O. MS. T 70/4, p. 27.

36 P.R.O. MS. T 70/163, 13 Sept. 1692, and T 70/18, July 1711.

37 P.R.O. MS. T 70/591, 1 Jan. 1712/13.

38 P.R.O. MS. T 70/1465, p. 44; Smith, *Voyage to Guinea* (London, 1744), p. 38.

39 P.R.O. MS. T 70/51, p. 240.

40 P.R.O. MS. T 70/15, fo. 24v, 4 Aug. 1679.

41 P.R.O. MS. T 70/1, fo. 20v.

42 P.R.O. MS. T 70/16, fo. 47r.

43 P.R.O. MS. T 70/108, 1683–4 (inside front cover).

44 India Office Library MS. East India Company Home Misc. no. 29, p. 135.

45 B.M. 8223 e/37.

46 P.R.O. MS. Adm. 106/66, 26 Oct. 1686.

47 P.R.O. MS. T 70/902, 17 March 1686.

48 P.R.O. MS. T 70/164, 6 Sept. 1700.

49 P.R.O. MS. T 70/60, p. 9.

50 Quoted from Davies, *Royal African Company*, pp. 136, 137.

51 P.R.O. MS. T 70/51, fo. 44v, postscript to a letter.

52 P.R.O. MS. T 70/18, July 1711.

53 P.R.O. MS. T 70/1465, 29 Feb. 1728/9.

54 Smith, *Voyage to Guinea*.

55 P.R.O. MS. T 70/51, fo. 11, 5 April 1698, Directors to Thomas Corker, Sherbro.

56 P.R.O. MS. T 70/52, p. 332.

57 P.R.O. MS. T 70/1, fo. 36.

58 P.R.O. MS. T 70/590, p. 162.

59 *Esmeraldo de Situ Orbis*, pp. 77, 139 and 189.

60 P.R.O. MS. T 70/2, p. 12.

61 E. W. Bovill, *The Golden Trade of the Moors* (Oxford, 1958), p. 30.

62 Hakluyt Society, 2nd ser., vol. LXXXVI, i, p. 153, Ramusio, *Navigazioni e viaggi*.

63 Quoted from C. A. Gordon, *Life on the Gold Coast*, by F. Wolfson, *Pageant of Ghana* (Oxford, 1958), p. 127.

64 P.R.O. MS. T 70/361, 5 Sept. 1683.

65 P.R.O. MS. T 70/361, 1 Nov. 1683.

66 P.R.O. MS. T 70/362, 1 Jan. 1720/1 and T 70/60, 21 Dec. 1721.

67 P.R.O. MS. T 70/1465, 8 Aug.

68 P.R.O. MS. T 70/176, p. 7.

69 C. P. Beaver, *African Memoranda* (London, 1805), map.

70 National Maritime Museum, Greenwich, MS. 53/035.

71 P.R.O. MS. T 70/51, p. 265.

72 P.R.O. MS. T 70/365, 6 June; T 70/362, 31 Dec. 1721; T 70/10, fo. 54r (1679).

73 P.R.O. MS. T 1/lvii, no. 58.

74 P.R.O. MS. T 70/60, 9 Feb. 1720.

75 P.R.O. MS. T 70/50, fo. 24v, Aug. 1686.

76 P.R.O. MS. T 70/62, p. 147.

77 P.R.O. MS. T 70/1465, p. 3.

78 P.R.O. MS. T 70/53, p. 144.

79 P.R.O. MS. T 70/1, fo. 20v.

80 P.R.O. MS. T 70/51, p. 265.
81 P.R.O. MS. T 70/11, fo. 167.
82 *Esmeraldo de Situ Orbis*, p. 85.
83 B.M. MS. Cotton, Otho E viii, fo. 220v.
84 P.R.O. MS. T 70/16, 14 Feb. 1687/8; T 70/11, fo. 168 and 15 Jan. 1694/5 and 16 April 1696.
85 P.R.O. MS. T 70/51, p. 265.
86 P.R.O. MS. T 70/53, fo. 133.
87 B.M. 1202 g 2 (3).
88 Smith, *Voyage to Guinea*, p. 44.
89 P.R.O. MS. T 70/15, fo. 53v, letter Barbados to London.
90 P.R.O. MS. T 70/51, p. 237.
91 P.R.O. MS. T 70/52, p. 378.
92 P.R.O. MS. T 70/362, 4 April 1722.
93 P.R.O. MS. T 70/362, 4 April 1722; T 70/53, fo. 133; T 70/362, 1 July 1722.
94 Smith, *Voyage to Guinea*, p. 33.
95 Wolfson, *Pageant of Ghana*, p. 5.
96 Astley, *Voyages*, vol. II, p. 376.
97 Coelho, *Duas Descricões*, p. 74; Purchas, *His Pilgrimes*, vol. II, p. 502.
98 P.R.O. MS. T 70/1, 4 Aug. 1673.
99 P.R.O. MS. T 70/360, 19 June 1678.
100 P.R.O. MS. T 70/10, 25 June 1678.
101 P.R.O. MS. T 70/360, 16 Jan. 1678/9; 24 Aug. 1680.
102 P.R.O. MS. T 70/16, fo. 24r.
103 P.R.O. MS. T 70/1, fo. 42.
104 P.R.O. MS. T 70/10, fo. 55.
105 P.R.O. MS. T 70/10, fo. 54r.
106 P.R.O. MS. T 70/361, 18 May 1682.
107 Barbot, *Description of the Coasts*, p. 99.
108 P.R.O. MS. T 70/590.
109 P.R.O. MS. T 70/350, p. 34.
110 B.M. 816 m 11 (23).
111 *Ibid.* (13).
112 P.R.O. MS. T 70/10, fo. 4r.
113 P.R.O. MS. T 70/1, fo. 31r.
114 P.R.O. MS. T 70/10, 6 March 1681.
115 P.R.O. MS. T 70/11, fo. 158.
116 P.R.O. MS. T 70/591, 3 June 1713.

117 P.R.O. MS. T 70/11, 14 March 1684/5.
118 P.R.O. MS. T 70/18, 10 Nov. 1710.
119 P.R.O. MS. T 70/11, 1 Aug. 1687 and 15 June 1688.
120 *Ibid.* fo. 160.
121 *Ibid.* 15 June 1688, 12 Feb. 1688/9 and 22 July 1690.
122 Barbot, *Description of the Coasts*, p. 106.
123 P.R.O. MS. T 70/877.
124 B.M. 816 m 11 (22).
125 B.M. 8223 e/39, e/47.
126 B.M. 816 m 11 (23).
127 P.R.O. MS. T 70/51, fo. 75r.
128 P.R.O. MS. T 70/53, 14 Sept. 1720.
129 P.R.O. MS. T 70/52, p. 376.
130 P.R.O. MS. T 70/60, 9 Feb. and 30 Sept. 1720 and 23 July 1721.
131 P.R.O. MS. T 70/66, fo. 52v.
132 *Voyage to Guinea*, p. 65.
133 P.R.O. MS. T 70/3, p. 89.
134 P.R.O. MS. T 70/362, 1 Jan. 1721/2.
135 P.R.O. MS. T 70/3, p. 89.
136 P.R.O. MS. T 70/4, fo. 1.
137 *Voyage to Guinea*, p. 57.
138 P.R.O. MS. T 70/362, 1 Jan. 1720/1.
139 P.R.O. MS. T 70/591, 4 Sept. 1713.
140 P.R.O. MS. T 70/1465, p. 46.
141 *Ibid.* 15 July 1728.
142 *Ibid.* 31 Aug. 1728.
143 *Ibid.* 16 March 1728.
144 *Ibid.*
145 *Ibid.* p. 45.
146 *Ibid.*
147 Smith, *Voyage to Guinea*, p. 64.
148 P.R.O. MS. T 70/1465.
149 P.R.O. MS. T 70/176, p. 3; *Commons Journal*, vol. XXVIII, pp. 273–89.
150 N. Owen, *Journal*, p. 104.
151 Golberry, *Travels in Africa* (London, 1803), vol. II, pp. 177f.
152 Smeathman's plan is printed in C. B. Wadstrom, *An Essay on Colonisation* (London, 1795), p. 207.

CHAPTER IV, pp. 120–57

1 *Description de l'Afrique*, ed. A. Epaulard (Paris, 1956), vol. I, p. 10, vol. II, pp. 462, 466, author's translation.

2 Fernandes, *Description de la Côte Occidentale d'Afrique*, pp. 77 n., 81, 83; Pereira, *Esmeraldo de Situ Orbis*, pp. 83, 85, 99, 101.

3 *A Provisional History of the Limba*, V. R. Dorjahn and A. S. Tholley, *Sierra Leone Studies*, N.S. vol. XII, p. 273.

4 Y. Person, *Les Kissis et leurs statuettes de pierres dans le cadre de l'histoire Ouest Africaine*, unpublished MS., I.F.A.N., Dakar.

5 Fernandes, *Description de la Côte Occidentale d'Afrique*, p. 37; see Westermann, *Languages of West Africa*, vol. II, p. 31.

6 H. R. Palmer, *The Carthaginian Voyage to West Africa* (Government Printer, the Gambia, 1931), p. v n.

7 *I.F.A.N. Bulletin du Comité d'Études Historiques et Scientifiques* (1930), p. 26, M. Saint Père, author's translation.

8 Leo Africanus, *Description de l'Afrique*, ed. A. Epaulard, vol. II, pp. 477, 478; D'Almada, *Tratado breve dos Rios de Guiné*; see below, p. 141.

9 B.M. Cotton MS., Otho E viii, fo. 27 r. This MS., partly destroyed by fire, probably describes Hawkins 3rd voyage.

10 Hakluyt Society, 2nd ser., vol. LXXXVII, p. 378; see also Mgr J. Cuvelier and l'Abbé L. Jadin, *L'Ancien Congo* (Brussels, 1954), pp. 21, 344, 351; F. Guerreiro, *Relação Annual das Coisas...*, vol. III, p. 255; F. Coelho, *Duas Descricões...*, p. 230; D'Almada, *Tratado breve dos Rios de Guiné*, passim; *Ethnographic Survey of Africa*, W. Africa, vol. II, p. 77.

11 D'Almada, *Tratado breve dos Rios de Guiné*, ch. xv.

12 Hakluyt Society, 2nd ser., vol. CXIII, pp. 105, 108; *Fenton's Journal*, ed. E. R. G. Taylor. Fenton says Farima had a vassal, *Jarima*, on the north shore of the river.

13 Coelho, *Duas Descricões...*, p. 220.

14 See Guerreiro, *Relação Annual das Coisas...*, vol. II, pp. 205, 207 and vol. III, pp. 243, 250, 253–5, 273; Purchas, *His Pilgrimes*, vol. IV, p. 2, vol. IX, p. 266; *Sierra Leone Studies*, O.S. vol. X, pp. 38 f. For similar marriage alliances as part of peace negotiations in the eighteenth century, see J. Matthews, *Voyage to Sierra Leone* (London, 1788), p. 116.

15 B.M. Cotton MS., Otho E viii. fo. 208 r.

16 Hakluyt Society, 2nd ser., vol. CXIII, p. 108, *Fenton's Journal*.

17 *Sierra Leone Studies*, O.S. vol. XI, p. 54.

18 Guerreiro, *Relação Annual das Coisas...*, vol. III, p. 270. Author's translation.

19 *Ibid.* pp. 252, 267 and vol. II, pp. 207, 202.

20 Guerreiro, *Relação Annual das Coisas...*, vol. II, p. 208.

21 *Sierra Leone Studies*, N.S. vol. IV, p. 244.

22 Coelho, *Duas Descricões...*, p. 74.

23 Hakluyt Society, vol. LVII, 1878, *The Hawkins Voyages*, ed C. R. Markham, p. 16.

24 See Hakluyt Society, 2nd ser., vol. CXIII, pl. VIII.

25 Bovill, *Golden Trade of the Moors*, p. 83.

26 D'Almada, *Tratado breve dos Rios de Guiné*, ch. xv.

27 *Ibid.*, author's translation.

28 *Sierra Leone Studies*, O.S. vol. III, p. 37.

29 B.M. Cotton MS., App. xlvii, fo. 37 v; *I.F.A.N. Bull.* vol. XV, no. 2, p. 702, R. Mauny.

30 *A Provisional History of the Limba*, ed. V. R. Dorjahn and A. S. Tholley, *Sierra Leone Studies*, N.S. vol. XII, p. 274.

31 The United Africa Company

News, *Historical Notes on Port Loko*, ed. J. C. D. Soloman. December quarter (Freetown, 1952).

32 *Sierra Leone Studies*, N.S., vol. XI, p. 134.

33 Astley, *Voyages*, vol. II, p. 378.

34 *I.F.A.N. Mémoires*, vol. XXX, pp. 72 and 142.

35 H. O. Newland, *West Africa* (London, 1920), p. 87; F. W. H. Migeod, *Mende Language* (London, 1908), p. 162; according to S. W. Koelle, *Karo = Gallinas, Polyglotta Africana* (London, 1854), p. 3; Ogilby, *Africa*, p. 381, the Gola-Vy, High Quoia and Folgias very closely resemble the *Karou*.

36 P.R.O. MS. T 70/360, 22 Nov.

37 Barbot, *Description of the Coasts*, pp. III and 122. This is largely copied from Ogilby's *Africa*.

38 See also *Sierra Leone Studies*, O.S., vol. XXII, p. 106 n.

39 See also Astley, *Voyages*, vol. II, p. 530.

40 *Description de l'Afrique...traduite du Flamand d'O.* Dapper (Amsterdam, 1686), p. 273.

41 Astley, *Voyages*, vol. II, p. 533, after Barbot.

42 Barbot, *Description of the Coasts*, p. 123.

43 P.R.O. MS. T 70/1465, fo. 4.

44 *Ibid.* 25 March 1728/9.

45 P.R.O. MS. T 70/590, fo. Ir, 18 July 1713; T 70/11, 15 June 1688, 15 Jan. 1694/5 and 8 Dec. 1698.

46 P.R.O. MS. T 70/587, fo. 1; T 70/361, loose leaf at end of volume, 16 Dec. 1682; T 70/1465, p. 23; T 70/60, 18 July 1723 and 31 Aug. 1728.

47 P.R.O. MS. T 70/591, loose folio, 15 March 1715/16; T 70/590, 24 Nov. 1699.

48 *Sierra Leone Studies. Reprints bearing on the Work of the Monuments and Relics Commission* (Government Printer, Freetown, 1953), p. 30.

49 Owen, *Journal...*, p. 76.

50 *Ibid.* p. 90.

51 Smith, *Voyage to Guinea*, pp. 52 and 75.

52 P.R.O. MS. T 70/360, 1 Aug. 1678.

53 Ogilby, *Africa*, p. 370; Sieur Villault, *A Relation of the Coasts of Africk called Guinee...* trans. (London, 1670), p. 36.

54 P.R.O. MS. T 70/1465, 22 March 1729.

55 Coelho, *Duas Descricões*, p. 74, and Astley, *Voyages*, vol. II, p. 322.

56 P.R.O. MS. T 70/590, 22 Oct. 1698; 591, 1 Jan. 1712/13; 362, 1 Jan. 1720/21 and T 70/362, 1 Oct. 1723, respectively.

57 P.R.O. MS. T 70/649, p. 15; 650, p. 26.

58 P.R.O. MS. T 70/648, p. 97.

59 P.R.O. MS. T 70/591, 3 July 1713 and 18 July 1714; T 70/649, p. 44.

60 *Journal*, pp. 29, 46, 47, 53 and 92.

61 *Voyage to Sierra Leone*, frontispiece.

62 *Africa*, p. 401.

63 A. Gouilly, *L'Islam dans l'Afrique Occidentale Française* (Paris, 1952), *passim*.

64 *Sierra Leone Studies*, O.S., vol. III (1919), p. 30.

65 *Journal*, p. 92.

66 Colonial Office, Sierra Leone, Despatch no. 332, 1886, p. 38.

67 *Ibid.* p. 28.

68 Guerreiro, *Relação Annual das Coisas*, vol. III, p. 244; Wadstrom, *Essay on Colonisation* (London, 1795), p. 41 n.; Astley, *Voyages*, vol. II, p. 145; Fernandes, *Description de la Côte Occidentale d'Afrique*, p. 151 n.

69 *Travels in the Timannee, Kooranko and Soolima Countries* (London, 1825), pp. 68 and 194.

70 *Sierra Leone Studies*, N.S. vol. IX, pp. 26f.

71 Sierra Leone Government Archives, 24 Sept. 1825, Treaty.

72 *A Description of the Manners and Customs of the Liberated African* (London, 1843), pp. 163, 164, 178.

## CHAPTER V, pp. 158–72

1 *Description de la Côte Occidentale d'Afrique*, p. 93.
2 *Tratado Breve dos Rios de Guiné.*
3 Purchas, *His Pilgrimes*, vol. IV, p. 2.
4 Smith, *Voyage to Guinea*, p. 58.
5 *Sierra Leone Studies*, O.S., vol. XIV, p. 15.
6 *Travels in the Timannee, Kooranko and Soolima Countries*, p. 79.
7 *The Tour of Africa* (London, 1821), vol. II, p. 497.
8 *Notes Africaines*, no. 52, p. 101.
9 Golberry, *Travels in Africa*, vol. II, p. 183.
10 *Voyage to... Sierra Leone*, p. 4.
11 C. Hutton, *Tour of Africa*, vol. II, p. 519.
12 Laing, *Travels in the Timannee, Kooranko and Soolima Countries*, p. 129.
13 Hakluyt Society, no. LVII, *The Hawkins Voyages*, ed. C. R. Markham, p. 16, from Hawkins's second voyage, 1564.
14 B.M. Cotton MS., Otho E viii, fo. 27r.
15 *Tratado Breve dos Rios de Guiné.*
16 N. Thomas, *Anthropological Report on Sierra Leone* (London, 1916), p. 31.
17 T. Winterbottom, *An Account of the Native Africans in... Sierra Leone* (London, 1803), vol. I, pp. 156 and 158.
18 *Sierra Leone Studies*, N.S., vol. VIII, p. 244—W. R. E. Clarke.
19 B.M. Add. MS. 28788, fo. 7v. 'Ilz vont toujours armés de coutteaux qu'ilz portent pendus à leur ceinture... d'autres aussy portent de petis arcs et des flêches.'
20 Winterbottom, *Account of the Native Africans...*, vol. I, p. 160.
21 *Description de la Côte Occidentale d'Afrique*, p. 95.
22 P.R.O. MS. T 70/1465, p. 48.
23 See E. Elisofon, *The Sculpture of Africa* (London, 1958), p. 19.
24 *Travels in the Timannee, Kooranko and Soolima Countries*, p. 32.
25 *Sierra Leone Studies*, N.S., vol. XI, p. 128—P. Savin d'Orfond.

## CHAPTER VI, pp. 173–89

1 *Journal*, p. 71.
2 B.M. MS. 1045, fo. 6 (2).
3 *Bulletin Agricole du Congo Belge*, vol. XLVIII, p. 743—E. L. Andriaens.
4 *Journal of the Linnean Society* (1955), pp. 302f.
5 See Col. Office, Sierra Leone, no. 6, 1881 (pamphlet).
6 G. C. Valliant, *The Aztecs of Mexico* (London, 1956), p. 28.
7 Cf. Jobson, *The Golden Trade*, p. 30, for fishing in the Gambia.
8 *Sierra Leone* (London, 1843), p. 127.
9 D. Paulme, *Les Gens du Riz* (Paris, 1954), p. 45.
10 F. R. Irvine, *Fishes and Fisheries of the Gold Coast* (London, 1947), p. 25.
11 *Report on the Fishery Resources of Sierra Leone* (Government Printer, Freetown, 1928), *passim*.
12 Irvine, *Fishes and Fisheries of the Gold Coast*, p. 27.
13 B.M. MS. 28788, fo. 7r.
14 Barbot, *Description of the Coasts*, p. 112.
15 Pereira, *Esmeraldo de Situ Orbis*, p. 61. Author's translation.
16 *Ibid.* p. 73.
17 *Some New and Accurate Observations on the Coast of Guinea*, p. 7.
18 Afzelius, *Report to the Directors*; Bosman, *Description of Guinea* (London, 1721), p. 271.
19 Fernandes, *Description de la Côte Occidentale d'Afrique*, p. 95.
20 *I.F.A.N. Bulletin*, vol. XV, no. 2, pp. 706, 711 and 791.
21 Hakluyt Society, 2nd ser., vol. LXXX, pp. 42 and 138.
22 *Ibid.* vol. LXXXVI, p. 149.
23 *Ibid.* p. 109.
24 Bosman, *Description of Guinea*, pp. 277–81.
25 Wolfson, *Pageant of Ghana*, p. 56.
26 Hakluyt Society, 2nd ser., vol. LXXXVII, ii, p. 344.
27 *Ibid.* vol. LXXXVI, p. 161; *c.* 1540.
28 *Voyage to Sierra Leone*, pp. 58 and 106.

29 *Some New and Accurate Observations on the Coast of Guinea*, p. 7.
30 Matthews, *Voyage to Sierra Leone*, p. 56.
31 Astley, *Voyages*, vol. II, p. 537.
32 *Ibid.* p. 319.
33 *Ibid.* p. 312.
34 *Voyage to Sierra Leone.*
35 Hakluyt Society, 2nd ser., vol. LXXX, p. 42, *Voyages of Cadamosto.*
36 *Description de la Côte Occidentale d'Afrique*, p. 137.
37 Hakluyt Society, 2nd ser., vol. LXXX, p. 157; the Anonymous Pilot.
38 Fernandes, *Description de la Côte Occidentale d'Afrique*, p. 97.
39 P.R.O. MS. T 70/1465, p. 29, 15 May.
40 Cf. W. Fagg, *Afro-Portuguese Ivories* (Kegan Paul, 1959), *passim.*
41 Astley, *Voyages*, p. 317.
42 B.M. Cotton MS., Otho E viii, fo. 26 v.
43 Cotton MS., App. xlvii *passim.*
44 *Voyage to Sierra Leone*, p. 38.
45 Fernandes, *Description de la Côte Occidentale d'Afrique*, p. 97.
46 F. R. Irvine, *Plants of the Gold Coast* (Oxford, 1930), p. 187.
47 Matthews, *Voyage to Sierra Leone*, p. 48.
48 *Some remarkable particulars concerning...the Colony of Sierra Leone...from the Registers and Reports of the Church Missionary Society* (Retford, 1821), p. 6.

CHAPTER VII, pp. 190–4

1 Quoted from L. G. Johnson, *General T. Perronet Thompson, 1783–1869* (Allen and Unwin, 1957), p. 40.
2 *Ibid.* p. 47.
3 B.M. Add. MS. 12131, *Mr James Strands Journal of Occurences.*
4 *Sierra Leone Studies*, N.S., vol. XII, p. 257.
5 Johnson, *General T. Perronet Thompson*, p. 54.
6 The Sierra Leone Association, a Paper read by the Hon. S. Lewis, Freetown, 6 August 1885—B.M. 8155 df 3.
7 E. W. Blyden, *Christianity, Islam and the Negro Race* (London, 1888), p. 234.

# INDEX

All African proper names have been indexed as they appear in the text; thus Alhaj Salieu Swarray, Bai Farima, Betura—though this last evidently represents a form of Bai Tura. Sierra Leone kings and warriors appear under Sierra Leone; all rivers under Rivers.

# *Index*

# Index

D'Almada, Alvares, 9f., 13, 128f., 158

D'Andrade, Dr Gaspar, Governor of Santiago, 14

D'Anville, cartographer, 63

Da Costa, —, 131

Da Gama, Vasco, 3

Da Sintra, Pedro, 6, 30, 112

Dakar, 178

dancing, 10, 92, 162

Dapper, Olphert, 25f., 63, 146, 152

Davis, Howell, 53f.

Davis, Robert, 73

De Faro, Rev. André, 68

De Jaille, M., 113f.

De Laun, Admiral, 74

De Marees, Piet, 181

De Peralta, Rev. John, 68

De Pontdevèze, Captain, 70, 113, 116

De Ronda, Rev. Augustin, 68

De Ruyter, Admiral, 50, 66, 96, 143

Deforo, *see* Folgia

Demurrage, 85

Denmark, 37

Derby, Signor, 108

Devenport, Laurence, 52

Dieppe, 35

disease, 45f., 73f., 103

Dominya, 126

*Dondaghs*, 145f.

Drake, Sir Francis, 16f.

dyes, 19, 38, 44, 91, 93, 160

Ebos, the, 194

Egypt, 28

El Mansur, Emperor of Morocco, 153

elephants, 29, 120, 185

Elizabeth I, Queen of England, 17, 33, 40

Elmina Castle, 3, 11, 15, 26, 30, 47, 62, 64

England

  challenges Portugal in Africa, 18, 31, 36f., 40

  experiments in local industries by her companies, 92f.

  financial crisis in, 42

  privateers from, 16, 35, 41, 128

  settlements from in Sierra Leone, 21, 24, 26, 96, 98f., 115, 119, 143

  trade declines in, 36

England, Captain, 53

Fabian, William, 36

Fabule, Vai warrior, 144

Fars, 154

Fenton, Edward, Admiral, 16f., 64, 134, 140, 186

Fernandes, Alvaro, 1

Fernandes, Valentim, 3f., 27, 123, 158, 171, 185

Fernando, Sittel, 126

Fernly, Captain, 111

feudalism, 148

Fez, 121

Finch, William, 4, 159

Fipping, Thomas, 73

fish-curing, 139, 177f.

fishing, 16, 126, 175f.

Florida, 47

Folgias, the, 144f.

Fort Thornton, 119

Fourah (Foro) Bay, 48, 112

France

  attacks English settlements, 69f., 96, 113

  challenges Portugal in Sierra Leone, 65

  privateers from, 35

  proposes settlement in the Sierra Leone river, 104

  rise of, 32

  settlement from: in Senegal, 26; in Sierra Leone, 48, 113f.

  trade of in Sierra Leone, 22

Franks, Richard, 51

Frederick, King of Prussia, 170

Freeman, John, 90

Freetown, 187

French Bay, 114

Frenchman's Bay, 48, 53, 119

Frobisher, Martin, 36, 64

Fulani, the, 7, 61, 89, 127, 131, 141, 164, 166

Fulani warriors, 154f.

*funde*, 141, 173, 189

Futa Jallon, 124f., 154f.

Futa Toro, 128

Gambia, the, 26, 37, 39n., 51, 53, 62, 70, 71, 88, 90, 175, 179

Gambia Island, 48, 113f., 163

game traps, 186f.

Gamble, Captain Samuel, 60, 90

Gao empire, 144

Gbandes, the, 124, 168

# Index

Gbande country, 142
George Island, 112
Ghana, 30, 124, 139, 175
Gibson, Henry, 71, 93, 103
Givi, the, 25, 145f.
Golas, the, 127f.
Golberry, S. M., 161
gold, 6, 11, 17f., 19, 30, 40f., 47, 73, 156, 159
Gold, Robert, 73
Graham, John, 53
Granada, 32
Grant, Alexander, 190
Gregory, Thomas, 41
Grindas, the, 130
gromettoes, 73n., 88f., 97, 111
Guerin, Sieur, 71
Guinea, 141, 175, 182f.
gum, 19
Gun, Robert, 59
guns, see especially 49, 99, 101, 112n., 172

Hakluyt's Voyages, 18
Hallsa, Captain, of New York, 61
Hamlin, Jean, Captain, 53
Hanno, 28
Hanse merchants, 36
Hawkins, John, 13, 18, 30, 35, 37, 40, 139, 165
Hawkins, William, 36, 39, 46
Heartsease, Samuel, Captain, 104
Heath, Henry, Surgeon, 98
Henry the Navigator, 1f., 30
Henry VII, King of England, 33, 36
Henry VIII, King of England, 40, 49
Herodotus, 28
Heron, Philip, 97
Heyn, Piet, Admiral, 47
hippopotamus, 120, 186
Holditch, —, 106
Hondo, the, 25, 145f.
horses, 131, 140, 166f., 187
Houston, Dr James, 74f., 94, 173, 182
Hutton, Catherine, 161

idols, 4, 6n., 10, 120, 122, 141
Ignacio, Rev. Father, 68
Iles de Los, 49, 60f., 97, 115, 132
India, 3, 10f., 17, 174, 185
Indians, American, 174, 182
Indonesia, 174

interlopers, 15, 39, 48, 50f., 59, 70, 80, 112, see also England, France
Islam, 3, 30, 32, 120f., 154f., 190
Islamic dress, 164
Isola Rossa (Plantain Islands), 2
Isola Salvaza (Banana Islands), 2
Isoletta di Scanni, 3
Italy, 1, 33
ivory, 17, 19, 25, 40, 47, 51f., 77, 81f., 118
ivory carving, 185

Jacas, the, 130
James, 'Jubly', 113n.
James II, King of England, 79f., 102
Jassily, 89, 98
Jatts Isle, 89, 98
Jerome, Signor, 84
Jesuits, 19f., 67, 159, see also Barreira, B.
Jobson, Richard, 37
John II, King of Portugal, 62
John Thomas, 22f., 150, see also Sierra Leone, kings
John's factory, 105
Johnson, the Rev., 187
Jones, Hugh, 81
Joseph, Rev. Signor, 68
justice, 9

Kailahun district, 168
Kamara, clan name, 129
Kanfori Domin Konteh, Susu king, 125f.
Kano, 121, 128, 139
Kapez, see Tyapi
Karamoko Alpha, see Alpha Ibrahima
Karoodoboe-Monou, 25
Karos, the, 144f.
Keeling, William, 18, 96n.
Kenya, 174
Kiatamba, Vai warrior, 144
Kirby, Captain Roger, 85
Kirkham, —, 77
Kissis, the, 124f., 162, 168, 174
Kissi language, 130
Kittam, the, 157
Kittam country, 100
Kittam factory, 52
Knox, Abraham, 95
Koi, 145
kola nuts, 17, 189
Kombo Smart, 171
Konkaw Island (Cogu), 96

# Index

# Index

naval warfare, 49f., 55
Netherlands, the
  attack on Tasso Island, 50
  attempted settlements of in Sierra
    Leone, 49, 65
  challenge to Portugal in Africa, 13,
    25, 36
  garrison in Cape Verde, 43
  overseas expansion, 19, 33
  prosperity of, 33, 38, 144
  sailing directions of, 15
  settlement of: at Cape Mount, 43;
    at Gallinas, 26, 28; in the Sierra
    Leone river, 48, 66
  trade of in Europe, 33
  trade of in India, 26
  trade of to Sierra Leone, 22
  West Indies Company of, 43
nets, 177, 186
New York, 61
Newton, John, 57, 101 n.
Nigeria, 128, 153, 155
*nomoli*, 141
Nongobah Bullom chiefdom, 4
Nova Scotians, the, 118, 191, 193
Nylander, Rev. G. R., 7

*Obe Vrig*, 4
Ogilby, John, 63, 152
Ogle, Captain Challoner, R.N., 55
Ormond, slaver, 113, 191
Oswald, Richard, 190
Owen, Blayney, 57
Owen, Nicholas, 57f., 70, 151, 155,
  173, 183

Pa Kargbo, Temne warrior, 142
Palha, Paulo, 131
palm oil, 41
Parker, Captain, of Liverpool, 76
Penwell, Marmaduke, 84, 107
Pereira, Balthasar, 65
Pereira, Pacheco, 3, 6, 8, 30, 62, 123
Philip II, King of Spain, 35
Philip III, King of Spain, 14, 35, 65
Pierce, Edward, 48f., 69, 78, 94, 97f.,
  108
*Pili*, 153
pirates, 53f., 106f., 138
Pirates' Bay, 55, 114
Plantain Islands, 2, 57, 101
Platt, Joshua, 101, 103
plunge-baskets, 175

Plunkett, Robert, 56, 75, 95, 103f.,
  105
poisons, 176f.
poor relief, Freetown, 187
Porequere, Sofa warrior, 143
Porter, —, 98
Portugal
  abandons Sierra Leone, 11, 13, 26,
    39, 49, 64
  accounts by, of West Africa, 123
  African trade of before and after
    1530, 36f.
  annexed by Spain, 34, 37
  confiscation in of English property,
    36
  first explorers from, 120, 125f.
  fleets of in West Africa, 1f., 7f., 14
  importers of food to Africa, 178f.
  Lagos, 1, 2
  Lisbon, 3, 32, 34
  missionaries from, 67
  possessions overseas, 11f.
  renegades from, 12, 16, 30
  rise of, 32
  royal administration of overseas
    trade, 11, 34
  settlement of: in Cacheo, 53; in
    Sierra Leone, 11, 22, 62f., 65
  State taxes in, 34, 47
  trade of, 92
  treaty with England, 38
Press Gang, 60
Principe Island, 55
private traders, 80, *see also* interlopers
Pye, Captain, 112

Quiah, 155
Quilliga, *see* Gallinas
*Quimanora*, 8
Quojas, the, *see* Givis

Rackham, Captain, 54
Raynal, Abbé, 183
Reed, Captain, 112
Rhodesia, 28
rice empoldering, 139
Richardson, —, 77
rivers
  Bitombo, Bintombo, *see* Sierra
    Leone river
  Boom, 101
  Bunce, 7
  Casamance, 1

208

# Index

# Index

# Index

Smeathman, Dr Henry, 119, 173
Smith, Richard, 105
Smith, William, 55, 75, 104f., 184
smuggling, 12
Smythe, Rev. John, 173
societies, 4, 10, 153, 162, 163n., 175, 175n.
Sofas, the, 143, 172
*Sokonɔ*, 153
*Solategi*, 127
*Songé*, 153
Songhai emperors, 125, 127, 129, 144, 153
Soninke kingdom, 124
Sonni Ali, 127
South America, 13
Sous, Bay of, 29
*Sowah*, 153
Spain
  annexes Portugal, 34, 36
  attempted fortification in the Sierra Leone river, 65
  bullion trade of, 34f.
  considers fortifying Sierra Leone, 20, 65
  in South America, 13
  rise of, 11
Stocks, Ned, 18
Stubbs, John, 54
Sudan, the, 123f., 141
sugar cane, 19
sugar plantations, 37, 121
sugar refining, 43
*Sumbas, see* Manis
Susus, the, 6, 123f., 161, 166f., 176, 194
Swan, Samuel, 192
Sweden, 37, 41
swivel guns, 112n.

Tagrin Point, 20f., 57, 62f., 129
Talangsan, 154
Tamiso, 142
*Tangomoas*, 12
Tasso Island, 5, 21, 50f., 94, 96, 98, 143, 182
tattooing, 139n.
Tecuyema, 172
Tekrur, 129
Temnes, the, 4, 6, 9, 62, 64, 119, 123f., 146, 161, 194
Temne language, 6, 124
ten per cent duty, 80f., 100

Tenes, the, 152
Thoma, Signor, 84
Thompson, Captain, 119
Thompson, Governor P., 191
Thurloe, Thomas, 46, 77
Timbuctoo, 121f.
Timna, 5, 21f.
Tintam, John, 36
tobacco, 160
tolls, 86f., 121
Tombo Island, 5, 62, 67
tow, 19
'trades', 12
trading companies
  Committee of Merchants trading to Africa, 112
  Company of the Adventurers of London, 41
  Company of the Merchant Adventurers, 39f.
  Company of the Merchants trading to Guinea, 41, 96
  Company of the Senegal Adventurers, 41
  East India Company, 42, 96
  Gambia Adventurers, 100
  Hudson Bay Company, 42
  Liverpool Company, 61, 113
  Royal Adventurers, 44, 96
  Royal African Company: charter, 78f.; chief agent, 76; commissions, 77; deserters, 52; equipment, 86f., 97f., 100; exports, 96; informers, 81; journals, 148; officers botanical collections, 173; plan to build in the Sierra Leone river mouth, 104; private trade by officers of, 81f.; recruits, 71f.; slaves, 88f.; surgeon, 74f.; *see also* 26, 42, 48, 50, 54, 57, 70f.
  Royal Company of France, 20
  Sierra Leone Company, 190f.
  South Sea Company, 85
  West Indies Company, Netherlands, 26, 43
  *see also* 15, 31, 34, 39f., 42f.
transport charges, 85
tribes, *see* Bullom, Temne, Mende, etc.; *also* Sierra Leone, kings
Tucker, Abraham, Henry, John, Peter, 149
Tuft, —, writer, 106
Tumba, *see* Tombo

# Index